Praise for Gregg Olsen's True Crime

"A wonderfully researched book . . . searing and brilliant. A must-read for true crime aficionados."

—Ann Rule on *If Loving You is Wrong*

"Through meticulous reporting, Gregg Olsen has masterfully reconstructed a fascinating turn-of-the-century story of medical malpractice and murder. Olsen is a top-notch writer."

—Michael Connelly, bestselling author of *The Law of Innocence,* on *Starvation Heights*

"A rapid-fire page-turner."

—*The Seattle Times* on *A Twisted Faith*

"Olsen has done a superior job in not only researching and assembling the obscure and tangled facts of the case but also in telling the story in a mesmerizing manner that leaves the reader both haunted and fascinated by what they have read."

—*The Plain Dealer* on *Abandoned Prayers*

"[Olsen and Morris] paint a portrait of systematic dysfunction . . . truly chilling moments . . . engrossing."

—*Kirkus Reviews* on *If I Can't Have You*

"Olsen brings his considerable narrative skills to this true-adventure tale."

—*Booklist* on *The Deep Dark*

"A powerful narrative of one family's tragedy."

—*Publishers Weekly* on *If I Can't Have You*

"An excellent book."

—*Library Journal* on *The Deep Dark*

"Explosive."

—*National Enquirer* on *If I Can't Have You*

"Olsen brings an eye for atmospheric detail to a forgotten terror tale that nearly slipped into oblivion."

—*Publishers Weekly* on *Starvation Heights*

"Gregg Olsen weaves his story deftly, managing to bring alive a wide cast of characters, all headed for and contributing to a tragedy driven by faith."

—Stephen Singular, *New York Times* bestselling author of *When Men Become Gods,* on *A Twisted Faith*

"A literary and journalistic achievement of the highest order . . . Gregg Olsen reinforces his standing as one of America's great crime reporters."

—Jack Olsen, author of *Salt of the Earth* and *Hastened to the Grave,* on *Starvation Heights*

"Gregg Olsen's work is absolutely top-notch, masterful. With [*Cruel Deception*], Gregg takes his rightful place among crime masters: Ann Rule, Jack Olsen, Joseph Wambaugh, and Joe McGinniss."

—Dennis McDougal, author of *In the Best of Families* and *Mother's Day*

ALSO BY GREGG OLSEN

NONFICTION

If You Tell

A Killing in Amish Country

If I Can't Have You

A Twisted Faith

The Deep Dark

If Loving You is Wrong

The Confessions of an American Black Widow (Bitch on Wheels)

Starvation Heights

Mockingbird (Cruel Deception)

Bitter Almonds

FICTION

Lying Next to Me

Beneath Her Skin

Dying to Be Her

The Hive

Snow Creek

Water's Edge

Silent Ridge

A Wicked Snow

A Cold Dark Place

Fear Collector

Heart of Ice

Victim Six

Closer Than Blood

The Bone Box

Shocking True Story

Now That She's Gone

Just Try to Stop Me

The Sound of Rain

The Last Thing She Ever Did

The Weight of Silence

The Girl in the Woods

ABANDONED PRAYERS

An Incredible True Story of Murder, Obsession, and Amish Secrets

GREGG OLSEN

ST. MARTIN'S GRIFFIN
NEW YORK

Published in the United States by St. Martin's Griffin, an imprint of St. Martin's Publishing Group

www.stmartins.com

ISBN 978-1-250-82397-7 (trade paperback)
ISBN 978-1-4299-0752-1 (ebook)

Our books may be purchased in bulk for promotional, educational, or business use. Please contact your local bookseller or the Macmillan Corporate and Premium Sales Department at 1-800-221-7945, extension 5442, or by email at MacmillanSpecialMarkets@macmillan.com.

First published in the United States by St. Martin's Paperbacks

Second St. Martin's Griffin Edition: 2021

10 9 8 7 6 5 4 3 2 1

For Gary and Danny

ACKNOWLEDGMENTS

The Amish do not wish to be involved with the modern world—yet many helped me because of their desire to see the truth come to light. I thank the many whose names do not appear in this book, but who were vital to the development of this story.

I owe considerable thanks to the Gingerich family, whose courage and love for their daughter and grandson were strong enough to allow them to open their homes and hearts to an outsider looking for the truth. In addition, I am exceedingly grateful to Liz Chupp, who made her personal diaries available, thus clearing up much of the haziness of Stutzman's past.

After a little more than two years of work, there are many others to whom I owe a debt of appreciation:

Ohio: Dennis Webb, the Canton *Repository* reporter, for his enthusiasm for the story; Lyndon Spigelmire, who provided much background from the archives of the Wayne County Public Library; Wayne County sheriff Captain Jim Gasser for his encouragement; and researcher Suzanne Myers for her help and interest.

Nebraska: Thayer County sheriff Gary Young, the Reverend Jean Samuelson, and state patrol investigator Jack Wyant, who shared personal observations and details of the investigation; court reporter Don McIntyre for his precise hearing transcript; and the people of Thayer County—all of whom are a part of this story.

Colorado: detectives Tony Archuleta and Bill Perreira of the Durango Police Department for the information they shared on their murder investigations; and *Louise Hanson*, for her courage in telling what she knew about Stutzman and his relationship with Danny.

Texas: David Alvarado, supervisor of criminal courts, Travis County District Clerk's office; reporter Kellye Norris; and Travis County assistant district attorneys Marianne Powers and Carla Garcia and defense counsels Connie Moore and Debra Hunt.

I am also indebted to my perceptive editor, Charles Conrad, whose guidance with the book's structure and content was invaluable; and literary agent David Black and his associate David Means for the support and encouragement they gave a first-time author.

Closer to home, much gratitude to Tim Burns and Karen Palmer and others at *Trailblazer*; and Rudy Yuly, whose support in 1988 kept this story alive.

As for Eli Stutzman, who declined my many requests for interviews, I still ask the question muttered by Gary Young and others countless times: *Why?*

Gregg Olsen
July 1990

AUTHOR'S NOTE

I have attempted in this book to reconstruct actual events by relying on police reports, grand jury testimony, court transcripts and trial evidence, as well as more than three hundred interviews conducted over a two-year period.

To protect the privacy of many people who played a part in this story, I have used pseudonyms. All names which appear in italics when first used in the book are pseudonyms. All other names are real.

PROLOGUE

The early morning was as dark and arctic as the inside of a locked freezer as Eli Stutzman's AMC Gremlin came down U.S. 81 through Thayer County, Nebraska. Wind cut through the car and snow scuttled across the road.

The season was frigid. Indeed, winters in southeast Nebraska can be exceedingly cold and drawn out, with snowfall often lasting into March. Forecasters had predicted an especially cold winter that year, but Eli Stutzman didn't care. He had no intention of staying in that region, which locals boast is the exact geographic center of America.

Stutzman was on his way to the home of a Kansas man he had met through a magazine's personal ads. The man was someone he could suck off, lie to, use for a place to crash and a meal. He might even be able to get some of his money. But, most important, the man was someone he could practice his story on. He was someone Stutzman didn't know.

The smoky, sweet taste of chewing tobacco filled his mouth; country music, coming over the radio, filled the car. Having driven all the way from western Wyoming, where he had stopped to pick up his son, Stutzman was tired and his eyelids drooped. However, the cold air leaking in from a broken window, plus the business at hand, kept him wired.

He had business in Thayer County. He needed a place

to get rid of Danny. He knew the kind of place he was looking for—the same kind of place he had dumped the other body: off the main highway, in a roadside ditch. Remoteness and no ID had been his protector then.

Would it work again?

His faded gray car sped through the county's biggest town and county seat, Hebron, situated in the center of the rural valley of the Little Blue River. Christmas lights glowed from condensation-streaked windows of storefronts. Leaving the Hebron city limits, the Gremlin continued south on 81.

With what he had in mind, Stutzman hoped he wouldn't be noticed, but he was. At 4:36 A.M., in a routine check of out-of-state cars, a Thayer County sheriff's deputy ran the Gremlin's New Mexico plate, HPG 183. Nothing came up and the deputy went home. He didn't get close enough to see the glazed, soulless look of Stutzman's eyes or the other passenger in the car.

Stutzman knew what he'd say to people when they asked about his son. Skiing was the answer that had come to him the week before. *"Danny wanted to stay in Wyoming skiing with friends."* The lie came easily. Lies always had. Questions could be answered with canned, pat responses as though all of his speech were programmed.

"But missing Christmas with his father?"

"He loved to ski."

"But, Eli, Danny hadn't seen you all summer!"

"You know kids. Danny wanted to ski."

Though his words were scripted and he practiced them in his head over and over, Stutzman usually failed with delivery. The expressions on his rigid face and in his blue eyes seldom tracked quite right with the words.

Look sad now, Eli, you've got to get rid of the boy.

Your wife is dead.

Your roommate is dead.

Don't forget the story about your partner at the ranch. Don't forget who you told which story. Most important, look sad—turn on the tears, if you can.

Through darkness as black as truck-stop coffee, Stutzman went east off 81 and turned south on a farm road north of the village of Chester, just shy of the Kansas state line. He searched for a suitable place, headlights reflecting off white snowbanks. When he opened the door, the air bit him through his red plaid flannel shirt and down vest. Danny wore a thin blue sleeper Stutzman had picked up in a New Mexico K-Mart.

The boy, of course, wouldn't need extra clothing.

PART ONE
Heartland

"What kind of a barbarian would do this to their kid?"

—Thayer County Sheriff Gary Young

CHAPTER ONE

December 24, 1985

It was time for a haircut. Chuck Kleveland felt the annoying fringe of sandy hair crowding his ears and knew that with the approaching holidays he couldn't let it go much longer. He kissed his wife, Kathy, swallowed his last bit of coffee, and put his shotgun in the gun rack of his '83 Ford pickup. He planned to do a little hunting on the way to the barber in Hebron.

It was 10 A.M., Christmas Eve.

Kleveland, age 44, pulled out of the driveway of his ranch-style home in Chester, a dozen miles due south of Hebron. Chester, a tiny town whose skyline consists of a pair of grain elevators, is within spitting distance of the Nebraska–Kansas state line. To nonresidents, the town doesn't seem like much, except maybe a good place to gas up or pick up a pack of cigarettes.

Hebron and Chester used to be the kind of nice, friendly prairie towns where people spend their entire lives. Now they are the kind of towns young people abandon for careers in Omaha—or, if they can bear to pull away from the heart and soul of their parents' and grandparents' birthright, they move away even farther, to one of the coasts. Family-owned farms have grown more scarce; a few are fallow.

Kleveland was of the generation—the *last* generation, some claimed—that still envisioned a good life on the bleak prairie of rural Nebraska. Although he had studied business at the university in Lincoln and lived in New York for a couple of years, Kleveland had returned to Chester, where he owned and ran Foote's Truckstop in Chester and a similar business in Kearney, a couple of hours to the west.

Kleveland drove east on Harlan Street before turning north on U.S. 81, a trace of snow mottling the road's shoulder. He could have stayed on 81 and been in Hebron in fifteen minutes, but instead he made a quick right on a farm road bordering a local corn grower's spread. Kleveland knew the field was a good place to find orange and gold ring-neck pheasants—stray grain kernels littered the ground and provided fodder for game fowl. His wife had another Christmas menu planned, but she would make room for the pheasants on the holiday table. Kathy Kleveland liked the way her husband fixed them.

He took a left and drove north, squinting as he scanned the slightly hilly terrain. The icy earth bristled with hard, dead cornstalks, their frosty surfaces sparkling in the cold, even light. No birds were startled into flight by the noise or movement of the cherry-red pickup.

The jangly sound of steel guitars from a country music radio station broke the bleakness of the morning.

From the corner of his eye Kleveland saw a small bit of blue against the brown and gray field. The color was out of place in the dull winter landscape. He braked to a stop and backed up to get a closer look. When he stepped from the cab, the 30-below-zero wind chill slashed through his parka. Standing at the edge of the roadside drainage ditch, he looked into the field and immediately spotted what had attracted his attention. Partially hidden in a brambly nest, the spiky remnants of yard-tall prairie grass, was a dead body.

It appeared to be a little girl dressed in a blue, one-piece blanket sleeper. Her hand was glazed over with ice and her body lay flat and stiff on the frozen ground. The child's dark hair was clean and neatly parted, but her head was tilted back, so Kleveland couldn't quite make out her face.

From his vantage point on the roadside, it appeared that the child's hand had been placed over her heart.

Kleveland had seen enough. He did not move closer to the small corpse, which lay only fifteen feet from the roadside. He didn't want to mess up any footprints or other evidence, and he sure as hell didn't want to be *part* of any evidence. He studied the field, then looked down the length of the dirt road. He wondered if whoever had left the child was still around, watching, as he walked back to his still-running pickup. Picking up the mike of his commercial two-way radio, installed to communicate with his truck-stop fleet of tank wagons, he called his bookkeeper in the office at Foote's.

"Joyce?" His voice was steady. "I think I found a dead body out here. Call the sheriff." He stopped short of giving the exact location. There were plenty of police scanners in the small, neatly painted homes in Thayer County. Kleveland knew that if word got out—and in Chester and Hebron one could bank on that—bystanders would be out at the scene in five minutes.

"I'll be on the highway, a mile north of town," he said.

Kleveland stared at the corpse. He had seen dead bodies before; he had picked them up when he worked as a volunteer for the local ambulance service, and he had found his mother when she died at home. But this was different, and unsettling in a different way.

You don't put a child's body out in a ditch, he thought, *unless you've got something to hide.*

Kleveland drove back to the highway and waited for the sheriff on the northwest corner of the square-mile grid where he had found the body.

CHAPTER TWO

Wayne and Holmes counties, in the Ohio Amish Country, are aligned vertically, with Wayne to the north. The landscape is pastoral, with steel and wood buggy wheels slicing through the rich earth like cleavers through paraffin. Whitewashed picket fences and farmhouses mark the line where nature ends and man's influence takes over. Yet, in Amish Country the demarcation is subtle. Fields are still plowed with horses; oat, corn, and hay crops are rotated; the land is cared for with the love and respect that outsiders reserve for humankind. No telephone poles, electric power lines, or television antennae clutter the sky.

Although adult Amish dress in black and white, their world is one of vivid color. Farms are planted in a quilt of green. Amish girls are allowed the deep hues of aqua, purple, and celery for their long dresses, secured by neat rows of straight pins instead of buttons. The men, however, are allowed hooks and eyes as clothing fasteners. Buttons are considered worldly, even militaristic.

Since draft horses are used for plowing, farms are appropriately small, with few topping eighty acres. The twice-daily milkings are done by hand. Most Amish farmers own fewer than ten dairy cows. Due to the antiquated milking methods, and the people's refusal to pasteurize, Amish milk is sold solely for cheese-making.

The Amish, descendants of Dutch and Swiss Anabaptists—"rebaptisers"—might have drowned in their own blood, so much had been spilled during the Protestant Reformation. The first Amish came to Penn's Woods in America in the 1730s; a century later, they migrated across the Alleghenies to Ohio, where the world's largest settlement continues to thrive.

Tourism bureaus would have people believe that all Amish people are the same, cut from the same nondescript pattern, but that is not the case. However, all do live by strict interpretation of the Bible. The Amish believe in adult baptism, nonresistance, and separatism from the world. Many of the forty different sects are named for their founding bishops—Troyer, Beachy, Swartzentruber, and so on. Different groups have their own ways, their own quirks. Yet, nearly all resist change. "Where is it written in the Bible that we should change?" they ask.

The Swartzentruber Order founded settlements in the Ohio villages of Apple Creek, Kidron, and Fredericksburg. This ultraconservative group took the most rigid stance against change, curling up like potato bugs to shut out the modern world.

While the rules of Scripture never changed, the *Ordnung*—the rules of the Order as set by the church's district bishop and its members—did. The *Ordnung* accounted for some of the differences among Amish church districts; for example, the fact that some men are allowed only three-inch hat brims while others are allowed four or even five inches, and the fact that some could use farm machinery with rubber tires while other were permitted only wooden or steel ones.

As other Amish orders slowly made concessions to some modern ways and methods, the Swartzentrubers remained true to centuries-old traditions. They were considered "low Amish." Those who used some modern conveniences were considered the antithesis; when an Amishman left for the modern world, others said he "went high."

Strips of deep purple and blue fabric used as wicks float loosely in the base of the gas mantle lanterns Amish use to illuminate their homes. Kerosene burns fast, and its smoky vapors discolor and stain walls and ceilings. The smell of the burning fuel, along with the aroma of hearty foods cooking, fill Amish homes.

Many Amishwomen use pressure cookers to preserve chicken and beef, although some of the more progressive rent freezers in town for storage. This practice is less common among the Swartzentrubers than higher Amish. Still, at the end of winter, many wonder where all the food has gone. "A whole cow should last us the winter, but with nine kids it doesn't," they say.

Photographs are banned, and Amish girls play with dolls that have no faces. Such representations are in conflict with the commandment forbidding graven images. Small boys play farmer, sometimes using old batteries to mimic milk cans. The batteries are for flashlights, a convenience the *Ordnung* allows.

At home, the Amish family speaks a dialect of German and Swiss with a little English mixed in—outsiders call it Pennsylvania Dutch, or Deutsch. It is only during dealings with the outside world that the Amish speak English to *Englischers*, or non-Amish.

The Amish seem nearly communal, with several branches of a family often sharing a farm. The *Grossdaadi*, or "grandpa house," is a smaller dwelling, often attached by a breezeway, where the grandparents live. In Amishland, grandparents never suffer the humiliation of a rest home.

Church is held every other Sunday in the homes of the congregation members. It is an all-day affair, starting about 9 A.M. and going into the afternoon. The words of the preacher, spoken not in Deutsch but in "high German," are often unintelligible. The Amish hymnal, the *Ausbund*, is better known for its bloody recounting of the lives of the martyrs than for its melodies. Hymns are long and dirgelike and, to children, tedious.

On Sundays no work is done, no money exchanged. The only chores permitted are those involving the care of animals.

The "in-between Sundays" are for visiting, a favorite pastime in a world without telephones.

Like a collection of scattered, great white boxes, the Eli H. Stutzman farm sits on a grassy hill above Welty Road in Apple Creek. The ruts of buggy wheels reveal that the home is Amish. No power lines mar the clear Ohio sky. The middle initial on the mailbox is an essential clue in discerning who resides there—the *H* stands for Harvey, Eli H. Stutzman's father. With families sometimes having a dozen or more children, such initials are a necessary kind of brand. Stutzman's roots were in the Amish settlement outside of Berne, Indiana, although his father moved the family to a farm a mile or so from Kidron in 1929.

When Eli H. Stutzman was 18 years old his hand got caught in an antiquated sorghum press. Infection set in and he lost some fingers. He was fitted with a hook and thereafter was known as One-Hand Eli. Such a nickname is essential in a world with so many named Eli, Levi, and Amos and a proliferation of the last names Miller, Swartzentruber, and Yoder.

Stutzman married Susan Miller, and in exhausting succession that left her with a stooped back and a stretched belly, the Amishwoman bore him thirteen children. The fourth child, a son named Eli, was born on September 28, 1950.

Eli E. (to avoid confusion with his father, the family called him Eli Ali) was a bright child with a slight stutter. He showed an early interest in horses and a disdain for farm-work, and he enjoyed being the center of attention.

Said a cousin: "Eli always thought he was a little too good for the rest of us."

School friends remembered Stutzman as a boy who could break the rules and convincingly place the blame elsewhere. By 6 or 7, it was apparent that the Amish boy was a habitual liar.

Years later, Susan Stutzman would clutch her hands to

her breast and shake her head. Try as she could, she could not find a reason why her son was untruthful. "If I could understand . . . he was always that way . . ." she said.

Once, Eli and his brother Andy played with a cart to which they had attached a small gasoline motor, taking turns riding the contraption down the hill by the barn. When the engine fell off and broke a pulley, they had to come up with a story for their father. It was Eli who covered it up.

"Eli learned how to lie then," Andy later said.

When the boys hooked up a couple of heifers to the same little cart, their father found out about it and confronted them. Eli again came up with a tale. "I think he lied *too* good," Andy said.

However, Eli's father wasn't fooled by the boy's lies. Although the stories were detailed enough and told with great sincerity, the elder Stutzman saw them for what they were.

One-Hand Eli was a minister in his church district. He had been chosen by lot, as the Amish have done for centuries. (Copies of the *Ausbund* are arranged on a table. Selected men each choose a hymnal, one of which contains a slip of paper with a verse. The man who gets the piece of paper is the one they believe God has chosen to preach His word.)

A small, gray-haired man whose hair was just a bit longer than that of some of his neighbors, the senior Stutzman held great faith and unyielding belief in the old ways. He would not accept any misbehavior by his children. A whipping was his swiftest and most effective remedy for disobedience.

As a father, he had a responsibility to ensure that his children followed the *Ordnung*. As a minister, he was under tremendous pressure to see that his children, more so than others, toed the line.

His problem was the son named for him, a bright but rebellious boy who had an eye for horses, money, and the modern world. At home or at school, Eli Ali found new ways to get into trouble. The incidents were small at first, but grew with age. The more his father held him down, the more he tried to break away.

A neighbor of the Stutzmans remembered the young Eli: "He didn't seem to work as hard as the others when we were out in the field or at a husking. Eli didn't feel well or he had some excuse—or his mind was on something else."

As the boy grew toward manhood, it seemed the Amish neighbor was right.

The Dog House, a rundown little Wayne County beer joint, was a popular hangout for Amish boys going through *rumspringa*, the equivalent of sowing wild oats. The fun was generally harmless—a couple of beers and a few laughs at the ways of the old folks. Young Eli Stutzman belonged to the Wild Westerns, a group of rowdy Amish youths who frequented the Dog House.

The boys in Stutzman's circle souped up their buggies with decals and bumper stickers. Radios were tucked out of view and country music blared from inside. Sometimes pranks were played. Buggies were torn up or trashed in a pond or a field. Once Eli stole a boy's bicycle. Mostly, it was done in fun.

However, Stutzman, whom many considered popular, later told friends that there were times when he had been treated as an outcast by some members of the Order. "Some boys who didn't like me hung a dead, skinned cat in my buggy," he claimed, although he had thrown out the carcass before anyone else saw it. "I don't know why they didn't like me," he added.

Rumspringa is also the time of dating, and the Amish girls liked Eli Stutzman—especially his eyes, which were as blue as new denim. He was small and slim, standing about five feet six inches and weighing 140 pounds. Dressed in his white shirt, black coat, and broadfall pants, he was perfectly proportioned—compact and solid. His brown hair hung over his ears in the kind of severe Prince Valiant that was the cut of the Swartzentruber Order. His wild and rebellious streak was his biggest plus. For the Amish, who value and insist on conformity, Eli Stutzman was fun to be around. He was different from the others.

Among the higher Amish, bundling, the courtship custom of an unmarried couple's occupying a bed without undressing, was seen as an archaic and dangerous invitation far too tempting for young people. The Swartzentrubers, however, held tight to the tradition, but not without a price. Out-of-wedlock pregnancies occurred occasionally. After all, birth control was not only against the Bible, it was in violation of the *Ordnung*.

Gossip among the Swartzentrubers frequently targeted girls who bundled "too hard." If such talk could be substantiated, the girl's dating was curtailed and monitored by her parents.

Amish adolescents learn little about sex from their parents, and there is no Amish school program to give even basic information. The teenagers learn by watching farm animals and by asking those whom they trust. Occasionally, boys get their hands on forbidden men's magazines.

Amish parents supervise "singings" for the youth. These co-ed gatherings take place in barns and include Amish songs and food. Sometimes they are wilder than that, with Amish boys smuggling in beer and transistor radios.

It was at a singing that Eli Stutzman met 16-year-old Ida Gingerich. For Ida, the attraction was immediate. She got the feeling, she later told her sister, that Stutzman liked her, too.

The daughter of Amos and Lizzie Gingerich, Ida was a beautiful girl with wide-set hazel eyes. When she laughed, dimples creased her cheeks. Her ash-blond hair was thick, with a slight wave—but no one outside her family knew that. She wore it like all the other Swartzentruber girls—rolled under, pulled back, and tucked under a bonnet. It was written in the Bible that only her husband could see the glory of her hair. And for Ida, that could only be Eli Stutzman.

The Gingeriches, like the Stutzmans, were Swartzentrubers, although they lived in a different church district. The Gingeriches were a warmer family, with great concern for one another. It wasn't that the Stutzmans didn't love one another—they simply didn't show it.

Eli and Ida dated for the next four years. Everyone assumed that after they joined the church—a requirement for marriage among the Amish—they would marry. It was Ida who first confessed her sins and knelt before the church to join the Swartzentrubers. Stutzman followed her baptism with his own.

In the fall of 1971 Stutzman, who only had a standard eighth-grade education, began work as a teacher at the one-room Maple Grove School.

Although neighbors believed that One-Hand Eli was pleased with his son's growth into adulthood—he was a member of the church, and he had a steady girl and a job as a schoolteacher—word came out that unease and rebellion continued at the Stutzman farm. Many who knew the family wondered why the minister couldn't control his son. Some felt that the minister was not sufficiently loving to his boy and was too harsh a disciplinarian.

When Eli was 21, he moved from his parents' farm to a farm across the road, run by an Old Order Amishman named Mose Keim. Keim, whose church was less restrictive than the conservative Swartzentrubers', knew that Stutzman had had some trouble at home.

Keim and his wife, Ada, wanted to help, but neither wanted to be embroiled in the middle of Stutzman family trouble. "Everyone liked Eli," Keim said later. "We didn't know how he was going to turn out."

Soon word got out that Stutzman had gone to the school board for a raise. He told Keim he hadn't named a figure, but he felt he needed more than the $140 a month he claimed he was earning. He also told Keim that his father thought he was trying to become more worldly by asking for more money.

"The truth was, I feel, that his father could no longer control his son," Keim said later. "But he still wanted to show who was boss."

Another neighbor shared similar feelings years later. "Old Eli tried to have his son's salary go directly to him, instead of to his boy. That is not any way for a father to be. Eli was 21 and should have been allowed his own money."

One-Hand Eli visited his son several times at Keim's, each time telling him he was wrong to leave home and must return immediately. The young man refused. He told Keim that his father had even gone to the school board to see that the raise was not given.

For young Stutzman, the pressure was too much. On February 12, 1972, he collapsed, without warning, as he was on his way to his upstairs bedroom to dress for a Saturday-night date with Ida Gingerich.

For Mennonite osteopath Elton Lehman, the tiny Ohio village of Mount Eaton was the perfect location for a family practice. There, although it was only a half-hour drive from Canton, he could still be a country doctor—the kind who knew all his patients' and their children's names and said hello in passing.

When the Amish needed a doctor, they made the trip to town and tied their horses to the clinic's hitching post. For patients too ill to travel, Dr. Lehman still made house calls. Even so, the doctor was often the last resort. Wary of modern medicine, the Swartzentrubers frequently employed home remedies before seeking the doctor's opinion.

Dr. Lehman had grown used to the Amish and their abrupt ways. The men dressed in black and white seldom said thank you. The women almost never spoke. Sometimes bare feet tracked mud and farm debris into his tidy office on Chestnut Street. But none of that mattered, since the Amish paid cash and on time. And they trusted him. A few Amish patients had even invited the doctor and his wife into their homes for dinner—a true indication of acceptance.

Dr. Lehman had heard the rumors about Eli Stutzman and his mental problems, so he was not surprised when he was summoned to Keim's farm that Saturday night. He found Stutzman in bed upstairs in a depressed and nervous state.

One-Hand Eli was there also, looking troubled and concerned. "My son is having more nerve problems. He is out of control," the senior Stutzman said in a hushed, concerned voice. "I don't know what to do to help him."

Young Eli remained in bed until Sunday evening, seeming to drift in and out of consciousness. Although his father had wanted him returned to his farm, Dr. Lehman recommended that he stay put until his condition improved.

As the weeks passed, Keim doubted that Stutzman would recover; his nerves seemed shot. He called in a woman who did foot reflexology, a technique some Amish favor over traditional medicine. The woman gasped when she tried to work on Stutzman's feet. "They are so sore, I cannot touch them. There is nothing I can do," she said.

Keim next took Stutzman to chiropractor Morton Bissell in Brewster, Ohio. Bissell showed the Amishman how his nerve pressure had tightened the "plates of his skull and caused them to shift abnormally." He prescribed some pills and arranged for a number of treatments.

At his Apple Creek farm, Keim did what he could do to help, at times even bathing the man. When he massaged his neck, it felt as taut and rigid as 8-gauge wire. He wondered how Stutzman could survive with such tense muscles and nerves.

But there was more. One day shortly after the collapse on the stairs, Keim found Stutzman crying in the barn. When he asked him what was wrong, Stutzman told him that ever since the breakdown he had had a constant erection that was both painful and embarrassing. Keim didn't know what to do to help the young man. He considered asking Dr. Lehman about it, but dismissed it as too private a matter.

"It seemed to go on for months," Keim later recalled. "Somehow that breakdown affected his sex."

It was at about that time that Keim and his wife discovered several notes that Stutzman had written on scraps of paper and left in his bedroom. The words, written in English, included references to Satan and Hell. Keim and his wife wondered if he had left them for their benefit, and if so, why?

One morning Keim found Stutzman downstairs, dressed and standing in the kitchen, his long Swartzentruber hair cut shorter and crudely. This was particularly disturbing to the farmer. "Eli, what in the world did you do to yourself?" Keim asked.

Stutzman ignored the question and said he wanted to go to Keim's church. That was fine with Keim, yet still he wondered why Stutzman hadn't had someone else cut his hair.

Next, Stutzman had his Swartzentruber-style buggy outfitted with a more sophisticated dash than the conservative Swartzentrubers permitted.

Even though Stutzman never went across the road to tell his family what he was up to, his father got wind of the changes.

The rumors ran wildly through the Amish community. Word was out that trouble still plagued the Stutzman family on Welty Road.

While out on the house call three months before, Dr. Lehman had seen that the young man was a time bomb waiting to explode, so it was no real surprise when One-Hand Eli came to his office for help in mid-May 1972.

The Amishman's concern was obvious and, to the doctor, seemed genuine.

"My son is no better," the old man said. "What can I do to control him?"

Dr. Lehman weighed the solutions. He told the Amishman that he could call Fallsview Hospital in Cuyahoga Falls, Ohio. If his son would go for treatment voluntarily, arrangements could be made quickly.

There was one alternative. The doctor hesitated slightly before suggesting it.

"If he resists, however, we could have the sheriff pick him up and go through probate."

The Amishman showed little emotion. He nodded to Dr. Lehman and left the office.

The day was warm and the field was dusty as Eli Stutzman and his mammoth horse-drawn harrow broke and smoothed Keim's field for planting. Mental problems had forced him to give up his teaching position, although occasionally he seemed well enough to do farm work. Stutzman seemed best after his appointments with Bissell, the chiropractor.

Keim watched from the yard as a sheriff's car pulled up the lane and two deputies approached him.

"Is Eli Stutzman working for you?" one of the deputies asked.

"He is over in the field."

"We have to talk with him now."

The officers left and a few minutes later returned with Stutzman, who was frantic.

"They're going to take me away!" Stutzman told Keim.

"Why?" Keim asked the deputies.

"We can't say, but we've got orders," one of them replied.

With that, they shoved Stutzman into the backseat of the sheriff's car.

Keim, both frightened and outraged, ran across Welty Road to the Stutzman farm, only to find that the old man and his son Andy had gone to Wooster, the county seat.

To Keim, it was all too clear who had set Stutzman up with the sheriff's department.

"Tell your husband I don't think much of what he has

done!" Keim told Susan Stutzman, whose shocked expression indicated that she had not known of the sheriff's visit.

Later that day, Keim learned that Stutzman had been taken to Fallsview Hospital and One-Hand Eli had rushed up to Cuyahoga Falls on the bus with a suitcase of clothes.

Keim had the feeling that Stutzman's father planned to commit his son and then go pick him up to bring him back home, where he could control him. What kind of a father could do that to his son? he wondered.

After three days in the hospital, Stutzman returned to Keim's farm, saying he was disgusted with his father and brother for having put him in a mental ward. He reasserted that he wanted to leave the Swartzentrubers and join Keim's Old Order Amish district.

Eli attended church a few times, then his interest seemed to wane. To Mose Keim, it was becoming more apparent that the young man had severe mental problems.

At that time Keim caught Stutzman in a number of lies, most of them pertaining to his whereabouts when he left the farm. Stutzman claimed he had Amish friends in Ashland—yet no one in Ashland had seen him there. Even worse, some whispered that they had seen Stutzman in a car, driving through the community with some friends who obviously weren't Amish. One Sunday, Stutzman entertained several *Englischers* at Keim's place when Mose and his wife were away. On August 12, 1972, Keim's barn burned to the ground a half hour after Stutzman had caught the bus for Ashland. Although Keim never believed that Stutzman had set the fire, others did.

When Stutzman told him he had sold his buggy and bought a bicycle and planned to leave the Amish, Keim was sorry about the young man's decision to leave the faith. However, he was not sad to see Stutzman leave the farm. Too many things had happened, and Keim had three children of his own to care for. Besides, he reasoned, there was nothing more he could do for Eli Stutzman. He had tried everything.

Others tried to help. To 24-year-old Amishman Joe Slabaugh, an occasional visitor to Mose Keim's farm after Stutzman's breakdown, Eli Stutzman was the kind of rowdy young troublemaker who became angry, even belligerent, whenever he was caught doing something he wasn't supposed to do—especially if going to the bishop was threatened. Stutzman tested the limits of the *Ordnung* at every opportunity, or so it seemed. When Slabaugh heard that Stutzman was having trouble with the Swartzentrubers, he figured that in time he would cool off and return to the fold.

Slabaugh, who was working as a carpenter in Apple Creek, searched for the right words to comfort Stutzman, yet let him see that he should come back to the Swartzentrubers. Stutzman insisted that he was happier without the rules of the Order and especially without his father, but it didn't show on his face. When Slabaugh left after a visit, he felt that what he had heard about Stutzman was true: he *was* crazy.

The Old Order Amish had two sanctions that were effective in keeping renegade members in the church. One was to *bann*, or excommunicate, a sinful member from the church body; the other, called *Meidnung*, was the practice of shunning or avoiding members who had been banned. Members could not accept services or goods from a banned Amishman. The measures were harsh, but they often worked and brought back the wayward.

The summer of 1972 was sweltering, and the confines of the Amish church meeting only intensified the heat. Amish men, women, and their obedient children sat lined up on wooden benches and listened respectfully to the preachers and bishop, although many of them could not understand the words of the sermon spoken in High German.

Joe Slabaugh was in church the day Stutzman was expelled and put under the *bann*. The church took council and asked the members whether Stutzman should be excommunicated for his disobedience and desire to leave the Order.

Slabaugh wanted to say something on his troubled friend's behalf, but he feared that if he did, he too might be put under the *bann*. So he sat quietly while it was done.

Slabaugh felt Stutzman had left the church because of something he wanted out of life, not to cause hardship for his parents, as some gossiped. Other boys were making peace with the church, and Slabaugh hoped his friend would also.

When the news about Stutzman reached Ida, she curled up on her bed and cried. Ida's sisters and mother tried to comfort her, but nothing worked. *Eli was going to be her husband. What would happen to her now?*

Since Stutzman could get work outside of the Swartzentrubers, he didn't have to suffer the financial hardship that forced some to return.

The breakdown and the lies had been worth it to Stutzman. He wanted out of the Amish and was glad to leave. If he couldn't take meals with his father, so what? He was free.

CHAPTER THREE

The Thayer County Sheriff's Department is housed in an ugly, squat cinder-block building in the considerable shadow of the massive limestone courthouse. The department's name, however, is painted on the front door in the kind of golden swash usually reserved for boutiques or cafes. On the morning of December 24, 1985, hot mulled cider simmered in a pot next to the coffeemaker in the back room. Paper plates heaped with homemade Christmas cookies covered the counter. Sheriff Gary Young and his chief deputy, Bill McPherson, expected an easy day that Christmas Eve. After all, most days were easy in the Thayer County Sheriff's Department; a few traffic violations and occasional burglaries and drunk-and-disorderlies were the only offenses that occupied their time. There hadn't been a murder in the county since a Chester woman shot her husband and dumped his body in a hog pen more than a decade ago.

At 9:30 A.M. a call came in from Ortman's Cafe. Some "crazy lady" had been at the restaurant all night. She was upset, "talking strange," and they wanted her out. Young told McPherson to respond. It wasn't so much an order as a reminder that it was McPherson's turn to respond to a call. Although Gary Young was the sheriff and the ultimate authority of law and order in Thayer County, he ran his operation with an easy, team-oriented approach. He and the dark-haired, mustachioed McPherson were the nucleus of the team.

Bill McPherson and the Reverend "Whistling" Bill Anderson, a self-appointed jail chaplain, were "smokin' and jokin' " in the office by the dispatcher's desk when the call came in. Anderson, a Methodist minister who had made a second, albeit small, congregation of the drunks and hotheads who drifted through the four cramped cells in the sheriff's office, had come in to see if anyone was in need of special prayer or, better, needed to be saved on Christmas Eve morning.

"Why don't you come with me out to Ortman's? We've got a crazy out there and you can talk to her," McPherson suggested. The minister agreed and they left to answer the call.

Gary Young had finished a twenty-one-year career in the Air Force before starting his law-enforcement career in Thayer County in 1978. Elected sheriff in 1981, he was a round man with a round face. His head was topped with a swirl of dark brown hair. Soft-spoken, yet tough when duty called, Young, age 47, left his office to pick up some last-minute Christmas presents for his three children. He munched on a cookie as he headed out the back door.

At a few minutes after 10:00, a more unsettling call was dispatched to Young's car radio: Chuck Kleveland had found a body—a child's body.

Young shook his head, refusing to believe it for a second. Then he reached for the radio and instructed the dispatcher to call Dan Werner, the county attorney and coroner. Young picked Werner up at his office in the small building south of the station, and together they drove to Chester.

The stocky, middle-aged woman with bleached, black-rooted hair was certifiable, a conclusion that took McPherson and the Reverend Anderson only a moment to reach. Patience and gentle questioning brought out her story. A truckdriver had dropped her off in Hebron after picking her up on the interstate and "messing" with her.

And, she said, she had killed someone.

She said she had been traveling for some time. Yet, her pink sweatpants and white top were clean, suggesting that she hadn't been on the road very long. The Reverend Anderson did his best to calm the woman, while McPherson talked with the Ortmans, who had made the complaint.

A call from the dispatcher interrupted the scene. Sheriff Young was 1097 with the coroner. He wanted 9321 to meet them.

The police code 1097 meant that Young was at the crime scene. "With the coroner" wasn't code, but it indicated to McPherson that someone was dead. The code 9321 was McPherson's radio number. Another deputy was en route to handle the crazy lady. The Reverend Anderson stayed behind.

McPherson turned on the red lights and peeled south to Chester. When he approached the scene, Young instructed him to park his car on the county-road intersection a mile from the junction of 81 and 8.

"This is a security area. Don't let anyone come down that road." Young said little else. Department policy was such that homicides—and at this point Young could only guess that this was the case—were never discussed over the radio.

McPherson waited. He knew it had to be bad, but he didn't know what it was all about. He wondered about the woman back at Ortman's. Whom had she killed in Chester?

"It's over there."

Kleveland pushed Gary Young toward the child's body; the sheriff just couldn't see it amid the brambles. While the wind blew air cold enough to freeze nose hairs, Young moved closer and saw the child's hand—the same clue that had given Kleveland the unmistakable impression that it was for real.

The child's head was tilted back, to the west, so Young couldn't make out her face. Her legs were stiff and parted like the cold blades of an open pair of scissors, and though there had been three or four inches of snow three days earlier, most of it had melted. A few snowflakes clung to the pale blue garment.

"Jesus," Kleveland said. "What in the hell happened to the kid?" Kleveland half-expected an immediate answer from either the sheriff or the county coroner.

Young shook his head and walked around the body to get a look at the child's face, or what was left of it. The soft tissues of the nose and the mouth had been scraped away. Exposed nasal cartilage centered the face with a chalky triangle. The eyes—perhaps blue, although they were cloudy and dark—were closed to thin slits. The child's left hand wasn't really over her heart, as Kleveland thought he had seen. It was resting over her lower abdomen. The child's right hand was tucked under her body. Sharp violet lines marked her neck and bruises discolored her forehead. Young wondered if the girl had been beaten and strangled. Yet, the girl had been placed carefully. Young figured that whoever had left her wanted her to be found.

Carefully watching each step before his feet touched the stone-hard ground, Young climbed back to the roadside to where Dan Werner was waiting.

"Well, is it?" Werner asked.

Young, still watching where his feet landed, nodded.

"Shit," Werner said, surprising the sheriff. Dan Werner, as straight as his sandy hair, a regular churchgoing family man, never cursed.

Young had the dispatcher call the state patrol and send for the crime van up in Lincoln. He had never before handled a murder case and wasn't too proud to call for immediate help. He told the dispatcher to relay the information that they had a probable homicide—grotesque purple marks circled the little girl's throat.

"Advise the patrol that no one has touched the body at this point," he said, signing off.

Finally, Young told Kleveland he could leave. The truck-stop owner was none too happy to oblige. He promised he wouldn't say anything. "I'll keep my mouth shut, you can count on it."

"Whoever did this could still be here," Young told him as Kleveland pulled away.

By noon, locals were cruising the area. From where McPherson sat in his car, he couldn't see anything and it irritated him that so many people had come to take a look. It was Christmas Eve, for God's sake.

Finally, Young radioed McPherson to come. The deputy braced himself against the wind and climbed over the ditch to where Young and state-patrol investigator Dan Scott huddled.

"Do you recognize her?" Young asked.

McPherson edged closer. At six feet two inches, and standing three or four feet above the body as it lay in the ditch, he wasn't close enough to see much. He bent over. The child's body, which from the roadside had seemed larger, appeared smaller when he stood next to it. The child's size troubled him.

"Must be something wrong with the kid. Retarded or something," he offered.

"Why?" Werner asked.

"The one-piece sleeper. This kid is too big for jammies with feet. My girls wouldn't wear a sleeper like that past age three or four. She could be retarded or abused." Looking at the dead kid, McPherson felt like someone had punched him in the stomach. It was the first time in eleven years as a cop that McPherson had had to deal with a dead child as young as the one in the blue sleeper. When he was a policeman in Lincoln he had investigated the case of a 17-year-old who had committed suicide by sucking on an M-80. But this was a baby.

Like Young and Werner and the other deputies at the scene, McPherson didn't know who the child was. Her skin looked dark enough that she might have been Mexican. He tried to look beyond the torn and chewed face, the buck-toothed mouth without an upper lip to cover the base of the front teeth. He wondered what the girl had looked like before she ended up in the ditch.

The baby-blue sleeper was noteworthy in another way: it was clean and seemed brand-new. The white and blue striped cotton ribbing of the collar and cuffs were in flawless condition. McPherson, the father of three girls, was puzzled by the perfect condition of the sleeper's plastic feet. He knew, as any father would, that the feet on a child's sleeper are the first to wear out. But these feet were spotless. The child hadn't done much, if any, walking.

Nebraska State Patrol investigators Jack Wyant, Dan Scott, and Carl Nedley mapped out the details of the scene. Most of the sheriff's department wore insulated coveralls, and a few of the state troopers were lucky enough to have a pair. Those who didn't made trips to the car heaters every twenty minutes or so.

An imposing figure of height, weight, and credentials, Jack Wyant is a veteran of the state patrol and is considered both competent and gruff—although when he smiles his grin is as wide as a jack-o'-lantern's. During his career he'd worked the full range in Nebraska, from traffic duty in Fremont and Broken Bow to narcotics investigations in Lincoln. He transferred into criminal investigations in 1977. A burly man who chokes the handlebars on his Harley on weekends, Wyant keeps Winstons in his front pocket and a lighter in his right hand. Even in the subzero temperatures of that day, he found time to puff between shivers.

Wyant took critical measurements of the scene and mapped out the body's position, noting that it had been discovered approximately twenty feet west of the dirt road, which ran north and south. It was lying on a line from the head to the feet of west-northwest to east-southeast. The ditch, which drained through a culvert under the road to the adjacent field, was approximately two and a half feet deep at the point where the body had been discovered.

While investigators continued to search the scene for evidence, Dan Scott knelt down and unzipped the blue sleeper to see if there were any clues about the manner of death—maybe more bruises or cuts.

Scott carefully peeled back the fabric, which was loose against the frozen, dry skin. Finally, he pulled the zipper to the crotch.

"Hey, this is a boy!" he called out.

Scott also discovered that the boy was not wearing any underwear. The troopers who had children felt that this was peculiar. Their boys and girls always wore underpants with their sleepers. No one speculated what it might mean, but it seemed to have some significance.

The marks on the neck, of course, appeared critical.

Young told Wyant that he thought the child had been beaten to death or strangled. "Those purple lines look like ligature marks," he said.

Wyant, usually inclined to wait for the results of an autopsy, agreed.

"Who would murder a little boy and throw him in a ditch like so much trash?" Young asked.

The investigators rolled the boy over to see if there was any evidence underneath him. Nothing seemed remarkable, although Wyant noted that a small stick had been caught in the frozen folds of the boy's neck. The stiff child was wrapped in a sheet and zipped into a body bag.

The body had not been frozen into the ground; a slight indentation like a little cup or cradle remained where the child's head had rested. It was likely that rigor mortis had not yet set in and the body had been warm when put there. Although soft to the touch, a patch of snow under the boy's legs remained undisturbed.

Frozen vehicle tracks from a pickup truck were photographed. Normal procedure would have called for plaster castings, but the frigid weather ruled that out. Killers had been identified before on the basis of tread marks, but if the little boy's murderer had just been passing through via U.S. 81, there would be no telling where he had gone.

Sheriff Young arranged for Lon Adams to bring a hearse from Hebron to Chester and the dead boy was taken to Adams-Tibbett Funeral Home. Once there, the sheriff's department and the state patrol could regroup. With any luck they would wrap it up before Christmas Eve dinner.

In the hours that followed, there would be little physical evidence recovered from the scene. A Sneaker brand T-shirt, size 34–36, was found three-eighths of a mile northwest of the body by Trooper Al Wise, who was scouring the area on horseback. It was gray, with PANTHER WRESTLING emblazoned in black block letters. A pair of white cotton men's briefs were found at the Lutheran cemetery a half-mile southeast of the dump site. Those pieces of evidence were tagged and bagged and sent to the state crime lab for analysis.

Watching in his rearview mirror until he could see no more, Kleveland drove straight home. The haircut could wait.

After telling Kathy about the body he'd found he went down the hall to check on his children, Amy, Becky, and David. All three teenagers were given to sleeping late, especially on school holidays. He checked to see that each was safe. He had no doubt that things were going to be different in Chester this Christmas.

As if there could be a good time to pass away, sixty-year-old funeral director Lon Adams considered Christmas Eve a "bad time to die." The pain accompanying a sudden death is unbearable, especially at Christmas. His heart went out to those who had loved this boy and would find out that he had been strangled.

The investigators and the patrolmen had followed the

gray hearse to the funeral home, and their eight cars crammed the back parking lot behind the mortuary. The boy in the black body bag was set on a porcelain table in the embalming room. Investigators hovered, speculating about the cause of death over the din of the old furnace, only inches from where the body lay in the cramped, mint-green room.

It was well past lunchtime but no one was hungry. There was too much to do, too much to consider. That afternoon, the funeral home was the liveliest place in town.

Both of the mortuary's phone lines were put into use as calls were placed to local officials who might be aware of a missing child. This seemed doubtful to Gary Young, who had a feeling that this child did not belong to anyone from Thayer County. More photographs were taken as the body was pushed back and forth like a rolling pin. An investigator climbed up on a chair to get a better overview Polaroid shot of the body. The local school superintendent was called in, but when he looked at the body he drew a blank.

Back in the sheriff's office, a teletype about the Chester victim was transmitted to all states crossed by U.S. 81: North Dakota, South Dakota, Nebraska, Kansas, Oklahoma, and Texas. Later, a report was dispatched to law enforcement in Missouri, Iowa, Colorado, and Wyoming.

Phone calls to the media were made, although the timing and the holiday work schedules kept cameramen and reporters from coming down for interviews. A brief news item based on the phone call was scheduled for the 10:00 P.M. news in Lincoln.

A few more visitors arrived at the funeral home. Among them were a sheriff and his deputy from neighboring Republic County, Kansas. They were ushered across the mortuary's sunflower-yellow shag carpet, through the casket and monument showroom done up in silver- and gray-flocked wallpaper, and into the embalming room. When they saw the boy, they shook their heads; they didn't recognize him either.

Although it was freezing outside, Adams told one of the troopers he could leave the mortuary's front door open to allow officers to come back and forth from County Attorney Dan Werner's office, which was next door.

"We don't have crime like you have up in Lincoln," Adams half-joked to a trooper.

"Doesn't look like that in your back room," the officer shot back.

So small it still closed down for lunch hour, the tiny State Bank of Chester had been a meeting place for the locals for years. It was the kind of place that symbolized Chester and its people: small-townish and proud of it. Bank president Harold Porter still typed his correspondence on a manual Royal—not because he didn't like change and refused to upgrade to an electric or, God forbid, a word processor, but because the typewriter still worked.

As had been her routine, United Methodist minister Jean Samuelson stopped in the bank the morning of December 24 and was immediately hit with the story of the dead boy. The news drained her. It didn't seem possible.

People in Chester now looked to Samuelson to make some sense out of what was happening on U.S. 81 just a mile from town.

Throughout the afternoon and evening rumors spread through town. People were afraid that some terrible child killer, a pervert probably, had come through town and murdered a little boy. Some even wondered if the child's pajamas indicated that the boy had been stolen from his bedroom. A ritual killing was also suggested.

"Chuck Kleveland says the child was wiped clean as could be. They washed him before they dumped him. His hand had been placed over his heart!"

Samuelson felt the fear build and searched for words to console her parishioners. When it was time for her 7:00 P.M. Christmas Eve service, the minister stood before her congregation of farmers and their wives and children and spoke about the little boy Kleveland had found that morning.

"Here we are celebrating the birth of a child and there is a dead child in our midst," she told them.

With a couple of hours to go before the midnight service, Samuelson went home to the seventy-year-old parsonage on the northwestern edge of town. On the back of a Christmas postcard she wrote the words to a song.

Who are the children, the ones with no one to care?
Our Lord says they are everywhere.
They are in the cities.
They are in the towns.
They are on a country road . . .

It was dark outside, and the darkness brought an even greater chill when Lon Adams took the body to Lincoln General Hospital, where it would be stored and defrosted for the autopsy now scheduled for the day after Christmas. The body was put into a vault secured with a combination lock.

The assemblage of police officers, state troopers, and regular Thayer County sheriff's personnel had rapidly dissipated after the body was taken to Lincoln. A few phone calls came to the sheriff's department after the late news broadcast, but nothing was definitive. One by one, the men working the case went home to their families feeling angry, disoriented, and totally unprepared for the holiday.

With thoughts of a killer on the loose, Jack Wyant drove up to his in-laws' home outside Lincoln for Christmas Eve dinner. Cops like Wyant like to say they get used to dealing with murder. They don't, really. Especially when it's a dead kid.

When Chief Deputy Bill McPherson went home to his family in Hebron, his girls' eager, smiling faces made him think of the boy in the pajamas. He left his children in the living room and went into the kitchen. His wife held him while tears came.

Gary Young was among the last to leave the office. As he walked to his car, he heard the bells of Sacred Heart Catholic Church chime parishioners to Christmas Eve Mass. It was five minutes before midnight. He went home and watched Mass on television, and all he could think of was the boy Chuck Kleveland had found in Chester.

Sheriff Young spent all of Christmas Day in the office except for a family dinner at his sister's in Byron, eight miles from where the victim had been found. The Young clan gathered and exchanged gifts as they always had, but for Gary it was not the same. The image of the little boy haunted him.

In some ways, the celebration seemed frivolous, maybe even trivial. It certainly didn't feel right. He left after dinner and went back to the office. The day had been a blur. He knew he would be in a better frame of mind once the autopsy was done. He had to be in Lincoln first thing in the morning. The autopsy was scheduled for 9:30.

CHAPTER FOUR

On August 23, 1972, Liz and Leroy Chupp, a New Order Amish couple living at Stoll Farms in Marshallville, took Eli Stutzman in, giving him room and board in exchange for chores. When Stutzman arrived at the sizable dairy operation in hilly, northeastern Wayne County, he was a young Amishman who seemed unsure of himself, as though he had had few dealings with the outside world.

When Ed Stoll's wife, Bonnie, first saw Eli Stutzman, her heart went out to the small-framed young man. When he came to the door—his face partly shielded by a wide black felt hat—she knew instantly that he was from a low Amish group. His skin was pale, almost chalky. The blue of his eyes seemed to be the only color on his body.

She had heard that he'd had a rough time with his father, who had thrown him out and put him under the *bann* for owning a radio.

" 'You!' " Stutzman said his father had screamed at him. " 'You are out! You are no longer my son!' "

Bonnie Stoll had also heard the story of the skinned cat.

Stutzman kept unusual company for an Amishman who had just left the Order. One of his closest friends was Jim Taylor, a deputy sheriff with the Wayne County sheriff's office. Taylor and Stutzman occasionally went out for late-night "coon hunting." They never caught anything; if they had, Liz Chupp, who'd kept a diary since she was 12, would have noted it in her journal.

Another who seemed to be a close friend was Morton Bissell, the chiropractor from Brewster whom Stutzman said specialized in herb teas.

Stutzman was open and honest about his mental collapse at Mose Keim's farm. But now his story had changed from the salary increase he sought, to a story that he must have thought the New Order Amish would feel more sympathy for. He said he had been under pressure from the Swartzentrubers because he had encouraged his pupils to speak English during recess, which was strictly forbidden by the conservative Order.

He was glad to get away and start a life of his own, he said.

Stutzman was delighted when Liz Chupp helped him order non-Amish clothes—particularly underwear, since the Swartzentrubers had forbidden it because of the clothing's worldly elastic waistbands—from the Penney's catalog. On September 10, days after he got a driver's license, he bought a 1970 Oldsmobile.

On his birthday, the Chupps presented him with a birthday cake and Stutzman seemed to choke with emotion. "This is the first birthday party I have ever had," he told them.

In time, Eli Stutzman, who helped with canning, painting, and cleaning—even when he didn't have to—became a part of the Chupp family.

"We felt lucky to know him," Liz Chupp said.

When he learned that the Chupps had taken in his son, One-Hand Eli wrote a terse letter to the New Order Amish couple.

"He wrote that he was sorry we saw fit to go against the church and interfere with the *bann*. 'This is not the Amish way,' " Chupp recalled.

The New Order Amish differed in areas of the *Ordnung*.

New Order homes frequently had phones, indoor plumbing, and electricity. They sometimes used tractors in the field, yet many, like the Chupps, used a buggy instead of a car for transportation. They disagreed with the harshness of the *bann*, although they understood its purpose.

They were considered "high" or "high-class" Amish.

Even though he was settled into an *Englischer's* routine at Stoll Farms, the Amish never seemed far from Stutzman's thoughts. On the evening of October 6, 1972, he wrote to an Amish friend that he had heard about some trouble in church—as more Swartzentruber boys left the fold.

Presumably for emphasis, Stutzman underlined the last sentence, which indicated that he hoped trouble in church was a thing of the past for him—at least for the time being. His Amish friend wondered if it was a hint that Stutzman would be coming back to church.

Stutzman wrote that he'd run into a friend who had told him how many boys had left the church. "Now just what is this world coming to?" he added.

As the days passed, Stutzman, as far as the Chupps could see, remained close to God and attended the Salem Mennonite Church. His evenings were spent at church functions or attending gospel concerts. For fun, Stutzman donned his Amish clothes and went to a Halloween party.

Abe Stutzman, Eli's first cousin, left the Amish and eventually found his way to Stoll Farms as a milker. On the weekends he and Eli went to country music shows in town or out for a few beers. Others who left the Amish at that time were Chris Swartzentruber and John Yoder. All the boys were Swartzentruber Amish, but since they had grown up in different church districts there had been little, if any, contact between them. Chris Swartzentruber had learned that Stutzman was working at Stoll's. Even better, Eli Stutzman had a car.

Eli Stutzman, Lydia Stutzman, and John Yoder formed an odd romantic triangle. John was in love with Lydia; Lydia was infatuated with Eli; and Eli—well, no one really knew how he felt about either of them. When he had the opportunity, it seemed he came between Yoder and Lydia.

Lydia Stutzman, a Conservative Mennonite, had a couple of dates with Eli Stutzman, although nothing serious ever developed. Once he took her to the Kentucky Fried Chicken in Wooster and ordered a single meal for the two of them to share. Other times they just drove around the community, listening to country music and visiting friends.

John Yoder was no saint, and no one needed to tell him that. But what Eli Stutzman was telling him seemed out of line. It was hurtful to Ida Gingerich.

"I got me a real good girl—that Ida," Stutzman boasted. "She lets me do everything when we're in bed."

As he listened to Stutzman detail his sexual involvement with Ida, Yoder felt sorry for the girl. Maybe Stutzman had forced himself on her. Or maybe she really did love him. But if he had any real feeling for her, how could he treat her this way?

Yoder liked Ida. He had dated her once—and nothing like that happened between them.

With the exception of his mother and one sister, Stutzman spoke little about his family. He almost never talked about his father, but infrequent comments—derogatory asides, actually—made it clear that they did not get along.

One day while they were passing the time at Stoll's, Stutzman told Eli Byler, a close friend who had left the slightly more moderate Troyer Amish Order before taking a job at Stoll Farms, that living with his father had been a "hellish nightmare."

Stutzman said he had once put a little button with an equine image on the bridle of his favorite horse. That kind of adornment wasn't allowed, but Stutzman as a teenager was determined to test the limits of the *Ordnung*. His father discovered the decoration and became furious and a shouting match ensued, yet the young man prevailed and the button stayed where he had fastened it.

Later, Stutzman was working as a hired hand on a nearby farm when officers of the Wayne County Sheriff's Department took him into custody.

"Because of that little button, my father told the sheriff I was crazy," he said.

Byler was disgusted, yet he understood. Stutzman's father was a preacher who had to set the standards for the community and uphold the rules of Amish life. But turning his son in to the sheriff and claiming he was crazy was outrageous and extreme—even cruel. Why was it better to say that his son was insane than to have the others in the church district think his boy's behavior was a reflection on his leadership at home?

Ida Gingerich continued to write to Stutzman after he moved in with the Chupps. She loved Eli and wanted him to see that he was wrong and should come back to her and the Amish.

Susan Stutzman tried to win her son back with Amish baked goods, but it was no use.

Stutzman was examined for the draft on January 22, 1973, and cleared for conscientious-objector classification the following day. To fulfill his obligation to the government—something many Amishmen refused—Stutzman applied for a job as an orderly at Massillon City Hospital in Stark County.

"He told us he didn't look forward to working at the hospital, he preferred farm work," Leroy Chupp later said.

On Valentine's Day, 1973, Stutzman told the Chupps he planned to ask *Ruth Zook*, whom he had been dating off and on since he left the Swartzentrubers, to marry him. Zook was a slightly overweight Amish girl who seemed to find her salvation in the bed of different Amish boys, instead of church. She was gossiped about by everyone, though the rumors were outrageous and not necessarily true.

"She once had twenty-one men in one night," John Yoder recalled, although he wasn't sure where he had heard it—from Zook or one of the twenty-one men.

A month later, Stutzman said Zook had turned him down, but he continued to date her. In April, Stutzman said he was going on a date with the ward secretary at the hospital.

"We wondered if he had gotten over Ruth Zook so quickly," Liz Chupp said.

Stutzman started working the 3:00–11:00 P.M. shift at the hospital. When he came home late, he said it was because he'd had to assist a patient. One of many Amish doing CO work, Stutzman made friends with several young *Englischers*. At the hospital, few could name a harder worker or a better-liked young man than Eli Stutzman. In spite of his simple education, hospital friends felt he held his own. He was especially good with patients who needed some extra care and consolation.

At the same time, Stutzman broadened his interests. In the spring and summer he attended Cleveland Indians baseball games, visited Sea World, saw the horses race at Northfield, and went to a Charley Pride concert.

He also went out at night regularly. Usually, he said he had a date with Zook.

Rebecca Yost, a Mennonite girl, thought Stutzman was handsome; he had the deepest blue eyes she'd ever seen. He seemed so sure of himself, so full of fun. Once at a party, he put a napkin on top of his head, like a woman's droopy head covering, and wandered around the room, breaking everyone up. Some said Stutzman should have been an actor.

Later, when Yost became pregnant, she narrowed down the list of potential fathers to Stutzman and another man. Stutzman gave her half the money for an abortion. He was dutiful, but he showed no remorse for his probable role in the pregnancy.

One weekend evening Stutzman gathered up a group of old friends to see a movie in Akron. When they arrived at a club, it was obvious that they weren't going to be seeing any movies that night. Stutzman had taken them to a strip joint. Stutzman sat near the stage as a half-dozen women performed. It was clear that Stutzman was not a stranger to this kind of entertainment.

Liz Chupp called the hospital when she discovered that Stutzman hadn't slept in his bed on the night of November 1. The personnel office told her that Stutzman had clocked out at 11:30 P.M.

"I'm sorry. I should have called," a sheepish Stutzman explained when he returned at 8:45 A.M. "But I fell asleep at a friend's place."

He also shared a bit of other news. His classification had now changed and he was no longer CO. He planned to tell Ed Stoll that he was ready to return to farm work. Three days later, he was on the dairy job.

If any of his close friends doubted that Eli Stutzman had odd ideas, they became believers at a birthday party in December 1973. John Yoder was turning 23, and Stutzman showed up wearing a brown plaid jacket, jeans, zippered boots and bearing a gift that would be remembered years later by those who attended.

Yoder unwrapped the small package and revealed a box containing men's red bikini underwear. Even the outside of the box seemed X-rated to the Swartzentruber boys in attendance, who had been raised without underwear of any kind.

Stutzman cozied up to Yoder on the living-room armchair and urged him to put the bikini on, but Yoder refused. He was embarrassed and didn't know what to make of the gift.

"Maybe it would be okay to give something like that to a girl," Yoder later said, "but to a man?"

In February 1974, the Chupps, Stutzman, and his friend Chris Swartzentruber made the 3,625-mile round trip to Orlando to see Disney World and Epcot. The week after they returned, Stutzman traded his Olds' for a new '74 Gran Torino. Friends wondered where he had gotten all the money.

Abe Stutzman left Stoll Farms for a job with a silo company in Greenville, Ohio, and Stutzman followed a month later. Before leaving, he told the Chupps he had gone to see his parents and had parked his car at a neighbor's so he wouldn't cause them more embarrassment. The visit was a disaster.

"My dad told me I'm not welcome at home anymore," he said.

Stutzman lasted barely a month on the silo-building job in Greenville. He returned to Stoll Farms on July 27, 1974, complaining that his cousin and the owner of the silo company were involved with drugs.

Liz Chupp doubted his story; Abe Stutzman didn't seem like a drug user to her. "We knew Abe, he was a good man. He wasn't using drugs that we could imagine," she said.

The situation became more confused when word came up from Greenville that it was Eli Stutzman who had been using drugs and had been fired because of it. The New Order Amishwoman, who was a trusting and faithful friend, found that hard to believe, too.

In late August a new employee was hired at Stoll Farms, a former Amishman named Henry E. Miller, whom Liz Chupp felt "had as much get-up-and-go as a lazy dog." He stuck mostly to himself, but in time Stutzman befriended him.

The following months would later become a blur. Years later Liz Chupp sorted them out with the help of her diary.

On September 5, 1974, Stutzman dropped a bomb when

he told the Chupps he had ordered a buggy and planned to return to the Amish within a year. It didn't make sense. Stutzman had just spent thousands on a new car. Further, he continually spoke of the rigors of the Swartzentruber world and how happy he was that he no longer had to endure their harsh, archaic ways.

The day after his out-of-the-blue announcement, Stutzman broke his collarbone in a farm accident. He told everyone that a cow had forced him into a wall while he was milking—although no one had seen it happen.

Jim Frost used to tell people he had dreamed of being a cop from the time he was 13. The dream came true. After graduating from Orrville High, he earned a law-enforcement degree at Cuyahoga Community College, quickly followed by an elementary-education degree from Kent State. After working as a dispatcher for the state patrol in Wooster, he was hired as a police officer in Orrville in 1967. He remained on the force for six years.

Brash and bright, at 28 he was elected sheriff of Wayne County. He was a local boy who had made good. People had expected that from Frost, an impeccably neat man with dark hair parted in the middle and a thin upper lip that was barely a line between his mouth and nose. He had a lovely wife who seemed to hang on his every word. Off duty, he favored cowboy hats and boots.

Although on the surface he was perfect, there was something secretive about the man. Indeed, he once told a reporter for the Wooster *Daily Record*, "I am very careful about what I do. I like to get away and go places where people don't know me, sometimes."

As sheriff, Frost's record was exemplary. Aside from some political trouble with a fellow officer when it came time for reelection, his only mistake centered around Eli Stutzman. In late fall, the sheriff's department, eager to catch some marijuana growers, put out the word that they needed some help in making a case. They even contacted the Amish for help, which was unusual in that the Amish prefer staying away from the *Englischers'* law.

Information that the Wayne County Sheriff's Department had gathered indicated that Earl, Lester, and Levi Miller were growing substantial quantities of marijuana among their potato- and cornfields. Gossip in town had it that the Millers' beautiful new house had been paid for in cash—something unheard of in a farm community where money was as tight as a clenched fist. The Millers allegedly dried pot in their barn and packaged it for sale in the basement of their farmhouse.

The Wayne County sheriff was not about to let the Millers get away with it. An undercover sting operation seemed the perfect solution.

Throughout the late fall, Stutzman seemed more secretive and preoccupied than ever, but no one could have guessed what was going on.

Stutzman moved from the Chupps' into Walter and Maryjane Stoll's on October 20. He said he wanted to move so that he could watch television and listen to the radio. Later, the timing seemed remarkable.

On October 30, farmer and alleged pot-grower Earl Miller answered the phone; it was Eli Stutzman on the line, saying he wanted to buy some marijuana to cure his headaches. He told Miller that when he was sharing a room with Henry E. Miller at Stoll Farms he smoked some and his headaches went away. It was Henry E. Miller—no relation to the Miller brothers—who had suggested he call.

That night, Les Miller gave Stutzman a small bag of pot. Stutzman offered money, but Miller told him to forget it—the pot was as green as lawn clippings. Stutzman persisted and set some bills on the kitchen table.

From the Millers', Stutzman rendezvoused with Jim Board, a Wayne County sheriff's detective working the case with Frost. Stutzman gave Board the little bag and said one of the Millers had gone into the basement to get it.

Stutzman didn't keep any of this secret. He told Liz Chupp what he had done at the Millers' and, even more surprising, whom he had done it for.

"He said he had purchased some marijuana undercover for the sheriff's department," she recalled.

On Halloween Day, Stutzman's friend from Stoll Farms, Henry E. Miller, was interviewed by Deputy Board.

Q. Who was the sale made to last night?
A. Eli Stutzman.
Q. What kind of sale was made and for how much?
A. He bought a small bag of marijuana for twelve dollars.
Q. Did you help set up the sale?
A. Yes, Eli called me, then later came to the farm and bought it.
Q. Whose idea was it to grow and sell the marijuana?
A. I don't really know whose idea it was to grow it, but Earl did the selling.
Q. Where is the unsold marijuana now?
A. I don't know.
Q. Who hid the unsold marijuana?
A. Earl Miller.
Q. When was the last time you saw the marijuana?
A. About two weeks ago, Sunday.
Q. Where did Earl get the marijuana that he sold Eli Stutzman?
A. He went down in the basement and came back up in about five minutes with it.

Stutzman's name was not on the arrest warrant, but his connection was obvious. The warrant stated that marijuana had been purchased the night before the sheriff showed up to serve it.

"You mean that goddamn Eli Stutzman is what got you

out here?" Earl Miller said when Frost waved the warrant in his face.

"I'm not saying who it is," Frost replied.

"What do you think we're running here, a grocery store where everyone comes and shops? Stutzman was the only one here last night."

Earl told the sheriff and his deputies to go ahead and look around. "You won't find shit."

Frost read the brothers their Mirandas and took them to the county jail in Wooster. Levi was released after questioning, but Les and Earl had to spend the night in a cell. It was not a complete loss: Earl Miller was glad that he didn't have to get up at 5:00 A.M. to milk.

The following night Levi Miller drove up to Marshallville to have a little chat with Stutzman. He found Stutzman in bed in his room. Miller wasn't there for small talk, and the look on his face must have made that evident to Stutzman.

"We want to know if you did this to us," Miller said.

Stutzman shook his head but said nothing.

"We've been treating you like a friend. We want to know if you screwed us," Miller insisted, trying to keep his voice low.

Stutzman denied it. He said he didn't know what Miller was talking about. His face went red and he kept a blanket wrapped around him as though it offered some protection.

Miller didn't touch Stutzman, although he thought a little force might loosen his tongue. He left with no more information than he'd had when he arrived.

The Sunday after the Miller brothers' arrest brought an unlikely visitor to their farm: Eli Stutzman. Stutzman complained that the sheriff's department had forced him into going undercover. He said he was sorry and wished that he hadn't done it.

"He said he was going to tell the judge he had been

pressured and tricked by the sheriff's department," Levi Miller said later.

Stutzman didn't say why or how he had been coerced, and the Millers didn't ask. Levi Miller thought Stutzman's participation stemmed from his desire to join the department—if he did a good job, they'd hire him.

They get to wear uniforms and carry guns. It might be a big deal to an ex-Amishman like Stutzman, he thought.

Later, when Miller gave it more thought, it all seemed so far-fetched: *How was Stutzman forced into making the buy? What did they have on Stutzman?*

Stutzman changed his mind a day later and said he was not going to recant. Once again he was siding with the Wayne County sheriff.

When Levi Miller found out, he flipped. "When he's talking to us, he's with us. When he's talking to them, he's on their side. Eli Stutzman doesn't have a mind of his own!"

On November 2, Stutzman told the Chupps that Henry E. Miller had called to warn him to stay away from the Millers' farm. "They're out for blood," he said.

Stutzman seemed shaken by the threat. He told Abe he had been making calls to the sheriff for help. "Someone has been making death threats," he said.

Stutzman showed Ed Stoll some of the dozen hand- and typewritten notes he'd received. The message on each was the same: *"If you talk . . . we're going to get you. There's no place to hide. We're watching you closely."*

Ed Stoll called the sheriff to report the threats.

"Eli was scared . . . and he had proof they were after him," he recalled.

The writer of the notes stated that he had seen Stutzman doing various chores around the farm—things that someone had to have seen. Stutzman was frightened. "Look, he saw me unload hay . . . they are close enough to see me!" he said.

The letters were postmarked Canton, but that didn't

mean much. Even mail from Marshallville was sent to Canton to be processed.

"Eli said he had been talking to the sheriff's department and they had just put him under protective custody. He was a witness in a drug case and the accused pushers were trying to force him to back down," Ed Stoll recalled.

A few times Stutzman took Stoll into the barn and showed him things that had been moved or disturbed—proof that something was up. "The pushers did this," Stutzman said. "I'm telling you, they're out to get me."

"You're just spooked," Stoll offered, trying to calm Stutzman. Deep down, the dairy farmer was also a bit worried.

November 19, 1974

Ed Stoll spent all day hauling corn from a barn to a storage building on the other side of the dairy. Stoll left Stutzman in the barn doing chores just after 5:00 P.M., when he took the last load.

The final load took about an hour, instead of the usual half hour. Stoll returned at dusk and found that the barn had been ransacked—bags scattered, hay bales knocked askew, feed bags spilled, and, more horrifying, blood splashed everywhere. It looked as though a dozen chickens had been slaughtered by a blind man. Gruesome arcs of blood stained the walls.

Stoll found Stutzman at the end of the barn, lying in a puddle of blood and surrounded by bloodied rocks.

"What took you so long?" Stutzman muttered weakly, blood dripping from his arms. His blue eyes were glassy.

"What happened?" Stoll asked as he hurried to Stutzman's side.

"Two guys jumped me and stabbed me. . . . I tried to fight them off. . . ."

In shock, Stoll ran to the house, cursing the Wayne County sheriff. Eli had as much as told them that this would happen.

"They are out to get me," he had said.

Abe was babysitting the Chupps' little girl, Marie, when Stoll ran into the house to call the emergency squad and the sheriff. By the time he made it back to the barn, Stutzman was on a stretcher. The color was drained from his face. Abe was sure that Stutzman was going to die.

For the second time in nine months, Sheriff Frost was on the scene, looking for evidence around Stoll Farms. Liz Chupp noted in her diary that Sheriff Frost had been out on January 29, investigating the theft of some hay bales from one of the neighboring farms.

Eli Stutzman was admitted to Dunlap Memorial Hospital, where he remained for five days.

By nightfall, a strange and frightening thing came to light. Before his attack, Stutzman said he had seen a strange car with out-of-state plates—West Virginia, he thought—driving up and down the road near the farm. Later, when he was in the barn, someone hiding in the hayloft threw a rock, hitting him in the head but not knocking him down. A second later, another man jumped from behind and cut him with a knife. Stutzman said that in the struggle he had stabbed one of his attackers with a pitchfork, but they had overpowered him.

Stutzman lost so much blood that he nearly died. Many said it was a miracle that Ed Stoll happened to be there to find him before it was too late.

The focus of the incident was immediately on the sheriff's department and not on Stutzman, the poor victim of their botched investigation. Ed Stoll, for one, was incensed and let the sheriff know about it.

"This man was coming to you for help. He told you someone was after him. You were supposed to protect him. You let this happen."

Rumors were confused and rampant. The story that emerged was that the sheriff's department had told Stutzman to buy the marijuana and had assured him that they would not go after the Millers for at least a week. Instead, within a few hours of the drug deal, the sheriff's department was at the Millers' farm with a warrant.

"That's how the Millers knew it was me," Stutzman told friends.

When Abe went to see his cousin at the hospital, he felt like Eli's big, protective brother.

Sheriff Frost, looking puffed up and important, stood in the hallway outside Stutzman's room.

"You aren't doing enough to catch the guys who hurt Eli!" Abe said, raising his voice. "You are just using him and throwing him out to the wolves. You're doing a lousy job of protecting your people."

Frost said nothing.

Some things didn't seem to fit. Those who saw the cuts on Stutzman's arms noticed that the wounds were clean, not jagged, as might be expected from a violent attack. Deep needle marks also marked his thin, white arms.

Chores were done and things were quiet at the Miller farm. Earl Miller noticed headlights flash in the lane at about 8:00 P.M. Sheriff Frost was back, this time poking around the Millers' cars, touching the hoods to see if the engines were still warm.

"Where have you guys been out to all night?" the sheriff asked.

They had just finished milking and were settling in for the night. "What's going on?" Levi Miller asked.

"We've got an attempted homicide. We're not fooling around here. Eli Stutzman was found up at Stoll's bleeding to death." Frost added that Stutzman had received death threats and was sure the Millers were behind it.

"So, like I said, where have you been tonight?" he asked again.

The Chupps saw Eli Stutzman at the hospital the day after the stabbing. Like a weakened, crumpled ball of a person,

Stutzman said two tall, long-haired men had attacked him. "They drove a Dodge Swinger," he added.

Liz Chupp asked about the bandages on Stutzman's wrists.

"I put up my arms to fend them off and they sliced me," Stutzman explained.

The following day, Mose Keim—the man who had nursed Stutzman through his nervous breakdown in 1972—called the Chupps with a vague warning. "Don't be too sure that what Eli Stutzman is saying to you is the truth. There were some strange things that went on when he lived with me," he said. "A lot of what he told me was not the truth."

Next, word came to Stoll's that Stutzman had had a mental collapse and was tied to the bed by hospital personnel. Strong tranquilizers were being administered to try to calm him. The ordeal had been too much. Liz Chupp said a prayer.

On November 22, when the truth came out, it shook everyone who had been sucked into Stutzman's carefully orchestrated tale of betrayal and brutality. Sheriff Frost went out to Stoll Farms, carrying the stack of threatening letters.

"Eli did this to himself," Frost said, seeming satisfied in cracking a difficult case. "He even wrote the letters."

Ed Stoll found the scenario hard to believe, but Frost compared the letters to some other writings made by Stutzman. The typed letters also matched a typewriter found in Stutzman's bedroom at Maryjane and Walter Stoll's house.

What kind of a man would do something like this? Ed thought at the time.

Beyond Stutzman's confession, there was more proof that it had all been a set-up. Investigators recovered a single-edge razor blade from the barn. In addition, they found a large IV needle used for cows. The needle had human blood on it.

Stoll felt used. The whole thing made him sick. "While

I was hauling my last load, Eli was running around the barn messing it up and squirting his own blood on the walls," he said.

It was true that Stutzman had worked in a hospital and boasted about his expansive medical knowledge. He had given plenty of IVs and he knew which vein would give the best show of blood. He had foreshadowed all of it by sending the notes to himself.

One thing Stutzman hadn't planned on was Ed Stoll taking such a long time with the last haul. The delay almost cost him his life.

"What took you so long?" Stutzman had said when Stoll found him on the floor. Now, to Stoll, the statement had a whole new meaning.

The Millers were never brought to trial because the prosecution's star witness was mentally disturbed—exactly as Stutzman had planned.

Before he was discharged, Stutzman sent for Rebecca Yost and asked her if she would come out to Stoll Farms and take care of him when he was released. Yost agreed.

On November 28, the Orrville *Courier* published a cryptic item on page 13:

> To clarify rumors in the Marshallville area, Wayne County Sheriff James M. Frost released information concerning an alleged aggravated assault Tuesday, November 19, at 6:45 P.M. The incident occurred in a barn on Co. Rd. 95 (Coal Bank Road) in Baughman Township. It is rumored that a 24-year-old man was assaulted and that the incident was drug related, Sheriff Frost stated.
>
> An intensive investigation by the sheriff's department revealed that the injuries to the male were self-inflicted. "There was no assault," Frost said. "This is a completely false complaint and was confirmed by the victim that it was his own doing," he continued.

> The sheriff's department normally does not release information on incidents which involve self-inflicted wounds. However, the release was made because of the department's concern about rumors in the Marshallville Community.

That statement was only part of the story. The truth of a former Amishman with mental problems being used as an undercover agent by the Wayne County sheriff's office would have been scandalous.

If Stutzman was ashamed or bothered by the whole business, it didn't seem so to others. From the day he came home he acted as though nothing had happened.

Maryjane Stoll felt sorry for the mixed-up young man and tried to get Stutzman to see a Christian counselor, but he refused, saying he wanted no part of any religion. Ed Stoll arranged for Stutzman to see a psychiatrist at the Wayne County Mental Health Department in Wooster.

Shortly after Stutzman was released from Dunlap, his father made the considerable buggy trip out to Marshallville. Stutzman told the Stolls to get rid of the old man, which they did. If One-Hand Eli had planned to bring his son home, he was mistaken.

Over the next few weeks Stutzman seemed to make progress, but Maryjane Stoll worried when he sometimes left for a day or two without saying where he was going. On occasion the time away stretched to several days.

Stutzman received an inordinate amount of mail at this time. Several letters—sometimes stacks of letters—arrived daily. Maryjane Stoll put them in his desk. Once, she found some things so disturbing and so strange that she didn't even know exactly what they were. She did know, however, that they had to do with sex.

She told her son Ed about the discovery. From her description he figured that his mother had run across a cache of vibrators and ticklers.

But that was not all.

Later, Mrs. Stoll found several magazines tucked under

Stutzman's mattress. The publications shocked and puzzled her. They contained graphic pictures of men having sex with each other. She burned them.

She never told anyone other than her son. Later, she might have wished she had.

On February 10, 1975, Ed Stoll fired Stutzman. Stutzman told the Chupps he had seen Stoll steal some parts from a farm equipment store and he had been fired because Stoll didn't want him around.

Of course, it was a lie.

CHAPTER FIVE

A straight shot north from Hebron via U.S. 81, U.S. 80 is Nebraska's main east-west route, stretching from Omaha to Scottsbluff. Gary Young punched the pedal on his '85 Crown Victoria patrol car, en route to the autopsy in Lincoln. Pushing 70 mph is easy in Nebraska, even for drivers who don't have the advantage of a badge. Highways are long, wide, and traffic-free.

Young was headed east on 80 to Lincoln to confirm what had seemed unequivocal back at the funeral home in Hebron: the little boy had been beaten and strangled before he was dumped in the field. He parked and found his way to the basement of Lincoln General Hospital.

The Clinical Evaluation Room—investigators called it simply the "autopsy room"—is a surprisingly bright and cheerful room at the end of a long, white corridor. By the time Young arrived, a crowd had assembled: Jack Wyant and a team of state patrol investigators, a forensic odontologist, a University of Nebraska anthropologist, and coroner's physician John Porterfield and his assistants Bill Cassel and Sue Carlson. The group's objective was twofold: first, to determine cause of death; second, to collect evidence that might assist in the identification process.

At nearly six feet six inches tall, the gray-haired Dr. Porterfield, age 58, was an imposing figure, yet his demeanor was far from intimidating. His voice carried the trace of an accent he had developed growing up in the hills of Missouri, although Nebraska had been his home for better than twenty years.

The evidence seal was cut, and the small, pajama-clad corpse was lifted from the 40-degree cooler where it had been slowly warmed. After a day and a half in the cooler, the dead boy had defrosted to the extent that his limbs were slightly flexible and his body tissues were no longer rock-hard.

In the bright light, it was obvious that the child's hair was blond, not dark brown or black as it had seemed in the field. The freckles on his face were also more distinct. The skin on the boy's hands looked wrinkled and wet, as though he had stayed in a bathtub too long.

The marks on the neck and head were darker and even more horrifying than they had seemed when Gary Young first set eyes on the body.

"Poor kid," someone said softly.

Wyant took a series of pictures, and over the course of the hour-long procedure, the staccato strobe of the investigator's camera never let up.

Gary Young stayed a bit to the side of the group and drew a deep breath. Young had observed other autopsies, so he knew the rules: stay out of the way—and listen to the doctor as he does the grisly job. Wyant took a decidedly converse approach. He liked to be in the thick of it. Wyant was a participant, not an observer.

The basics emerged quickly. With bone development as a primary guideline, Dr. Porterfield fixed the age of the victim at approximately 10 years.

"What would a 10-year-old be doing wearing pajamas with feet?" Wyant wondered aloud.

Sue Carlson stretched a tape measure the length of the boy and noted 131 centimeters (51.5 inches) for his height. The corpse's weight was estimated at fifty to sixty pounds. Porterfield told the investigators that the boy appeared to have been in good health and was well nourished and clean.

Wyant speculated that perhaps the boy's mother had

abandoned him because she could no longer provide for him. Desperate circumstances might have forced the mother into doing the unthinkable.

Credible or not, at least it was a story and it was better than nothing. *Sometimes a story leads to the truth*, Wyant thought.

Next, the doctor and his assistants measured and documented the animal activity that had left the child without a nose, right cheek, and upper lip.

"Field mice," Wyant offered, not one to hold back a comment or a question. Porterfield's staff knew to expect that from Wyant. There were investigators from the state patrol who never said a word during an autopsy. Then there was Jack Wyant, always at elbow's length, looking for the answer, voicing his opinion. Porterfield had learned that he was worth listening to.

Often he was right on the money.

The only possible identifying marks discovered on the corpse were a circular scar the size of a cigarette burn on the boy's right forearm and a small tan birthmark on the inside right calf.

The doctor moved on in a quick and mechanical manner. Finger-, palm-, and footprints were inked onto paper. Full-body X rays were taken. Finally, fingernail scrapings were taken from each digit and put into an envelope for analysis at the crime lab.

Bill Cassel made an incision through the child's chest and Sheriff Young could see that the body was still partially frozen. Ice crystals caught the light.

One by one, vital organs were removed, examined, and weighed. Porterfield noted some congestion in the lungs, which were still partially frozen. The stomach, he said, was contracted and empty. Fecal matter in the boy's large bowel indicated that at the time of his death, it had been at least two hours since he had eaten—although it could have been up to ten or more hours. The heart and kidneys were healthy and unremarkable.

Piece by piece, bit by bit, the little boy from Chester

was dismantled as though his body were a jigsaw puzzle.

Dr. Porterfield determined that the boy's anus was slightly dilated, leading Young and Wyant immediately to theorize that the boy had been sexually abused before he had been dumped in Thayer County. Yet, the doctor saw no signs of trauma in or around the anus. A swab was taken to test for the presence of semen.

Wyant was sure it would come back positive.

As far as determining who the child was, even his teeth offered no clues. Although he could have used some dental work, the dead boy had never had any fillings. It was unlikely that there were any records that might provide his identity. Dr. Sprague, the odontologist, made notes, and dental X rays were taken, but nothing was expected to come from them.

Wyant considered the prints from the child's feet the best chance they had for identification. Such prints are frequently standard hospital procedure with newborns, so he optimistically assumed they existed somewhere. Of course, it was the "somewhere" that posed the problem.

Dr. Porterfield examined the boy's battered and flesh-eroded head. The investigators in Hebron had thought the large and grotesque bruises on the child's forehead were caused by a savage beating.

"No damage to the skull," the doctor intoned, recording his findings on a chart.

This remark stunned the sheriff. He asked about the bruises, and the doctor indicated that they were likely the result of the cold temperature. In places where little or no fat exists between bone and skin, skin discolors rapidly.

Gary Young's opinion was that if the boy hadn't been beaten to death, strangulation had to be the answer. The pathologists pursued the option and looked for hemorrhaging in the neck muscles. The boy's head was propped up and a few minutes passed while they waited for blood to drain from the neck into the body. This procedure yielded no clues. Dr. Porterfield examined the child's hyoid bone—the small, wishbone-shaped bone on the neck that is frequently broken or cracked in cases of strangulation. It was intact. However, as he told Wyant and Young, that bone is extremely flexible in children.

Again, Gary Young was incredulous. If he hadn't been beaten or strangled, how in the hell had the child died?

No one knew the answer. Dr. Porterfield had virtually nothing to go on. Not being one to speculate as some of his contemporaries readily did, he preferred to let the evidence speak for itself.

But there isn't any evidence this time, Young thought.

Dr. Porterfield fixed the child's death at thirty-six hours before Kleveland's discovery.

The doctor then ruled that the cause of death could not be determined. He could see the look of disappointment and frustration on Young's face.

The mouth and rectal swabs, blood and hair samples, fingernail scrapings, and the sleeper were gathered and sent to the state patrol crime lab.

Young and Wyant left Lincoln General feeling cheated and defeated by the doctor's ruling. In his heart, the sheriff knew that a child just doesn't die without a reason. He had to go back to his county and tell his shaken community that they had no more information about the boy than they had on Christmas Eve. No name. No cause.

All they knew were some things that *hadn't* happened to the boy. He hadn't been beaten or strangled. Suffocation was still a possibility, but it was difficult to determine.

Gut feelings told the investigators that they were dealing with a murder. Circumstances pointed that way, but they needed physical evidence.

Porterfield was relatively new to the coroner's physician post, having held the spot only since the fall, but he was by no means inexperienced. He had been doing that kind of work for better than two decades.

But what had he missed? Had a clue passed him by?

Normal procedure calls for interment right after the autopsy. However, troubled by the mysterious lack of evidence, Wyant insisted that embalming and burial be delayed. He kept thinking—or hoping—that something might come up and another doctor could take a look at the body and provide an answer.

County Attorney Dan Werner agreed and arrangements were made to store the body at the funeral home in Hebron, although they did not have a cooler like the one in Lincoln and alternatives needed to be considered.

When released later, the initial findings from the crime lab revealed no semen captured by the mouth or rectal swabs, presumably eliminating the possibility of the crime being sexual in nature. The child's blood type was A, with a positive Rh factor. Finally, the lab indicated that the hairs found on the sleeper and on the T-shirt did not come from the dead child.

The last hope for bona fide clues in the baffling case seemed to be the trace-evidence analysis. Wyant stayed in Lincoln, and Young drove back to Hebron to continue the investigation. With fingers crossed, both waited for the results to come back from the lab. Everything was riding on a blue sleeper, a T-shirt, and some fingernail scrapings.

CHAPTER SIX

If the bloody incident in the barn at Stoll Farms had been a shock, Eli Stutzman's return to the Amish bordered on the unbelievable. Not a soul had seen it coming.

Stutzman despised and mocked the *Ordnung*'s arbitrary restrictions. "It's fine to hire a driver to ride in the car, but against the rules to actually drive a car," he once told a friend. "One bishop sets the rules deciding you can't have anything newer than 1900, the next bishop says 1910. They have an imaginary line and they keep moving it."

Stutzman scarcely—if at all—discussed his plans with Eli Byler when the two made a vacation trip to Florida in March 1975. When Byler asked about his plans, Stutzman said his brother Johnny had told him that Ida had been waiting for him when he was in Marshallville. Stutzman wanted to do right by Ida.

On March 18, Stutzman spent three hours visiting Liz and Leroy Chupp in Holmesville. He said he planned to sell his car and get rid of his *Englische* clothes.

That spring, Stutzman moved to *Elam Bontrager*'s farm. The choice was an odd one for a man who professed a rededication to the Amish world and life. Bontrager was a man many Amish considered of dubious character. They claimed Bontrager wore Amish clothes to give the appearance of honesty and integrity. He used the black hat, they said, to make money. He also drank too much and, worse, traded race horses. Many figured it was the horses that had lured Stutzman to Bontrager's farm.

If Eli Stutzman wanted to rejoin us, why did he move in with someone like Bontrager? they wondered.

In order to return to the church, Stutzman had to give members of the community the impression that he was going to live the Amish life. Promises were only words. To the Amish, to believe was to see. There were signs that Stutzman's intent was false: some said his hair was still too short, too modern; it was taking him too long to grow it to Swartzentruber length. However, he was given the benefit of the doubt. He was a man with mental problems. Maybe he would do better once he came back to the church.

Stutzman's family—especially his father—felt tremendous relief when the young man, submissive and repenting, asked his brother Andy to take him to see Bishop Abe Yoder for confession. He said he was ready to return to church membership.

Ida Gingerich, who at the time was working at her cousin Gideon Gingerich's farm, thought Stutzman's return was an answer to years of prayer.

Others weren't so sure. Mose Keim, for one, was skeptical when he heard that Stutzman had come back to the Amish essentially to marry Ida Gingerich.

"I don't believe Eli is mentally fit to marry anyone," Keim told his wife. The Amishwoman agreed.

It was summer when Stutzman made his confession in church at the home of Enos and Lovina Swartzentruber of Apple Creek. The confession was kept private. Later, when pieces of the puzzle were put into place, none of the Amish spoke about what had been said in Enos and Lovina's home. It was between God, the church, and Eli Stutzman.

When the Amish hitched their buggies and departed that afternoon, none knew the truth about the man they had welcomed back. Nothing was known about the drugs he used, the abortion he was party to, and the sex toys Maryjane Stoll had found in his bedroom.

The Amish told themselves that Eli Stutzman was going to live a clean life. "At least that is what we hoped," Dan Gingerich later said.

Their hope was wasted.

On August 31, 1975, Stutzman called Eli Byler for a ride to see the Chupps, who lived too far for Stutzman to take a buggy. Byler understood. He knew that once an Amishman had experienced the freedom of coming and going as he pleased, it was difficult, if not impossible, to go back to the old ways. It was especially hard to give up car travel.

Stutzman was concerned that the Amish would see him get into Byler's car, so he arranged to be picked up under a bridge near Bontrager's farm.

Keeping secrets and covering tracks in the Amish community was not easy. But Stutzman was good at it. He had been for years.

Despite all his problems, Stutzman was hired by the school board to teach at the Cherry Ridge School. Surely the school board would have hired another teacher had someone been available. Then again, the Amish are among the most forgiving of people.

Later, when defensiveness came into play, a member of the district said: "Eli was a good teacher—a better teacher than a farmer."

Before the end of harvest, Eli Stutzman, Ida Gingerich, and church leaders prepared for the couple to be "published"—or announced to be married. The wedding was planned for October 6, but something went wrong and the publishing was postponed.

Some wondered if there was another woman.

Although Stutzman had professed his devotion to Ida—

it was, after all, the reason he told Byler he had come back to the Amish—he continued to be seen with Rebecca Yost. Ida, of course, had no idea about any of that. If she had known, the Amishwoman would not have stood for such an obvious slap in the face—no matter how much she loved Stutzman.

Figuring out the relationship between Stutzman and Rebecca Yost was easy for the Amish neighbors who saw the young *Englische* woman and her Amish boyfriend.

"Maybe both of them were getting what they wanted? I'll scratch your back if you scratch mine?" one of the Yosts' Amish neighbors said later of the relationship.

As October approached and the Amish farmers finished the backbreaking work of the harvest, news of trouble with Eli Stutzman and Ida Gingerich's blood tests emerged.

"I think maybe it is God's will. Maybe He is telling me it isn't a good idea to marry Eli," Ida told her sister Lydia when the test failed a second time.

Naive about medicine, none of the Amish knew the purpose of the tests. The Amish assumed it had something to do with the physical makeup of the person and problems the children might develop if born from certain parents. They did not wish to tamper with God's will—it was His decision who would bear children and what their health would be.

Early one October morning, Joe Slabaugh stopped by the Cherry Ridge School to visit with Stutzman before his pupils arrived for class. Stutzman confided that the wedding had been delayed because of failed blood tests. However, he didn't seem worried. The delay was only a temporary setback.

"If things go as planned, I will soon have a helper," Stutzman said, referring to his new wife. Somehow he knew that the tests would be approved. He didn't explain what his plan was.

Shortly after Rebecca Yost drove Stutzman to the Chupps' on November 8, he abruptly dropped her. Neighbors near her family's Apple Creek farm heard it was because Stutzman told people he had gotten Ida Gingerich pregnant and had to marry her. Such things happened, even among the Amish. With Stutzman's wild background, no one suspected it was a lie.

At the Gingerich farm, his plan became clear. It was his old standby, in fact. He suggested perpetrating a fraud. Stutzman told Ida that he knew a doctor who could take the blood and "fix it" so that they could get married. It seemed dishonest and Ida refused to go along with it.

A short time later, the desperate groom rushed into the Gingerich home waving a piece of paper and bursting with incredible and exciting news. "We have passed the test!" he told them. "I drank some herb tea my doctor prescribed and it fixed my blood!"

Amos Gingerich, a bit more savvy than some, pulled Stutzman aside and asked him if his story was true. Stutzman looked the man in the eye and told him that indeed it was.

"You were not being tested for syphilis?" Gingerich asked.

"Oh, no. My blood was just not right, but now it is," he explained.

The answer fell flat, but there was little Gingerich felt he could do. He wondered where Eli Stutzman had gotten syphilis. Gingerich knew that Ohio tested only for venereal disease.

Eli Byler also doubted the herbal tea story. He figured that Stutzman must have gotten some help through one of his contacts in the hospital where he had worked as an orderly. Maybe someone had pushed the papers through as a favor, he thought.

Abe Stutzman heard that it was One-Hand Eli himself who had persuaded a doctor to sign off on the blood tests. Abe thought the problem was some kind of genetic incompatibility, and he doubted that the elder Stutzman would let anything stand in the way of getting his son married to a good Amish girl. Marriage would fix the rebel for good.

The old man doesn't want to lose his grip on Eli, Abe thought.

Later, when Amishman Henry Yoder asked Stutzman where he could find the doctor who had prescribed the herb tea, Stutzman said the doctor had moved away. "I don't know where he's gone to," he said with a shrug.

December 25, 1975

Many thought that Eli Stutzman and Ida Gingerich's wedding day would never arrive. Barely a year before, Stutzman's close friends would have laughed at the idea of their friend returning to Old Order ways.

Preparations had begun weeks before the wedding day. Lizzie Gingerich and her children had spent many days cleaning and preparing the house. Since there had been so many false starts with this wedding, the family was glad to see it finally come to pass.

A week before the wedding, Stutzman went to see the deacon to request a *Zeugniss*—the required letter from the church indicating that he was in good standing as a member. The deacon presented Stutzman's intention to Bishop Abe Yoder, whose signature was also necessary. Although Bishop Yoder signed it, one can only speculate how willingly he did so. The bishop had seen Stutzman in and out of the church, in and out of trouble.

But all of that was in the past now. Many thanked God for watching over Stutzman and helping him to mend his ways. He was a man who always needed help.

"In some ways," Ida told her sister Lydia before the wedding, "I think Eli is a weak man. I know that I can be a help to him."

Final arrangements for the ceremony took place in the darkness the morning of the wedding. Stutzman arrived early to behead two dozen chickens for the wedding meal, a tradition of the more conservative groups.

Mary Miller, a friend of Ida's, didn't think the bride seemed happy. She wondered if Ida had heard the same thing she had: Eli Stutzman still had his driver's license.

A hymn from the *Ausbund* was indicated by page number and the ceremony began. The couple wore black, although the bride's cap was white. Stutzman wore his hat during the ceremony.

Bishop Yoder asked the couple if they had remained pure before their marriage. Both said they had.

For a wedding gift, Amos Gingerich gave the couple several beautiful pieces of oak furniture he had made himself: a bedroom set, a dry sink, and a hutch. Although Amish don't allow themselves pride—pride leads to vanity—Gingerich knew he had done a good job with the carpentry. The honey-toned wood glowed.

Other gifts were displayed at the Gingerich home. However, most of the gifts would be received after the wedding, during the time the new couple would spend visiting relatives and friends before setting up house on Elam Bontrager's farm.

A few weeks later, Ida learned she was pregnant.

Eli Stutzman really was trapped, now.

David Amstutz, age 45, had business dealings with many of the Amish, including Stutzman's good friend and landlord, Elam Bontrager.

It was through his connection with Bontrager that Amstutz met Eli Stutzman. Bontrager warned Amstutz that Stutzman was obsessed with sex. "Eli's hard all the time," Bontrager said.

Still, Amstutz was unprepared for what happened one night when driving Stutzman back to Bontrager's farm.

"I'll give you twenty dollars if you let me give you a blow job," Stutzman said.

Amstutz pushed him away.

"Twenty-five dollars," Stutzman persevered.

Amstutz told him he was crazy, but Stutzman increased his offer to sixty dollars, forcing Amstutz to kick him out of his cab. Both had been drinking a bit, but Amstutz, like

Stutzman, had a wife at home. He wasn't interested in having sex with a man. The idea was revolting. Stutzman obviously had a taste for it—enough that he was willing to pay someone for it.

In what all of the Amish hoped was a better situation, the newlyweds moved from Bontrager's to Ida's cousin Gideon Gingerich's fifty-eight acre farm.

From the beginning, however, there was trouble. Ida confided to Gideon that her husband often left her alone, causing her to wonder and worry where he went at night.

Englische friends kept a safe distance from the newly married Amishman. They didn't want to cause him trouble with church leaders, who continued to watch for a slip-up.

Late one August afternoon, John and Lydia Yoder expected to find Eli Stutzman at home. Ida, now in the final weeks of pregnancy, greeted the Yoders warmly.

"Where's your husband?" John Yoder asked in Deutsch.

Ida hesitated slightly, but, perhaps because she knew Yoder from years ago, she made no excuses. "He's gone. He went away somewhere. I don't know where he is or when he will be back," she said.

Ida is used to being left alone, Yoder thought.

"I don't know what I would do if I needed to go to Bill-Barb's to have my baby. I wouldn't know where to find Eli," Ida said.

Bill-Barb was Barbara Hostetler, an Old Order Amish midwife who had helped deliver hundreds of Amish babies in her Mount Eaton home. Her husband's name was Bill, hence her nickname, Bill-Barb.

Perhaps thinking that she had said too much against her husband, Ida changed the subject. While she was one who could be direct and speak up, she knew an Amishwoman's place was in support of her husband. It was written so in the Bible.

On September 7, Stutzman arranged for a driver to take his wife to Bill-Barb's, where Dr. Lehman was waiting.

After an easy delivery, Dr. Lehman handed Ida Gingerich her firstborn, a son with blue eyes and downy blond hair. She named him Daniel, after her brother, although Eli also had a brother named Daniel. The baby's middle initial was E., for his father's name.

Stutzman surprised Dr. Lehman with two requests. He wanted Danny to have the complete series of baby vaccinations—something that less than five percent of the Swartzentrubers requested. Even more unusual, Stutzman wanted his son circumcised. Dr. Lehman had never had such a request from a Swartzentruber. When word got around, some Amish figured that Stutzman wanted the circumcision because he had been *Englische* for a while and kept some ideas from the modern world.

With a new baby, it was time for a farm of the family's own. Stutzman announced that he had struck a deal with Chris Swartzentruber's brother Daniel. The Amishman owned a ninety-five-acre farm on Sand Hill near Dalton and wanted $72,500 for it. On a handshake, the Stutzmans moved in. It was spring and Danny was 6 months old.

At the same time, Ida learned she was pregnant. Again, she hoped a child would fill the gap in the marriage. She was due by Thanksgiving.

To Eli Stutzman, another baby would not have been seen as a joy, but another impediment to his freedom. Another nail in the coffin.

As the air warmed with spring, problems at the Stutzman farm moved beyond silence and pretense. The trouble was no surprise to anyone. During late winter, word had gotten around the Amish that there were once again problems with Eli Stutzman. He continued trading race horses with Elam Bontrager—and others whom no one in the community knew. In addition, Stutzman's running around continued to take its toll on Ida's generally happy nature.

To see her daughter in such obvious pain was heartbreaking to Lizzie Gingerich. But she was only an observer of their marriage. It was not her place to come between a daughter and her life's companion. Her husband felt the same way. It was God who had joined Ida and Eli. Their marriage was in His hands.

Yet, while Ida was unhappy, Stutzman often put on a good front, acting the concerned and loving husband. He once asked Amos Gingerich if he would build some steps to the well, because Ida's heart was giving her problems. It was the first time Gingerich had heard of the condition.

Buds had burst, leaving tree branches looking as though they had been dipped into a million shades of green, the day Lizzie and Dan Gingerich went out to Moser Road for a visit. Baby Daniel reminded all of the older Gingeriches of the children who had come before him. With no baby pictures, of course, there were no means of direct comparison.

When it was time to leave, Dan Gingerich, age 15, went to hitch the buggy. He was still working on the reins when Ida and Lizzie, who held the swaddled Danny close to her cloaked breast, stood on the front porch to say goodbye.

Something was wrong with his sister and Dan strained to hear. Ida's voice cut through a choppy stream of tears.

"To cry like that was not like Ida. She was always the happy one," he later said.

"Eli's not doing very good," Ida said. "I don't know what to do about him. I try everything I can think of, yet nothing seems to work."

Lizzie moved closer to comfort her daughter, but it brought only more sobs. "Time will make it better, and prayer will help," she offered.

Ida shook her head helplessly. "But I can't handle him," she said.

Lizzie didn't know how to help. Finally, Ida dropped the essence of the problem. Her words had an edge to them; it was obvious that it was excruciating for her to speak them. "*I don't think Eli loves me*," she said.

Lizzie did not press her daughter for details and none were offered. On the ride back to the Gingerich farm, mother and son agonized over what had transpired. Dan wondered if it could be true that Stutzman didn't love his sister.

"If Eli didn't love Ida, why did he marry her?" he later asked.

The first week of May 1977, Eli and Ida Stutzman met with loan officer Richard Armstrong in the offices of Federal Land Bank in Wooster. FLB had tendered hundreds of loans for the Amish. Not surprisingly, Amish were seen as excellent credit risks. They usually put a lot of money down and had flawless credit histories unencumbered by charge cards and time payment plans. Further, the Amish standard of living was low—$10,000 a year was enough for a family of ten. A high income wasn't required to qualify for a loan.

To Armstrong, who had grown up in Wayne County farm country with Amish neighbors, the Stutzmans were a nondescript, simple Amish couple—a study in black, white, and blue.

Ida acquiesced to her husband's authority, offering few comments while the loan amount of $55,000 was discussed. Stutzman said he needed the loan to pay the mortgage contract on his farm with the previous owner. A typed note signed by Daniel and Sarah Swartzentruber deeding the property to the Stutzmans was produced to verify the intention.

Such a document would likely raise the eyebrows of any lender unfamiliar with the ways of the Amish. Who but the Amish, ever trustworthy as they were, would deed property and transfer it to another party without a mortgage to back it up? In essence, Eli Stutzman already owned the farm. If Stutzman had wanted to ignore his obligation to pay the Swartzentrubers, he could have.

This was not unusual, given that the Amish insist on keeping their affairs to themselves as they maintain their separation from the modern world. Why record business concerns with the court? Of course, there was a good reason, and trouble resulted when parties shunned modern legal procedures. If a borrower defaulted on a bank loan, the Amishman who sold the farm and was still receiving payments was left out in the cold. If their loan had not been recorded, they were the last in line when the proceeds from the sale of a property were dispersed.

If Armstrong noticed that Eli Stutzman was different from the other Amishmen he had met over the years, it was something about his manner. Eli Stutzman was a gentler, almost soft-spoken man. He was not as authoritarian as other Amishmen. He seemed less dominant, less than iron-handed. Perhaps Armstrong unconsciously picked up on the vocal nuances and accent of an Amishman who had spent time with *Englischers* after jumping the fence. Around town, some called those who left the Order "jerked-over" Amish.

Stutzman hauled out a shoebox and went over recent farm records. Ordinarily, FLB's procedure called for the review of three years of records, but since Stutzman had lived only a few months on the farm, the practice was waived. Regardless of the productivity of Stutzman's farm, the land would appreciate and the lender would have no difficulty getting its money out of it in the event of foreclosure.

If there was any trouble at home, Armstrong didn't catch any hint of it. If the couple did not seem especially close or warm toward each other, there was an easy enough explanation: they were low Amish.

Since Ida's name was on the deed prepared by Dan Swartzentruber's attorney, her presence and signature were essential for the execution of the loan. If Eli Stutzman wanted money, he needed Ida.

"Somebody is lying low for Eli Stutzman."

When Amos Gingerich first heard the vague rumor, he

didn't know what to make of it. His son-in-law was in some kind of trouble. The second time he heard it, he acted. He went to see his son-in-law at the Cherry Ridge School to warn him of the rampant rumors that somebody was out to get him.

"I'm not worried," Stutzman told his father-in-law.

Shortly after meeting with the Stutzmans, loan officer Armstrong made the trip to Dalton for the appraisal. It was an average property, especially suited to Amish horse farming—rolling hills, a creek, and some wooded acreage. The property contrasted with the type of land sought by *Englische* farmers, who prefer a treeless terrain and level land for cultivation. Amish prefer a mix, particularly wooded areas for hunting and lumber. They "buzz" some of their trees and mill lumber for outbuildings and houses.

The Stutzman property was fine. With escalating land values in Wayne County during the 1970s, it was apparent to Armstrong that FLB wouldn't be at risk. Besides—and this never escaped the loan officer's mind—this was a loan to an Amishman. Those were usually risk-free, although Armstrong had heard of cases in which Amish with perfect credit and payment history became delinquent with their final payment. This seemed out of character until he learned the reason. Amish families who acquire *Englische* farms keep the electrical power until the farm is paid off—a requirement of the loan. Some use the electricity, although it is forbidden by the *Ordnung*. For those who do, electricity can be as addictive as a drug. In those few such cases, the church intervenes and pays off the loan. Power lines are severed, and meters are smashed with hammers or rocks.

On July 7, the loan was approved. A check for $55,000 was cut for the Stutzmans, essentially the borrowers, when Daniel Swartzentruber was the seller. The procedure was a bit peculiar. Usually, money is dispersed to the seller. At that time, however, loan money did not have to be used for the reason stated on the loan application.

Dan Swartzentruber continued to receive regular payments. He was unaware that the Stutzmans had arranged the loan. If there was another purpose for the loan money, it was unknown to Ida Stutzman. She would never have signed her name to a document that was misrepresented.

The reason stated for the loan, however, was as clear as the sunny summer morning when they picked up the check: "Pay mortgage contract on the farm with the previous owner."

Years later, Armstrong wondered if giving the money directly to the Stutzmans was such a good idea. "It was pretty much a standard practice then," he said.

Swartzentruber Amish girl Anna Hershberger was only a teenager when she died of cancer the first week of July 1977. Ida and Danny Stutzman went alone to the funeral.

Her family talked about it that night: "Ida didn't seem herself. Something was on her mind. It wasn't right that Eli didn't come with her and the baby."

Anna's funeral was to be the last time many saw Ida. Later, the Gingeriches were left to wonder if there was a reason why Stutzman hadn't shown up. "Maybe it was that he couldn't face us," Dan Gingerich said.

July 11, 1977

The sky over Wayne County was dark and stormy as Abe Stutzman's little brother—also named Eli—who had been hired that summer to work on Eli and Ida's farm, hoisted himself up a ladder to pick apples for his cousin Ida. Eli Stutzman had business to take care of and had taken the buggy into town earlier in the day. Ida spent most of her time inside doing the woman's chores she had been raised to do.

Jagged streaks of lightning and the echo of approaching thunder broke the stillness of the late afternoon, and livestock shifted nervously as they hunkered under trees and sought safety inside the barn. The boy picked a few more apples, then retreated into the two-story farmhouse.

Farmers are used to such storms. *Englische* houses and barns are topped with the sharp spires of lightning rods. The Amish refuse to use rods, just as they refuse insurance. Such precautions interfere with God's will.

Baby Daniel, now 10 months old, slept in the crib. As required by the *Ordnung*, he wore a loose, white dressing gown and a cap on his head. At age two he would wear pants, and the cap would become a hat—a miniature of his father's.

Lightning continued to split the air like an ax crashing on an anvil, hard and with frightening fury. Sue Snavely, the Stutzmans' neighbor across the road, had forgotten how much she hated electrical storms. Only a few months before, the Snavelys had returned to Ohio after years away with the military. She waited for her accountant husband, Howard, to come home from his job at Republic Steel in Massillon.

Eli Stutzman guided the buggy up the muddy dirt driveway. With no windshield or storm front—forbidden by the Swartzentrubers because they resemble cars—his chest and bearded face had been soaked by the downpour. A tarp wrapped around his waist, however, kept his legs dry from the spray of the trotting horse. *Englischers* and those who left the Amish ridiculed the inconsistencies of the religion that allowed a plastic tarp as protection but not a plastic storm front.

Stutzman dropped the reins and excitedly called the hired boy to come to the barn. "Lightning hit the barn. I saw it hit from up the hill," he told the boy in Deutsch.

The boy hurried into the barn where Stutzman had motioned him. The barn, which abutted the road, was dark and cool. The boy watched as the man searched the roof line for the strike. Neither spoke. Finally Stutzman pointed to a timber high above them. "It hit there. See it?" he asked.

The boy focused his sharp eyes but saw nothing. He looked harder.

"It is there!" Stutzman commanded. A small chip on the peak of the inside of the barn caught the boy's attention, but if it had been there days before or even years before, he would never be able to say.

He nodded to his boss as he watched Stutzman climb a ladder up the granary. Stutzman called down that he had found where the lightning had traveled. He needed water, and the hired boy retrieved some from the well. From the floor, fifteen feet below, the boy watched Stutzman pour the water high on the corn-laden wooden granary. He still couldn't see what had alarmed Stutzman.

Amos and Lizzie Gingerich spent most of the day away from their Fredericksburg home visiting in Holmes County. The day had been uneventful, although there had been a good soaking and a thunder shower in the late afternoon.

Amos read from the newspaper and remarked on another member of the community who had passed away. Lizzie shook her head sadly and made a quick count of the number who had died in the recent months, more than a dozen. The last one from their district had been Anna Hershberger. Lizzie was saddened by all the deaths, yet thankful that her household had been spared.

"Where in the world is the next one going to be?" she asked.

There is no blackness like night in Wayne County. The lack of cities and the mist in the air create an impossible darkness that seizes everything. Ancient oak trees are shrouded in black. At night, there is nothing for anyone to see.

July 11 was a night some would later try to forget, and others would struggle with all they possessed to recall anything they could.

Tim Blosser, an attorney from Dalton who had met

Stutzman at the little sawmill across Moser Road in April, stopped by a little after 6:00 P.M. to help the Amish family prepare a will. When Blosser arrived, Stutzman told him of the lightning and, along with Ida, showed him a spot on the floor of the upper level of the barn that had been doused. Blosser saw where a window had been blown out and Stutzman told him that the lightning had done it that afternoon. Oddly, Blosser didn't see any shards of glass, but he did see some water-soaked embers among the hay on the floor—proof that a fire had smoldered there.

The hired boy hadn't seen any embers when Stutzman commanded him to get a bucket of water earlier in the evening.

"His wife seemed very happy that Eli had been able to extinguish the fire before it burned down their barn," Blosser later said.

If the attorney ever doubted Stutzman's honesty, it was only briefly when the Amishman said he had seen the lightning strike. The attorney thought such timing was remarkable.

Inside, while Ida rocked the baby in her arms, the men discussed the terms of the will Stutzman said he wanted. If Ida died, everything would go to her husband; in the event of his death, the estate was hers. If they should die simultaneously, Danny would get the estate. Amos Gingerich was named executor. The will would need to be typed and witnessed before becoming a valid legal document.

Blosser later recalled that he left the farm around 8:30 P.M.

As far as the hired boy knew, the rest of the evening passed quietly. The ticking of a wind-up mantel clock marked the hours. With the weak glow of kerosene lamps the only source of light, and with cows in need of milking before sunrise, the Amish retire early. That night was no different. Ida, Eli, and Danny slept in the small bedroom on the main floor. Before bed, Ida sang old German songs and cuddled her son. The curtains were drawn, but the windows were open to allow a cool breeze to circulate in the still, hot house.

Young Eli went to bed upstairs around 9:00 P.M.

If anything out of the ordinary happened between bedtime and the hours before midnight, no one was old enough to remember it—or lived to tell about it.

At midnight, the hired boy stirred. His eyes were drawn to the window, where a brightness shone. He went to the window. Below, he saw the gold and red of flames and a black plume rising from the barn. Dressing as he went, he raced down the stairs and called for Eli and Ida to wake. Light from the fire illuminated their room; curtains fluttered from the rush of hot air. Danny was asleep in his crib, but the Stutzmans were gone.

Why didn't Eli or Ida wake me with news of the blaze? the boy wondered. *Where are they? Why didn't they call for me to help?*

On the front porch, the boy ran into Stutzman. The Amishman's dilated pupils made his eyes seem black, only rimmed in blue.

"Go to Harley Gerber's! Have him call the fire department! Hurry!"

Young Eli ran past the south side of the barn, away from the flaming north side, his bare feet pressing the surface of the now-dry dirt driveway. Over his shoulder he saw Stutzman pull farm machinery from the barn. A box wagon and tools had already been moved.

As he turned the corner where Moser Road meets the driveway, the boy saw Ida, motionless on her back. Her eyes were closed. She was very still and only a step or two from the barn.

"Ida! Ida!" he called as he knelt beside her. "What is wrong? Ida, wake up!"

He touched her, but she didn't budge. Although most of the color was washed from her face, her left cheek and her left hand were pink from the heat. He could see that she was too hot, too close to the fire.

Thinking that he'd better tell Eli, the boy ran back and screamed that Ida was hurt.

Stutzman just shook his head.

He already knew.

"Go to Harley Gerber's now! Get the doctor, too!" Stutzman instructed.

"He seemed mad that I had not done what he told me," the boy later said.

Young Eli did an about-face. Passing Ida again, he wondered why Stutzman hadn't mentioned that his wife had been hurt in the first place. Why was Eli Stutzman more concerned about the farm equipment than his wife?

The crashing of splintering, burning timbers and the snap of crunch-dry straw riddled the night like gunfire. The frightened boy ran as fast as he could.

Ida needed help . . . *now!*

Across Moser Road, the sound of the fire ricocheted through an open window and woke Sue Snavely. She woke Howard, who pulled on a pair of pants and told his wife to call the fire department. As they ran downstairs, the noise woke two of their children.

The screen door slammed behind Howard Snavely as he ran across Moser Road toward the Amish family's front door. He assumed that the Stutzmans were unaware of the fire, since he saw no one outside. Just as Snavely reached the porch, Stutzman came around from the other side of the barn. Had the Amishman heard Snavely calling for them to wake up? Had he seen him run across the road? The timing seemed lucky and remarkable.

Stutzman was a fright. The bearded Amishman was frantic, disheveled, hysterical. He waved for Snavely to come. Snavely sensed that something bad had happened—something more terrible than the burning barn.

"We've got to get my wife out! She's trapped in the barn!" Stutzman cried out.

Adrenaline surged through Snavely's body as he followed Stutzman to the milk house on the south side of the barn. Amish dairy farmers used the little rooms, neatly lined in clay tiles, to keep milk cool and clean until haulers came to get it.

"We've got to get her out!" Stutzman screamed again.

Snavely noticed some stainless steel three-gallon buckets and a milk strainer in a heap outside the door. Panting for breath, Stutzman swung the door open, and Snavely saw Ida, dressed in her Amish clothes—including her small, starched black scarf—lying on her back. Her feet were next to the door, her head farther inside. The woman's pregnancy was obvious beneath her dark coat.

Stutzman muttered something about a heart attack as he lifted his wife up by her underarms. Snavely carried the woman's feet and legs. Her uncradled head hung down. The men carried her across the road to the night pasture.

By then Stutzman had calmed considerably. He was quiet, and his body no longer shook in frightened spasms. On impulse, Howard Snavely reached for Ida's wrist; he detected no pulse. Stutzman, who knew mouth-to-mouth resuscitation from his work at the hospital, did nothing.

Kidron fire chief Mel Wyss saw flames rising off the peaked roof of the barn as his fire truck topped Sand Hill. With the speed and efficiency of any big-city fire department, firemen started pumping water from a 1,500-gallon tanker—the small department's only such unit.

Bystanders arrived. A few Amish from nearby farms came by buggy, but most were *Englischers* coming by car. Elam Bontrager was on the scene, although later no one from the fire department could remember talking with him.

Snavely frantically called for Wyss to come across the road to the pasture. "We have an injury! Mrs. Stutzman is hurt!" he called.

When the fire chief looked at the woman, he knew she was dead.

Wyss, who as a Sugarcreek Township trustee knew

Stutzman well enough to recognize him on the street, approached the Amishman to gather information for his report. Stutzman was nervous and excited, and no one could blame him for that. Yet, his reaction seemed incomplete. He was oblivious to the condition of his wife.

Wyss noted a few milk pails in the vicinity of the milk-house doorway. The heat was too intense for him to enter, but it was clear and smoke-free.

Stutzman looked on, blinking at the yellow light of the blaze. He told Wyss that his wife had awakened him in the middle of the night and told him the barn was on fire.

"I told her to go call the fire department and she left for help. When I came around the barn and went into the milk house, I found her inside. She was lying inside on her back. She must have had a heart attack because of the smoke," he said.

The Kidron Rescue Squad arrived then. Of course, they were too late to save Ida Stutzman, but they still had a role: the Amish would ride to the hospital in their van.

Howard Snavely watched as the paramedics tried to revive Ida. After a few minutes, a young paramedic said softly: "She's gone."

Stutzman didn't hear the fatal prognosis. He was busy discussing with one of the firefighters the lightning bolt that he said had caused the blaze. His mind seemed to be on things other than his wife and the unborn child she carried.

Stutzman's seeming indifference to his wife's death was considered by some a normal reaction to the most horrible of circumstances. It was a case of shock, some would later say.

Some things were missed or went unnoticed. It was dark, investigators' eyes alternating between the dark of night and the bright light of the fire. It was hard to see certain things. No one gave the marks on Ida's face and mouth any consideration.

Sue Snavely, who didn't know that Ida had died, worried about the Stutzmans, although she barely knew them. The soft-spoken Amishman had been over to use their telephone a few times. Amish were hard to get to know. She wondered if their livestock had gotten out of the barn in time.

Returning from the Gerbers' place, young Eli ran up Moser Road and saw that Ida had been carried to the pasture on the other side of the road. Through the fence he saw her lifeless body. She looked exactly as she had when he'd first seen her slumped outside the milk house on the south side of the barn.

The boy figured that the paramedics had carried her across the road. He didn't know that it was Stutzman and Howard Snavely who had done it—*after* the boy had gone for help. He didn't know that it was after he ran to Gerbers' that a terrified Stutzman had screamed to Howard Snavely to help him get his wife out of the barn.

Neighbors took Danny to Elam Bontrager's home, a mile or so down the road. David Amstutz was dispatched to Fredericksburg to summon the Gingeriches to the hospital.

The flames threatened a shed, but firefighters were able to save it. The farmhouse was undamaged. The cherry tree that was so beautiful and smelled so sweet in the spring was scorched and wilted.

It took Wayne County sheriff's deputy Phil Carr ten minutes to get to Moser Road from Kidron, where he had been on patrol. He arrived at the Stutzmans' farm at 12:40 A.M. He was alone, although he knew from the radio dispatcher that Sheriff Frost had been alerted and was on his way. Carr, who had been with the department two years, was briefed by Mel Wyss. He conducted no interviews of his own. At the time, it didn't seem necessary.

As it had been obvious to Wyss, Carr knew that Mrs. Stutzman was dead. He observed the firefighting effort, which now focused on ensuring that the flames did not ignite the house or any outbuildings. Carr measured the distances from the barn to where the woman had been set that night. She now lay 103 feet west of the barn in the night pasture. Prior to that, according to where Stutzman said he had put her, Ida Stutzman had lain 56 feet from the barn.

Stutzman, shaken and disoriented, initially estimated that he had put her 30 feet from the barn. Such a discrepancy was understandable given the stress of the fire.

Wyss instructed Wes Hofstetter and another squadman to take Ida Stutzman to Dunlap Memorial Hospital. With as much grace as possible, the woman was put on a stretcher and covered to the neck with a sheet. Her husband didn't ask about her and gave no indication that he knew she was dead.

Although Stutzman's reaction seemed inappropriate, he was an Amishman. Amish don't show emotion.

But his wife is dead, Hofstetter thought.

The strobe of the lights flashed on the eight-mile drive to the hospital. No sirens wailed on the deserted roadway—no need for them at that time of morning. Stutzman sat in the front next to Hofstetter. Another squadman rode in back with Ida.

Sheriff Jim Frost arrived at the fire scene and moved on, staying at the farm only a few minutes. He left word that he was on his way to the hospital to interview Stutzman.

Another who showed up at the fire was Tim Blosser, the attorney who had been at the Stutzman house just before the fire. "You aren't going to believe this," he told one of the deputies at the scene. "I was here earlier in the evening helping the Stutzmans write their will!"

Dr. J. T. Questel was a slight man with white hair and a penchant for belt buckles big enough to cut him in two. One buckle was the symbol of the NRA, and the Wayne County coroner made no bones about his affiliation. He was a doctor, a farmer, and a man who hated crime and criminals with an unwavering passion. As coroner, he had seen too often what criminals can do.

Questel grew up on the Ohio–West Virginia border. After serving in the Air Force, he went to medical school at Ohio State, where he met his wife. Helen Questel was from Wooster, which was reason enough for them to settle in the Wayne County seat.

The couple made many friends in Wooster, including Jim Frost. "We both consider Jim to be like a son," Questel later said.

Nearly every coroner has a case that haunts him long after he makes his ruling. Reasons vary. Sometimes a piece of evidence doesn't fit. Maybe a statement doesn't jive with the crime scene. When Dr. Questel was called in on the death of an Amishwoman from Dalton, he came face to face with one that would haunt him for the rest of his life.

The fire was still smoldering when the coroner arrived at the scene. Dr. Questel was not required to inspect every death scene reported in the county. The woman was Amish, pregnant, and dead due to a violent situation—a raging barn fire. It warranted a look.

Deputy Carr briefed him on the Amishman's tragic story—his wife had died while rescuing milk cans. Stutzman indicated that his wife had a weak heart, the legacy of a bout with rheumatic fever when she was a teenager. She was unconscious when he found her and carried her outside the doorway of the milk house. Because it was too hot, he moved her again. Questel studied Deputy Carr's sketches of the scene.

The idea of a pregnant woman hauling milk cans from a burning barn in the middle of the night did not strike him as odd. Like other *Englischers* in Wayne County, Questel had always considered the Amish industrious and thrifty. If they could save something from ruin, they would.

No one—not Sheriff Frost or any investigator—told the coroner about Stutzman's history of violence and deception in Marshallville. No one mentioned that setups had been the Amishman's forte.

His headlights crudely slashed the darkness as David Amstutz drove up the drive to the Gingerich farmhouse. The car door slammed and Daniel was the first to answer the sound. He knew that a predawn visit could only mean bad news.

"There's been a fire at Eli's. Ida is dead and Eli is in critical condition," Amstutz called into an open window.

The confused and shocked Gingeriches asked about Danny, but Amstutz had no information on the baby.

Lizzie and Amos hurried out the door for a ride to the hospital. All they could do now was pray. God had chosen this time to take their daughter. Their son-in-law was near death. And no one seemed to know about the little boy.

Where was Danny? Was he safe? they wondered.

At Sand Hill, the Stutzman barn had been reduced to black ashes. Ida Stutzman was now only a memory, and her husband and son were alone. She was pronounced DOA, although it was clear to everyone that she had died hours earlier than 1:47 A.M., which was the time recorded for her death.

The Gingeriches searched for answers to the tragedy. Of course, there needn't be a reason beyond the ultimate truth: God had chosen her. On the way to the hospital, Amos told Lizzie of the time he had gone to Cherry Ridge School to warn Stutzman that somebody was out to get him. Amos speculated that the fire was a result of a vendetta.

At the hospital, they met with Stutzman's parents and Elam Bontrager. Stutzman sat on a chair, seeming disoriented and shaken—of course, no one would have expected anything else.

"Ida woke me," Stutzman told them.

"Why did she wake you? What woke her?" Amos Gingerich asked.

"She heard something pop. Something exploded in the barn." Stutzman added that he and Ida had run to get help. Later, when she didn't return, he had gone to the milk house looking for her. "When I walked in a little, I kicked at something—it was her feet," he said.

Stutzman said that Ida's heart had failed. She had probably had a heart attack in the milk house. It had been too much work for her, and too much smoke.

The explosion that Stutzman said his wife had heard puzzled the Amish. Some wondered if Stutzman might have had some gasoline or kerosene cans in the barn. But young Eli, the hired hand, couldn't recall seeing any gas cans in the barn. The same was true for kerosene. "Why would he have kerosene in the barn?" young Eli later said. "It wouldn't make sense—it was stored in the shed."

In the basement morgue at Dunlap Memorial Hospital, the Wayne County coroner donned a striped white smock and began examining Ida Stutzman's body. J. T. Questel drew blood for carbon monoxide analysis, and, since Sheriff Frost had said that the Stutzmans had Valium in the house, blood would be sent to a lab in Cleveland to screen for traces of the drug.

Most of the woman's burns were on her left side, the side closer to the barn. Ida's left breast was exposed; Questel noted that her nipple had been burned to a parchmentlike hardness. Some of her chest had blistered like blow-torched house paint. The left side of her face was also severely burned—not from flames, Questel thought, but from the intense indirect heat of the fire. The left side of her abdomen was parched enough to cause slippage of some skin. Some burns were rimmed in white, then red.

Ida Stutzman's nylon head scarf had melted in a number of places; there the fabric had soldered itself to her neck.

Her navy-colored jacket was also scorched. A more direct flame would have ignited it.

When Dr. Questel loosened her dress he could see that the dead woman had suffered extensive burns underneath her clothing—which was not unusual given the extreme heat. Her cotton dress would have provided no protection. Questel noticed mud smears on her dress, which was not unusual since the milk house was a cool, wet place. Additionally, he noted that her right fingers had been scorched to a deep red, as was the base of her palm. The center of her palm, however, was still white and unburned. Her hand was frozen in a loose clench. It appeared to him that she had grabbed something extremely hot. But that was only a guess.

Long scratches cut across her forehead from the bridge of her nose to just above her left eyebrow. A bloody laceration from the corner of her mouth was also noted in his report. Blood seeped over her gums and between her teeth.

The coroner's series of Polaroids were the only photographs ever taken of Ida, as her Order strictly forbade photography.

If she hadn't been Amish—*Amish don't commit murder*—or if Frost had given Questel the critical background on Stutzman's life in Marshallville, he might have looked at Ida's death a little differently. Later, when he reviewed the case, some things proved puzzling.

Ida's left breast had been exposed, which would suggest that she hadn't had time to pin her dress when she ran out of the house to fight the fire. However, if her husband had told her to go to the neighbors', as he had stated to Wyss and Frost, the modest Amishwoman undoubtedly would have pinned it before leaving.

Her clenched hand was also a concern. The burns covered the entire fingers—not just the obvious contact surfaces. The natural response to grabbing something hot is to let go quickly. But her fingers had been roasted.

Most disturbing were the cut and scratches on her face and mouth. Ida Stutzman could have fallen and caused the cut. In fact, Stutzman had said that his wife had fallen in the milk house. But he was specific: *She was on her back.* How could she harm her mouth and scratch her forehead falling backward? In addition, the mud on the front of her dress was insignificant enough to suggest that she had not fallen or doubled over and then rolled onto her back.

The mouth is a very vulnerable and tender part of the human body. It was more likely that she had been struck by something or, in the most chilling scenario, beaten. When a boxer bleeds from a blow it usually is one planted on the mouth, or above the eyes.

The blood in her mouth and on her face was red enough to indicate to the coroner that the woman had been alive when the trauma that caused the cut occurred. As oxygen is depleted from blood, the color edges from cherry red toward dark brown.

None of this, however, was noted, filed, or discussed at the time.

A coroner's job is to interpret the condition of the body and determine the cause of death. Inexplicably, the sheriff's department did not report Stutzman's history of violence. The information was glaring in its omission.

Deputy Phil Carr did not know, nor did fire chief Mel Wyss. But Sheriff Frost knew it. It is unlikely that the events at Stoll Farms—the phony notes, the self-mutilation, the lies—would have slipped his mind.

Dr. Questel ruled death by natural causes, primarily cardiac arrest—the cause Stutzman had suggested when he told them that she had a weak heart from rheumatic fever. Additionally, the doctor noted that the stress of the burning barn had been too much for her and had contributed to her death.

The body was released to Wayne Spidell of DesVoines-Spidell Funeral Home in Mount Eaton.

After Frost left the hospital, where he had interviewed Stutzman, he went back to his office in the Wayne County

Justice Center and shut his door. Whether he had notes from the interview or typed the entry from memory is unclear. In either case, no one who knew him would question Frost's accuracy. Additionally, those who read his reports knew Jim Frost was reliable in his recollections and unsurpassed in his details. Others envied his ability—Frost could build a case on paper and each word he used was a steel nail.

On Case C950-77 he wrote:

> Eli related to me that this evening while he was coming home from Dalton, about late supper time, he thought he saw a flash of lightning strike his barn. He checked the barn and could not find any sign of fire. He then ate, milked the cows, and when he was done milking the cows, he went up to get some straw and found a spot on the top of the granary, which stores wheat, that appeared to have been burned by a lightning strike. Because of this, approximately every half-hour he checked the area on the west side of the barn, but never found any other evidence of fire. His wife, Ida, woke him in the night and stated, "There looks like there is a fire in the west end of the barn." They both ran outside and he asked her to call the fire department. She went around one side of the barn and yelled something back to him, which he could not understand. He tried to get things out of the barn; however, the fire was too hot and intense. As he went around the side of the milk house, he saw many items out by the side of the road that had been in the milk house. Upon checking in the milk house, he found his wife with her feet toward the door, lying in somewhat of a curled position. Blocking the door was a large milk vat filled with items from the milk house. He indicates the milk house was full of smoke, but there was no fire and no intense heat. He dragged his wife out of the

> milk house to the other side of the road with her left side toward the fire. He attempted CPR and mouth-to-mouth resuscitation, but was unable to revive her. After help began arriving, he noticed that the heat from the fire was apparently burning her face and arms. He got help to drag her further into a field away from the fire.

Rather cryptically, at the end of the report, Frost had typed a postscript. It sat on the page by itself, either for emphasis or as an afterthought: "Eli Stutzman sees Dr. Kahn and gets prescriptions for Valium from time to time."

Dr. Kahn was with the Wayne County Mental Health Department. It seemed unlikely that the events in Marshallville had slipped Jim Frost's mind, since he knew that Stutzman was seeing a psychiatrist.

The sheriff filed the report and did nothing to further the investigation of Ida Stutzman's death. Apparently, he felt that such an undertaking was unwarranted—at least that's what those close to him believed. None could ignore that the woman was of the Amish. Her husband was an Amishman, a farmer, a schoolteacher. Why should his story be doubted?

This file was put away and would be archived after the coroner's report made the cause of death official. Ida Stutzman's is the skinniest file in Wayne County. She was faceless in life, anonymous in death.

Eli Stutzman went to the Gingerich home at 8:00 A.M., disheveled and seemingly grief-stricken. Other than the pain on his face, there wasn't a mark on his face or body. When Edna Gingerich saw Stutzman she was surprised that he appeared so well.

"We thanked God that Eli and Danny had been spared," Ida's sister said later.

As though Stutzman was searching for meaning or justification, he gathered the Gingeriches and told them: "It was such a funny thing that we had just finalized our will. God had sent me up to Dalton to take care of the will just before He called Ida home. He was watching out for me and Danny. Our Lord, the one who died for us on the cross, works miracles."

It was true that Ida had been called home to God, but they wanted to know what had happened.

"Ida woke me at midnight, telling me the barn was on fire," Stutzman said. "We both went out. I went to the upper part of the barn. I told her to call the fire department at the neighbors'. She asked if she could save some things out of the milk house first. I told her she could, but hurry. When I was done in upper barn, I found her. She was in the milk house trying to put the vats out and she was overcome by smoke. Her feet were under the vats."

Further, Stutzman told them he had tried to resuscitate her for twenty or thirty minutes. None of them would have tampered with God's plan, but they could excuse Stutzman for his lapse. They knew he had learned CPR when he worked at Massillon City Hospital.

Stutzman said he had dragged his wife out of the milk house to the night pasture across the road—by himself—and had put her gently on the grass and tried to awaken her to life, but he had failed.

If anything didn't ring absolutely true to the Gingeriches it was the vats that Stutzman said Ida had attempted to carry from the milk house. As the steel vats were used as washing tubs for milk pails, it didn't seem likely that Ida would have bothered to carry them out. And if she had, wouldn't she have fallen *forward*—not backward as she had been found?

Waid Spidell had the perfect manner for a mortician—thoughtful, warm, and exceedingly sympathetic. All of these attributes served him well as a funeral director, the euphemism of his profession.

It was a few hours before daylight when Spidell arrived at Dunlap Memorial. The information was sketchy: A low-

Amish woman had died in a barn fire near Dalton. She was a member of the Swartzentruber Order. If Spidell had any qualms about going, it was because the dead woman was a Swartzentruber, which meant a home embalming.

A corpse in a darkened room with no running water was a gruesome nightmare for the mortician. Gravity drained the blood, and old-fashioned pumps were used to force preservatives into the body. The Swartzentrubers did not want their dead taken to a worldly funeral parlor. They were the only group that still asked for home embalming.

Stutzman, his parents, and in-laws were waiting for Spidell at the hospital. Their black attire accentuated the somber nature of the meeting. Even though the men had been in the room for some time, they still wore their hats. Spidell gathered information about the survivors for the newspaper.

Amos Gingerich wanted the embalming—"embamming," the Amish called it—done at home, but Stutzman spoke up. "Given the circumstances, you would probably like to do the embamming at the funeral home, wouldn't you?" he asked.

Spidell was surprised but grateful. He assumed that Stutzman set aside the tradition because the fire had damaged too much of the Stutzman home as well as the barn.

No makeup was applied to Ida Stutzman's face at the funeral home. Even the gash in her mouth was not concealed. Spidell dressed her in some clothes her relatives had furnished.

YOUNG AMISH MOTHER DIES
IN DALTON AREA BARN FIRE

The Tuesday edition of the Wooster *Daily Record* carried a front-page article and photograph of the fire. The article gave Stutzman's story of what had happened, including the lightning strike and his periodic checks to see if a fire had resulted. Ida Stutzman had gone into the milk house and was trying to recover milk cans when she was overcome.

The Amish assumed that if it was in the newspaper, it was true.

Dr. Elton Lehman was one of the first to be troubled over the reports of Ida Stutzman's tragic death. Lehman knew the Stutzmans as well as any non-Amish. The story was a bit unusual in that barn fires occurred frequently in the county, yet he couldn't remember anyone else having died in one. But it was not the unprecedented nature of the woman's death that would bother him in the end.

Dr. Lehman, who doubled his duty to the rural community as assistant coroner, made a call to Questel to discuss business, including the barn fire. During the conversation, the coroner said he had named heart attack as the cause of the 26-year-old woman's death. The statement brought a sharp response.

"Heart attack?" Dr. Lehman was incredulous.

"That's what killed her. It wasn't the smoke or fire," Questel said, not knowing that the woman's heart had been as strong as his own.

Dr. Lehman asked how the coroner had come up with that ruling.

"The husband told us," Questel answered. "Ida Stutzman had a weak heart. Always had. She collapsed in the milk house because of her heart condition."

Lehman was stunned. The case had been closed. Notes from the coroner and Polaroids of Ida's dead face had been locked up in the coroner's file cabinet. Everything neatly put away.

Eli told them Ida had a bad heart. It was Eli's word, Lehman thought. But he knew that Ida Stutzman hadn't had a weak heart. He had been her doctor since she was 16.

Why did Stutzman tell that story? he wondered. It didn't feel right, but he gave the Amishman the benefit of the doubt. Perhaps someone had gotten his story wrong.

Dr. Lehman, like Questel and the others, was unaware of Stutzman's history of deceit and violence.

Of course Sheriff Jim Frost was all too familiar with it, and after the barn fire he even talked about it. At a social gathering at his home, Frost told a friend he was skeptical about Stutzman's story of the fire. He said he felt Ida had been murdered.

"He [Frost] told me that he thought Stutzman had beaten his wife—possibly with a rock—and planned to put her in the fire to destroy the evidence. He was frustrated he couldn't find enough to pin it on him. There wasn't enough to go on," the Wayne County man said.

CHAPTER SEVEN

It was as if Chuck Kleveland had unwittingly tossed a stone into a very still pond the morning he found the dead boy. Rings of fear moved from Chester to Hebron to Deshler and crossed over state boundaries into Kansas and Missouri. Before the end of Christmas week, the paranoia was felt deeply and bitterly far from the ditch where the body had been dumped.

With nothing tangible to go on—no identity and no cause of death—from day one the investigation boomeranged from lead to disappointing lead, alternately giving Sheriff Young and Investigator Wyant hope and then mercilessly yanking it away.

Although the autopsy at Lincoln General failed to determine the cause of death, Young and Wyant considered the case a homicide. So what if Dr. Porterfield had been unable to come up with the cause of the death? County Attorney Dan Werner was unsatisfied and ordered another opinion. A pathologist from Scottsbluff, Nebraska, was called in.

The state patrol commissioned an artist from Washington County, Kansas, to sketch a composite of what the boy might have looked like before the rodents disfigured his face. The artist struggled with the nose—there was no telling if it had been long or short, broad or turned up. The two front teeth also posed a challenge. Was the child buck-toothed, or did his upper lip cover his front teeth? Several versions were tried and finally one was selected to represent what some locals now called the Christmas Child.

Flyers headlined WANTED: YOUR HELP IN IDENTIFYING THIS CHILD, were printed and circulated across Nebraska, then beyond. The results of such efforts were astonishing, if only for the sheer number of responses. In the first week of the investigation, more than 150 leads flooded Young's office.

However, one by one, the leads evaporated into nothing. The crazy lady at Ortman's was checked out and eliminated as the dead child's mother.

In the days after Christmas, Young's quiet little office on Third and Olive Streets had turned into a tornado of turmoil. Missing-children's agencies from coast to coast had been contacted and immediately inundated Thayer County authorities with possible names of the victim.

Young and his deputies were moved by the often sketchy stories that came with each child's name. So many kids were missing, and so many had been lost forever. Last seen: two years ago, four years, seven years.

Photographs also arrived by the fistful. Young reviewed dozens of snapshots of little boys who resembled the freckle-faced, gap-toothed victim. He also received many bearing no similarities—black, Mexican, and even some missing little girls.

Deputy Bill McPherson contacted Chuck Kleveland at Foote's Truckstop to determine who had been on duty that day. The two men who had worked the shift in question had no recollection of anyone getting off the bus. It was another dead end.

A woman called the sheriff after seeing the sketch in the local media. She thought the child looked like a boy she knew up in Havre, Montana. The woman told Young that there were several children in the family and that they'd had a great deal of contact with social services. Some of the children were learning-disabled.

"No kid wears a sleeper when they are this boy's age. Must be retarded or something."

It seemed farfetched, but Young followed up on the Montana lead. After a few phone calls, he learned that all of the children in the family were fine. It was another zero.

A grandmother from Van Nuys, California, got wind of the story and made a frantic call to the sheriff. She thought the little boy looked like her missing grandson, although she hadn't seen the boy in four years. Young took down the information, and after a series of phone calls he tracked down the child, now a sixth-grader.

Other leads offered cruel and false hope.

A photo and a report of a child believed to be the Chester boy was received by the sheriff. The boy's father was an escapee from a prison in West Virginia and rumor had it that he had returned to southeast Nebraska. The family had disappeared from their home in Humboldt, Nebraska, more than one hundred miles east of Hebron. The photograph showed a gap-toothed boy of the right age and coloring. He even had freckles. Young brightened. This one was bizarre, but it might be the one.

The state patrol was summoned to assist. A sneak attack seemed like the best plan. If the father had killed the boy, he'd surely run if he caught wind of the law's pursuit. Yet, word leaked through town that an escaped criminal had killed the boy.

Four patrol cars streaked down the highway to where they had learned the boy's family was living in Washington County, Kansas.

A knock on the front door of the tiny frame house and the great hope was gone in a second. Hearts sank when the escapee produced the boy in the photograph.

"Is this you?" an investigator asked the child, holding out a color portrait.

"Yeah," the kid answered. "I still have that shirt. I'll go upstairs and get it!" As he ran upstairs, he was eliminated from the potential victim list. The escapee was arrested and returned to West Virginia.

On December 31, the weekly Hebron *Journal Register* published its first article on the Chester boy. The headline of the lead article read:

FOUL PLAY STILL SUSPECTED IN DEATH OF YOUTH FOUND BY COUNTY ROAD NEAR CHESTER LAST WEEK
Humbolt, Nebr., Boy Found Alive in Kansas

Phone lines at the sheriff's office jammed so frequently that an additional line was brought in so the county attorney could reach Gary Young. In addition, when the volume of information required it—which was nearly daily during the first couple of weeks following Kleveland's discovery—meetings of the sheriff's department and state patrol investigators were held in the basement.

At the end of one bitter January day; Gary Young set up a conference call with Dan Werner, Investigator Wyant, and Dr. Blevins, the medical examiner from Scottsbluff.

Blevins told Young that he believed the boy had died from rapid freezing. Due to analysis of the material provided by Dr. Porterfield and the staff at Lincoln General, Blevins did not consider hypothermia or gradual freezing to have been involved.

Blevins told them that in some northern states, bodies are found after people have wandered off into frozen woods, by rescuers following a trail of clothing. As the victim's body temperature drops, they feel euphoric, then hot as though they are burning up. Clothing is shed in the snow.

The boy could have frozen to death, but it would have been rapidly.

Blevins said the dilated anus was another sign of the rapid freezing of the child's body. He called the marks on the boy's neck and forehead "freezer burns." It was possible, he said, that the boy was alive but unconscious when placed in the ditch.

Young shook his head. None of this made any sense.

There were no signs of violence on the boy's body. Judging by the condition of his body—clean and well nourished—he had to have been cared for and loved. How had he died? If the boy had been alive, then why was he put outside in the cold?

The implication of that question chilled him deeper than the blast of cold he'd felt in that field in Chester a couple of weeks before: *the boy had been alive when he was set outside.*

Something Blevins said about hypothermia played repeatedly in Wyant's mind: *"It's an easy way to die."*

The robin's-egg-blue sleeper was another long shot and this time the FBI stepped in to help. The brand was Toddlecare, manufactured by Regal. The sleeper was so new it still had the plastic thread used to secure the tags on the collar. An FBI investigator tried to link the sleeper's garment production unit number to the location of shipment. With that information, the scope of the investigation could be narrowed considerably.

On the morning of January 10, an FBI agent called Sheriff Young with a classic good news/bad news message. The good news was that the sleeper had been manufactured for K-Mart and that the particular garment production unit number had been shipped to one of two K-Mart distribution centers in July 1985. It had probably been on the sales floor in August.

"The bad news?" Young asked, not really wishing to hear any.

"The bad news," the agent went on, "is that one of the distribution centers services stores east of the Mississippi and the other serves the ones to the west. This one came from the western center. There's nothing more we can do to track the garment any further."

The phone call left the sheriff with the feeling that the only way they were going to find out the boy's identity was if someone came forward and told them his name. He wondered why no one had.

January 17, 1986
The sheriff's dispatcher took the call late in the afternoon. The caller had information regarding the unidentified boy. Jack Wyant got on the line.

The caller, a nervous man who refused to identify himself, stated that he wanted to come down to the sheriff's office in person. He knew plenty about the little boy abandoned in Chester. "I was there when it happened," he said.

Wyant pressed for details, but the man declined. He said he would be at the sheriff's office in five minutes, then he hung up.

After fifteen minutes of clock-watching, Wyant had Deputy McPherson call the phone company to trace the strange call.

It was tracked to a York, Nebraska, residence. After further investigation, the police learned that they were dealing with what Sheriff Young liked to call an 8-ball.

More leads were followed up. A 43-year-old Columbus, Nebraska, man came forward—somewhere in the back of his mind drifted the memory of something strange involving a man chasing a little boy near the Belvidere Corner off U.S. 81 north of Hebron. The date he had encountered the man and child was Sunday, December 22.

In an effort to see if there was anything to his vague recollection, Wyant suggested hypnosis. The man agreed.

Under hypnosis, the man recalled driving north on 81 while his wife and children slept. On the east shoulder he noticed a man and a young boy. As he got closer, he could see that the man had grabbed the boy and that they seemed to be involved in some serious talk.

The man was in his twenties; the boy appeared to be about 12 years of age. As he drove past the man and boy, the witness saw an older, full-sized car—a Chevrolet, he thought. Seated behind the wheel was another man, a little older and clean-shaven. The look on the driver's face was odd, an expression he couldn't quite peg. The witness wondered what was going on. He recalled watching the younger man and the boy run across the road to the west shoulder.

He couldn't recall any details of the license plates or the exact make and model of the car. The investigators excused him and indicated that they would bring the witness a vehicle-identification encyclopedia in the hope that the right photo would jog his memory.

A Greyhound bus driver from Omaha told the sheriff that he had picked up a boy on December 20, 1985, at Bosselman's Truckstop in Grand Island, northwest of Hebron. The bus driver said the boy had been running when he made contact with him. The driver took him to town, where he purchased a ticket.

Young listened with interest as the details became more clear and precise. The bus driver said the boy was wearing a gray T-shirt with PANTHER WRESTLING emblazoned on the front.

"I even kidded the boy about not being big enough to be a wrestler!" the driver said with a laugh.

Further, the boy had a sack of clothes with him and was last seen when the driver dropped him off around 8:00 P.M. at the Lincoln terminal.

By now Gary Young had learned the hardest lesson of law enforcement. It isn't that no one comes forward to help the police. Often it's simply the wrong kind of people who do. Some are crazy and some are just overly helpful. And as helpful as the news media were in getting the word out, the information they disseminated seemed to fuel the fantasies of the crazies.

The bus driver could have been either of those, and, Young also conceded, he could also be right.

But the lead was checked out. It went nowhere.

Each morning after stopping at Ortman's for breakfast, the sheriff went to his office, poured himself a cup of coffee, and tried to catch the killer. For a time, it seemed that

Thayer County's sheriff and his deputies had become the nucleus of a clearinghouse for missing children.

Days passed into weeks. Like a magician's perpetual string of kerchiefs, leads kept coming from and going to nowhere. A boy from Savannah, Georgia, was eliminated from the list of possible victims, as were ones from Orlando, Phoenix, Canada, and Mexico.

Some suggested that the boy had been abducted from his bed at his home. Both Young and Wyant discounted that theory. No one had reported this child missing. None of the missing-children's agencies or the FBI had any reports of abductions that fit the boy's case. The case of the frozen child, who some now called Little Boy Blue because of the blanket-sleeper, had to be handled in a manner opposite that of most missing-children cases. They had a body, but no name. Usually a case starts with the name and investigators scour the country for the missing.

Wyant and Young kept each other informed as necessary, but their contact tapered off as the case grew older.

The call from the crime lab in Lincoln couldn't have come at a better time. The last day of January 1986 found the Nebraska investigation fizzling and in desperate need of a boost. With the results of the lab report, Wyant and Young hoped they could pinpoint both the dead boy's identity and that of his killer.

The lab technician's microscope had discovered a large number of thin, half-circle-shaped blue paint fragments as well as red, white, and blue cotton fibers with the fingernail scrapings submitted by Dr. Porterfield.

Examinations of the blue sleeper turned up more of the paint fragments as well as some nylon and polyester fibers.

Only one soil grain was recovered from the sleeper's rubber feet. Abrasions were barely evident—even under extreme magnification. This confirmed that Wyant was right: The child had not walked to the site where his body had been found; he had been carried.

Further scrutiny of the sleeper showed that faint, brownish stains on the left foot and the inside front neck of the garment were urine. No urine, however, was detected in the crotch area. This meant that likely the child had been alive when he was dressed in the sleeper. Young surmised that when urinating the boy had dribbled a little on his toe, and when pulling up the sleeper a few drops had stained the neck area.

No semen or saliva stains were detected on the sleeper.

The fibers found on the men's underwear picked up at the Lutheran cemetery were not similar to the debris found on the boy's sleeper. The briefs tested positive for semen and urine, yet it was not conclusive that they were related to the case in any way.

It was the discovery of fragments on the gray wrestling T-shirt that immediately gave the investigators the needed shot in the arm—at least at first. As with the sleeper, there were fragments of blue paint and some nylon fibers on the T-shirt.

The clear and blue fibers found on the T-shirt and the sleeper were of the type found in carpet. The origin of the blue paint was less clear. Chemists determined that it was thinner and more brittle than the types used on cars and houses. It was possible that the paint was of the type used in toy manufacturing, although further analysis would be needed.

As Wyant saw it, the T-shirt had become a critical link in their case. Find the right Panther Wrestling team and it might lead them to the answer to the mystery.

It was a long shot, but it was all they had. But there was a bright spot. No other Panther Wrestling team they had encountered used that same logo of the panther looking over its shoulder. Most featured only the big cat's head.

Wyant and Young had discussed the T-shirt evidence on numerous occasions. The shirt had been recovered in the northeast corner of the field in a flat area. Yet, the terrain of the field itself was hilly and stubbled with the spiny remains of cornstalks. Young didn't think it was possible that the wind could have blown the shirt across the field.

"It must have dropped out of a vehicle and been blown into the ditch," he told Wyant.

The person who dumped the child had to have stopped, either before or after abandoning the child, and the T-shirt must have fallen out of his vehicle. Young felt that the killer must have stopped *before* the body had been dumped. He simply could not come up with a reason for the killer to have stopped afterward.

If the killer had stopped *before*, what was going on?

Wyant switched gears and began the process of tracking down the Panther Wrestling teams in Nebraska. As he compiled the list, he became discouraged. Dozens of such teams existed in Nebraska and probably thousands more nationwide. How would they find the right one?

On February 21, Gary Young met with Dan Werner and Lon Adams in the mortuary's garage to pick up the boy's body for another go-round with the pathologists. The back of the garage, surrounded by boxes and tools, had been the hiding place for the corpse. It was supposed to be a secret, but others in the county whispered that the child was kept in town in the kind of freezer homemakers use to store sides of beef.

Young's knife cut the yellow and black evidence seal and the silver duct tape that ensured no one would tamper with the evidence. *Evidence.* He knew that the boy's body should only be considered "evidence" in a criminal case.

Inside the freezer was the boy's naked body, sewn together with more stitches than a country sampler and swaddled in a plastic body bag. Fifty frozen pounds of someone's child. They carried the package to Young's police car and put it in the trunk. Gary Young did this gently, as though putting down a newborn for a nap.

Young drove the corpse to Lincoln for one last look, poke, and cut. Plans were now in the works to let the child rest. Some accepted that there would never be any answers in the mysterious case.

Gary Young was not among that group and he knew he never could be.

CHAPTER EIGHT

August 5, 1977

There wasn't an Amishman in Wayne County who wasn't aware of the barn-raising planned for Eli E. Stutzman, a widower and father of a young boy. At daylight they began coming, tools and supplies filling buggies. By midmorning a formidable crew of two hundred Amish had assembled, each with a job to do. In the house, women gathered to cook and visit. A big meal was planned for noon.

Curiously, Stutzman was absent from much of the actual work. Some passed it off as a part of the grief process—the bereaved man's need for solitude. They also knew that the trauma of losing a wife might be even more difficult for a weak or disturbed man like Stutzman.

The morning of the raising, a couple of neighbor boys saw Elam Bontrager go to a desk in the house and remove some pills from a drawer, then go upstairs to the bedroom where Stutzman was resting.

Maybe they were pills to settle Stutzman's conscience, Daniel Gingerich later thought.

Further, it was strange that Bontrager went right to the drawer for the pills before he even saw Stutzman. *Bontrager had to know exactly where the pills were*, Gingerich thought.

The first of the massive, wooden, pinned-joint post and beam framing was erected by 7:00 A.M., although some of the cutting and measuring had been completed before. Just after noon, the structure resembled a barn, walls were up, and two dozen Amishmen furiously drove nails through shakes on the roof.

It was an unbearable day for the Gingerich family. Ida's father would have cried all day if he hadn't been so busy. His daughter was on his mind. His son-in-law's story had some holes in it and he felt suspicious and wondered if others did, too.

Richard Armstrong, the loan officer from Wooster, was in the area and decided to stop by to say hello. He hadn't realized that the barn-raising was taking place, but when he arrived the framing was finished. His car was the only motor vehicle on the property.

"Where's Eli?" he asked one of the workers.

"He is in the house sleeping right now," the man responded.

This seemed odd to Armstrong. It was midday and Stutzman's barn was being built by friends and family . . . all these people here to help him and he was in the house sleeping.

Before evening, with the exception of a few finishing touches needed on the inside, the barn was complete. They left behind more than a handsome barn; it was a symbol of the strength and unity of their community. The labor had been free—given by the community as a token of their support for the troubled man. Stutzman ordinarily would have been charged for the lumber and hardware, but because of the tragedy and, maybe, because of his mental state, even that had been without cost.

As they left, however, some were uncomfortable about the design Stutzman had insisted upon. More horse stalls had been built than were needed for dairy farming.

The Firemen's Lounge is the name of the barbershop adjacent to the Kidron Fire Department. *Very adjacent.* In fact, the two share the same telephone number. Until he answered the phone, barber/fire chief Mel Wyss could never be sure if a caller wanted a haircut or the rescue squad. The barbershop was one of the community's best sources for information and gossip.

Stories started to drift in after the Stutzman barn-raising. Some even came from the Amish. Dan Hershberger and John Stutzman said they didn't like what was happening on the Stutzman farm; they thought he was just buying time, and that he wasn't going to stay with the Order. Sometimes word leaked out of strange goings-on at the Stutzman farm.

Eli Stutzman called John Yoder one Saturday a week or so after the raising; he wanted a ride.

Yoder drove down Moser Road and at the little T at the base of Sand Hill found Stutzman waving him over. Beside him was a hickory rocker. Yoder recognized the chair as Ida's.

"Don't tell anyone about this," Stutzman said as he loaded the backseat of Yoder's '71 Dodge Dart Demon. "I didn't want Susie to see me with the rocker. And I don't want anyone to know that I went into a car." (Ida's sister Susie was then staying at the Stutzman farm.)

Yoder understood how the Amish were—how they took delight in telling the bishop news about those who had strayed from the laws of the Order.

Stutzman told Yoder to drive to an auction house on Route 57 in Riceland. "It didn't make sense to me," Yoder later said. "Eli didn't need the money, and even if he did, he had other things that would bring a better price than the fifty dollars the rocker would get. It was as if he wanted to get rid of that rocker."

Why would he want to get rid of something that had belonged to his wife? The Amish are not unsentimental. Ida had rocked baby Daniel in that chair only a month ago.

Yoder knew better than to ask. He knew that Stutzman had been under strain since the fire. He also knew that

Stutzman had suffered a couple of nervous breakdowns.

When they arrived at the auction house, Stutzman took the chair inside. A few minutes later he came out and instructed Yoder to drive to Buehler's Mart in Orrville, where he purchased two cases of beer. Then they returned home.

Yoder expected to let his friend off on Moser Road so that Susie wouldn't see him in a car, but Stutzman told him to park in the drive next to a shed. He hid the beer inside and thanked his friend for the ride.

Buying beer notwithstanding, the whole trip puzzled Yoder. Why would Stutzman, who had said he was so concerned that someone might see him get into a car that he carried the rocker up the road, out of view, want to be dropped off in his driveway in broad daylight?

As the weeks passed, it became clear that Stutzman didn't want any reminders of his late wife.

He asked Amos Gingerich to build him a chest so that he could store Ida's clothes for Danny to keep when he grew up. "It is too painful for me to see them in the wardrobe," he said.

For some reason, the old man felt that his son-in-law was insincere. Stutzman had asked for the storage chest, but it didn't seem like he wanted it. "Did he just want to get Ida's clothes out of the way?" Gingerich asked later.

In the coming months, another concern was rekindled when race horses were delivered to the farm. The new barn could hold more of the expensive animals.

All of the Gingeriches did what they could to help Stutzman restart his life since God had called his wife home. Amos Gingerich sent his children over to help run the farm and take care of Danny. Some wondered if Stutzman would marry Ida's sister Susie.

Just after the barn was built, Gingerich gave Stutzman two thousand dollars. "You have so many things to buy to start over," Amos said, offering the money. When Stutzman hesitated, Amos said: "But, Eli, all of the expense!" Stutzman then accepted the money.

Dan Gingerich also stayed at Stutzman's farm, filling his days with farm chores and taking care of his brother-in-law, who now seemed to be afraid all the time. In fact, he seemed never to want to be alone, even at bedtime.

Amish often share a bed. It is practical—especially when a household has more than a dozen people. It makes little sense to have individual beds.

At that time, Stutzman complained of a bad back, so he spent little time, if any, doing regular farm chores. His routine was to stay inside, occasionally making a trip in the buggy to visit friends. He rarely took Danny along.

At noontime each day, Dan Gingerich brought in the mail and took it upstairs, where he and Stutzman would lie down and read through it. Stutzman was delighted by the money sent by strangers who had heard about the fire.

After Stutzman drifted off, Dan continued his chores. He felt sorry for his brother-in-law, but he wondered if Stutzman felt bad because he had lost his wife, or if there was another reason why he didn't want to be alone.

One day Stutzman told his brother-in-law that he had not cut himself up in Marshallville. It was a lie he said he had to tell, to end all the trouble. Dan didn't know what to believe. Each time Stutzman told a story, he seemed so sincere.

Another time, Stutzman confided his hatred of his father. "He was too strict. He wouldn't even let us boys smoke!" Stutzman complained.

Dan understood. He had worked for One-Hand Eli when he was 16 and had found the man too "sarcastic" and too unyielding and set in his ways. To One-Hand Eli, there was only one way—*his* way.

January 16, 1978

Amos Gingerich was stunned by the parallels between Stutzman's situation and that of a LaGrange, Indiana, farmer he read about in the Amish newspaper *Die Bot-*

schaft. Gingerich urged his son-in-law to write to the farmer, Harley Schrock, an Amishman whose wife had also died suddenly and tragically.

A week later, Stutzman mailed a 4-page letter written in an off-putting red ink to Schrock. In it he offered Schrock his condolences and, for the first time, he recounted the night of the barn fire in writing. It was around midnight, he wrote, when Ida woke him after hearing an explosion and seeing flames through a barn window. The couple hurried to the barn, but found it too engulfed in flame to save the old wooden structure. Stutzman described how he had in mind to save some tools and implements from the barn and when Ida asked what she could do to help, he told her to go to the neighbors to call the fire department. On her way, she asked if she shouldn't try to retrieve some things from the milk house and Stutzman told her she could—as long as it was not too hot inside the little room. Stutzman wrote that he then went about salvaging what farm equipment and livestock he could—a foal was saved, but a bull was taken by the flames—before returning his attention to the milk house. Just outside the milk house, he found strainers and other equipment, and the doorway blocked by a milk vat that Ida had been attempting to save. Inside, he made a horrible discovery: his beloved life's companion dead, her body slumped next to the doorway.

All of this was possible, of course. Yet Stutzman, eager to enhance the story's credibility, went further, as he had many other times in his life. He wrote that it was the doctor who had determined that Ida had died from a heart attack, and that other "officials" had determined that the fire might have been caused by lightning. The truth was that *he* had been the one to suggest both scenarios. He had told many people over the previous six months that he had *seen* the lightning strike with his own eyes—but now it was some nameless official who had identified the cause.

When he made his statement to Sheriff Frost, Stutzman reportedly indicated that he wasn't able to hear what Ida was saying when she left for the neighbors. But in the letter

Stutzman stated that he and Ida had a discussion about the milk house and what the Amishwoman could do to help.

Harley Schrock was touched by the letter and put it away in a safe place, unaware that it was Stutzman's most complete—and only documented—version of the night of the barn fire. Suddenly Eli Stutzman recalled details that had eluded him—and events and ideas that were patently untrue.

When he opened his front door, Chris Swartzentruber was shocked and delighted. At his door in Greenville, Ohio, was his buddy Eli Stutzman, dressed in his Amish clothes and grinning ear to ear. Swartzentruber hadn't seen Stutzman since his marriage to Ida Gingerich.

"How did you get here?"

Stutzman just smiled that old Eli grin and skirted the question. But Swartzentruber pressed him. "How did you get a driver's license? You're supposed to be Amish!"

Stutzman just laughed.

For Swartzentruber, the laughter stopped when Stutzman shared his tragic news about Ida's death in the fire. Swartzentruber offered his condolences, but was still curious about what had happened to Stutzman's wife.

"What was she doing in the barn?" he asked.

"She had gone into the barn near the hayhold to save some puppies."

The response caught Swartzentruber off guard. To Low Amish, a dog is not a pet, it is an animal. There would be a lot of other things more important in a burning barn than some puppies.

Stutzman said he had seen lightning strike the barn when returning from Kidron. Swartzentruber was skeptical. He had been up that way many times when his brother Daniel owned the farm. How could Stutzman see lightning strike the barn coming from Kidron? A bolt in the sky, maybe, but not a direct strike on the barn. What was Stutzman trying to pull now?

CHAPTER NINE

When Jean Samuelson came to Chester as pastor of the United Methodist Church, she brought with her a marriage as shaky as the railroad tracks leading out of town. Try as she and her pastor husband did, neither could make it work. As a minister she could chalk up the strain to God's Grand Plan; as a wife, that proved excruciatingly difficult.

The Methodist church was built in 1912 of red brick with clay from deposits found in Thayer County. When Samuelson first saw the facade it looked like an institutional building, maybe a school. Inside, of course, it was a church. Rich, red carpet and row upon row of gleaming oak pews filled the expansive room. A stained-glass dome topped the ceiling. More than 250 belonged, making it the biggest of the three churches in town.

Two months after his discovery, the dead boy continued to find his way into her prayers and thoughts. Samuelson felt a connection to the child, as though God was speaking to her through the tiny lifeless form in the blue blanket-sleeper.

When her parishioners came to her with stories of the indignity of keeping the body in a freezer, she felt the bond strengthen.

"Ambulance drivers are talking about the stinky body in Hebron."

"The poor child has been through several autopsies. If

I were his mother, I'd die if my baby had been subjected to that."

Her women parishioners urged her to organize a simple community service and burial that would put the child back with God.

People in Chester were aghast when they heard that the county attorney was going to order another autopsy.

"They keep looking for evidence that doesn't seem to exist. It's time to stop it. It's time to let the child rest."

Sheriff Young and investigator Wyant scheduled a press conference for Tuesday, January 28, 1986. An airbrush artist hired by the state patrol had mixed reality with fantasy by painting a nose, lips, and cheek on top of the morgue photograph. The child's teeth, however, still dominated the image, like two square, perfectly spaced white tiles. As was the case with the artist who had done the first composite, the features were a guess.

Young hoped the photo would be the impetus for more publicity, and, God willing, a lead that would finally go somewhere. That afternoon, 5-by-7 prints were mailed all over the country.

The time had come to bury the boy and the national media responded. Reporters wondered what the townspeople had called the boy. Samuelson received a letter from a Missouri minister and gave them the answer:

> "As a father of three children, including a 9-year-old boy, I was saddened and moved by the story in *USA Today* in which your community will bury the unknown boy, whose name is known only to God.
>
> I hurt for that little child. . . ."

Before closing, the man suggested the name "Matthew," which means "Gift of God." Samuelson felt the name fit.

. . .

Donations from the community and beyond came to Chester in support of their plan for the burial. A mother from Fairbury donated her son's size-8 suit. A widow gave up one of her family plots in Chester's cemetery. Lon Adams's wife, Dixie, arranged for the donation of a marker:

LITTLE BOY
ABANDONED
FOUND NEAR
CHESTER, NEB.
DECEMBER 24, 1985
WHOM WE HAVE CALLED "MATTHEW"
WHICH MEANS "GIFT OF GOD"

A space was left on the stone with the hope that someday the boy's real name could be engraved there.

Gary Young knew that the burial was important for the community's healing process. People wanted the uneasiness to end. But for him it was an unsolved murder, a tragedy that someone had forced on the community when they killed the little boy. The minister down in Chester could forgive that, but he couldn't.

Forgiveness, after all, was part of her job.

Offers to help solve the mystery of the dead boy continued to come from far away and from the most unlikely places.

Impressionist and stand-up comedian Fred Travalena was touched deeply by the story when he read about it in a Las Vegas paper.

Travalena felt compelled by God to help the sheriff and packed his bags for Nebraska. To Travalena, the story indicated that God had sent the child as a messenger of some kind: found on Christmas Eve, his funeral was planned for Easter. Travalena was even taken aback by the name of the town generating most of the stories—Hebron. It was the name of a holy place in the Bible.

It was as if the little boy were calling to him: *Find out who I am! Hurry!*

A press conference with Travalena was held and another composite of the boy was released. Accompanied by Young and Samuelson, the comedian drove out to pray at the dump site.

At midnight, several days after she learned that she would give the boy's funeral, Samuelson woke abruptly from a dream. A gut-wrenching feeling of fear and sadness gripped her. She saw tears at the roadside where the boy had been found. Whoever had left the child in Chester had left with great pain and a heavy heart.

In prayer, the minister asked, "Why do you keep speaking to me about this child? Why should I feel guilty? *Why should I feel guilty?*"

The answer that came to her was that the boy had been in her life many times. And she had been too busy trying to prove herself worthy to see him.

Suddenly, Samuelson felt that whoever had left the child had probably once been like him. He, too, was like a child who had fallen through the cracks.

The little boy's service was supposed to be a quiet, community funeral—a few flowers, some appropriate scripture, and hymns sung deeply from the heart. People in Chester talked about the service with great relief as Easter drew closer. The word, however, had gone beyond Thayer County.

Media calls became so incessant that Samuelson unplugged her telephone. Calls from the press inundated the church and the parsonage. CBS, ABC . . . call letters melded into one another. *People* magazine planned to send someone.

May 19, 1986

As expected, a flurry of activity followed the memorial-service story told in *People*. Most mysterious—or, Jack

Wyant initially believed, ludicrous—was the call from a Missouri woman who claimed to possess special gifts that could help the authorities solve the case of the Chester boy. The woman did not consider herself a psychic, but a person with a direct line to God.

She told Wyant that she felt that the boy was neither retarded nor mute, as had been speculated in the magazine. She said that she felt a connection to Kansas, and that through a vision she had seen a two- or four-lane highway—similar, Wyant wasn't surprised to learn, to the one pictured in *People*.

The woman shared a few other visions and impressions that seemed far from the reality of the case. She saw a white male, medium build, with brown straight hair and wearing slacks and a long-sleeved white shirt.

"He seemed to be spreading a flammable liquid near a building," she later wrote in her follow-up letter to Wyant. "I heard the word 'kerosene.' Next I heard the words 'Iowa' and 'Iowa farming community.' Next, 'Near a dairy farm.' "

She also said she saw a vision of land and a fence. The land sloped upward to the right, and a dirt road ran opposite the fence. She felt the place was close by the dairy farm.

The woman had no idea how it all connected, or if indeed it did. But she did have the distinct impression that the man she had described was the suspect in the case. She wanted no money, only the permission to use the Nebraska State Patrol as a reference on her résumé.

Wyant was polite to the woman and filed her letter in his case notebook—the first of two three-inch binders he would fill over the course of the investigation. He had heard stories of cases where psychics had helped out, but he had no firsthand knowledge of a psychic actually doing any good.

The months passed, and the holiday season brought snow, school concerts, and the case of a Grinch who stole Christmas light bulbs from homes and businesses in Hebron. It also brought the unshakable memories of the year before. For Thayer County, the memories could be recalled in vivid detail.

The Hebron *Journal Register* summed it up in a front-page headline:

ONE YEAR LATER AUTHORITIES ARE NO CLOSER
TO SOLVING CHESTER CHRISTMAS MYSTERY

The new year started off with County Attorney Werner requesting that another pathologist look into the case of the boy's death. John Porterfield had no problem with the state seeking another opinion, though he didn't believe the investigators were likely to turn up anything.

"To plow the same old ground again has never yielded anything I've ever heard of," he said.

Photographs, X rays, police reports, and microscopic tissue slides were shipped to the pathology department at the Saint Louis University Medical Center, a facility that handled more than one thousand autopsies a year. Wyant considered the Saint Louis facility to be the best in the region.

Dr. Michael Graham, the Saint Louis pathologist, had what Dr. Porterfield considered a major disadvantage: looking at a picture is never the same as looking at the corpse. Dr. Graham, on the other hand, felt that sometimes it's better to be an outsider and review the complete package—that sometimes things are clearer that way.

Like the rodent who didn't see his shadow, Jack Wyant might have wished he'd stayed in bed on Groundhog Day. He didn't much care for the news he received from Dr. Graham the morning of February 2, 1987. It was another strikeout. The 35-year-old assistant professor of pathology said that the cause of death could not be determined based on the available information.

He didn't fault the information provided. The reports

were clear, the slides excellent. But nothing in the package pointed conclusively to the cause of death.

Further, the anal dilation had been the result of the dying process. He could find no evidence that an object had been inserted into the boy's rectum. The low level of carbon monoxide found in his blood could be explained as having resulted from breathing tobacco smoke or car exhaust—the amounts were only trace, and by no means lethal.

Pathologists used drug screens to test for the more common lethals—barbiturates and alcohol. None turned up. Certain drugs, however, do not show up unless the lab knows what to look for. Such phantom drugs are a closely guarded secret—for good and obvious reasons.

Dr. Graham favored the view that the child had died a natural death, though not related to an upper-respiratory viral infection the boy may have had. Death due to a seizure disorder such as epilepsy was another possibility, but it too could not be established conclusively, since no medical history was available on the unknown boy.

Dr. Graham disliked leaving the case with a question mark, but he had done all he could.

CHAPTER TEN

Like the lights of a hundred cigarettes, fireflies bobbed up and down through the calm of the quiet night air as Dan Gingerich returned from visiting Abe Stutzman's parents, in Apple Creek. It was after 10:00 P.M., and since the lights were out, he assumed Eli Stutzman was asleep. Concerned that the noise of the buggy might awaken Stutzman, Gingerich brought it around into the upper driveway. Quietly, by the yellow glow of a kerosene lantern, he put the horse into a stall.

Just as he set foot on the gravel between the barn and the house there was movement at the bedroom window.

"Daniel, Daniel, where is my gun? Where is my gun?" Stutzman called from the window. His voice was full of fear. He begged Gingerich to get his gun and put it away in a safe place—a place where Stutzman couldn't find it.

Gingerich tried to calm the frantic man. "I'll take care of it," he promised.

"Hide it!" Stutzman pleaded.

Gingerich got the gun and put it in the barn.

When he returned, Stutzman explained that he was having horrible nightmares so frightening that he was afraid to close his eyes. One nightmare in particular was unbearable.

In his dream, he said, he knelt before Jesus Christ and confessed his sins. He asked if he would be saved if he took his own life. Jesus looked at him and said, "Yes, you will be saved."

Stutzman repeated his question again, just to make sure he understood, and again Jesus told him salvation would be given even if he killed himself. Stutzman had pulled the barrel of his gun to his face and just started to pull the trigger when the weathered hand of an old man reached from behind him and forced the gun away.

It was his father.

One-Hand Eli screamed at his son: *"You will not kill yourself! You will not!"*

The next day, Amos and Lizzie Gingerich came to the farm and learned of the nightmare.

"Take my gun away from the farm," Stutzman begged them. "I don't trust myself with it." They packed it in the buggy and took it to their farm for safekeeping. Their son-in-law was in frightening shape. What was going to happen next?

If Stutzman was telling everyone about his nightmare, it was nothing compared to what his twin brothers-in-law had endured. Something terrible had happened to the Gingerich boys, Amos and Andy, when they stayed overnight at Stutzman's. At the time neither boy had ever spoken directly of it—they only alluded to it years later when more information about their brother-in-law found its way to the formidable Amish rumor mill.

In bed late one night, Andy felt his brother-in-law pushing his pelvis against him. The 15-year-old turned away, thinking Stutzman was having a bad dream. Stutzman made soft sounds, almost a whine, but no words came. Stutzman pushed his pelvis against the boy and pressed his erect penis against Andy's back several times. Then he stopped.

The boy reasoned Stutzman had stopped because he knew Andy would not be part of anything so much against God's word.

Later, he learned that his twin, Amos, had gone through

the same thing. They knew that Stutzman was mixed up from Ida's death and that he had had problems in the past, but this kind of thing was totally forbidden. They were 15 years old, their sister was dead, and their brother-in-law had tried to have sex with them. How could they make sense of this?

"I wanted him to just leave me alone. I didn't know what to do—I thought he was trying some homosexual things to me," Andy later said.

July 11, 1978

The Gingeriches were held hostage by their emotions: the memory of Ida haunted them, as did Stutzman's disturbing behavior. No one wanted to push or confront Stutzman. The Gingeriches were afraid that Stutzman was slipping into an abyss of madness.

Exactly one year to the day after Ida had died in the fire, the inevitable happened.

Susie was the first to notice that Eli and Danny had not been home that night. The buggy was missing and Stutzman's bed had not been slept in. Stutzman had been acting so strangely lately, she was worried that something terrible had taken place. When he came home later that day, he went right up to his bedroom.

Later that afternoon, Andy Gingerich was tending livestock in the barn when he heard screams and scuffling sounds coming from the house. The next thing he knew, someone was running for the neighbor's to telephone for help, shouting, "Call the emergency squad! Eli Ali's gone mental!"

Upstairs in his bedroom, covered with a blanket and looking disheveled and wild, Stutzman was wavering between semiconsciousness and alert tirades.

"Where did you put the stones?" he demanded, pointing a finger at a bewildered and frightened little Danny. "*Where are the stones?*" He spoke loudly, his voice stern. He was sweating under the blanket, and his eyes rolled upward.

The Amish had gathered at the foot of the stairs, and

someone said that Stutzman had spent the night at the graveyard where Ida had been buried—or at least that he had babbled something of the sort.

When the emergency squad from Kidron arrived, the volunteer firemen heard howls and shouts from upstairs. Like a child, Stutzman was chanting the same thing over and over, starting and stopping without rhythm. The words were in Deutsch, and the firemen, although of Swiss extraction, couldn't understand them—the Amish tongue is its own language.

The chant in fact had something to do with stones or a stone. Some of the Amish wondered if he meant Ida's headstone.

The Stutzman farm was familiar to the squad members who had been there to fight the fire. When the Amish told them it was the exact anniversary of Ida's death, it all made sense. The Eli Stutzman they had seen the year before had been emotionless, but now he was a raging animal. Maybe he had bottled everything up inside, trapping his emotions for the big explosion they were witnessing.

The men waited at the bottom of the stairs while the Amishmen filled them in on what had happened. They heard what sounded like a hurricane lamp crash to the floor, and more screams.

Fire Chief Mel Wyss led the squad. He grabbed a quilt, proceeded upstairs with his men, and threw the quilt over Stutzman as he thrashed on his bed.

Stutzman struggled to break free. He was so wild and strong that it took four men to hold him and bind his legs and arms for the drive to the psychiatric ward at Dover Hospital.

"Watch that he don't bite," a squad member warned.

On the way, Stutzman continued to struggle. At least once en route, the squad pulled over to tighten his arm straps. He continued screaming until they pulled into the hospital parking lot, when he seemed to calm. Perhaps he had worn himself out, or perhaps he knew that screams wouldn't matter in a psychiatric ward.

Stutzman was admitted on July 11 and remained there for a full week.

The Amish community grieved for the disturbed young man. What if he did not pull out of this? What would happen to his little boy?

Twice the Gingeriches went to the hospital to visit Stutzman. Both times he seemed subdued, and afterward the Gingeriches felt he had not been happy to see them. They couldn't understand why. They loved Ida, too. They understood his grief.

A week later, Stutzman returned to Moser Road. He was on medication, and he had appointments scheduled with the psychiatrist for follow-up sessions.

If the Amish wondered whether he was going to be all right, their answer came, in part, during the first church he attended after being discharged from Dover. After only an hour of preaching, Eli rose, picked up Danny, and left.

Andy Stutzman saw that his brother was slipping away and made numerous trips to Moser Road to try to help him. Sometimes he brought ice cream or watermelon, and a few times he even stayed overnight. One time Stutzman refused to take the tranquilizers. Dr. Lehman suggested it might help to dissolve the pills into Mountain Dew or 7-up. Andy followed the advice, and as long as Eli drank it all, it worked.

One morning, however, Stutzman seemed to have taken a turn for the worse. He sent Andy to a neighbor's to call the doctor for more drugs. On his way back, Andy ran into Eli, who had left his bed and was walking quickly toward him.

"You're not going to put me away again? You're not going to sign me in to the mental hospital again?"

"No, Eli, I'm not going to sign you in unless you are mentally unaware and you don't know how to take care of yourself. Then I will have to. Do you understand?"

A week later, Stutzman started attending a Mennonite church. For the Amish, the pattern was all too obvious, and they were desperate to save him—and keep him Amish.

In an effort to help his brother, Chris Stutzman took Eli to Canistota, South Dakota, to the Ortman Clinic—a kind of chiropractic health spa that does considerable business with the Amish. Stutzman checked in on August 28, citing "sleep problems" as the reason.

He couldn't get over his wife's death, he told the admitting clerk.

He checked out on September 1. His brothers feared that the treatments hadn't done much good.

"We could see he still wasn't right," Andy Stutzman said later.

One Sunday when Stutzman was away, Susie Gingerich discovered her sister's suitcase. Something was inside and she became curious, but it was locked. She thought there might be some clothes that belonged to Ida that should be stored properly or given away.

Since she had the same kind of suitcase, she used her key. When she opened it she wished she hadn't. She wasn't sure what she saw—a radio or a cassette recorder. Whatever it was, it was against the *Ordnung*.

There was something else. Inside the recorder, Susie saw a wad of money. She didn't count it, but there seemed to be a great deal of it. Why, she wondered, was the money in her sister's suitcase?

When Stutzman returned home, Susie confessed what she had done. The troubled woman did not question him about what she had seen, but sought his forgiveness. She had violated their trust by looking someplace she should not have.

Stutzman forgave her and told her that the contents of the suitcase were things he had used to help ease the pain of Ida's death.

Later, after Susie had told Amos what she had done and how sorry she was, Amos asked Stutzman about the suitcase.

"It was something I had in the hospital. It made me feel better, but I don't listen to it anymore," Stutzman said.

Amos Gingerich wondered if the whiskey he had found in the cooler fulfilled the same purpose—to make Eli Stutzman feel better.

December 12, 1978

Stutzman stopped in to see Elton Lehman at his office in Mount Eaton. He said that he was having trouble with church again and, in fact, that he hadn't been to church in six weeks.

"The church hasn't agreed on its problems, so we haven't had communion for two years. I want to take communion," he said.

Dr. Lehman felt sorry for the young man.

"He was so troubled and yet so spiritual. He wanted to have communion and he couldn't. It didn't seem fair to him. He was upset about it," Lehman recalled later.

"My psychiatrist has told me to leave the church. I don't know what I will do," Stutzman told the doctor.

Just before Christmas, Stutzman called his cousin, Abe, and asked if he and Danny could come visit after the holidays. He also shared startling news. He had sold all of his dairy cows and was leaving the Amish. He also had a new job where he couldn't take his son. Could he leave Danny with Abe for a couple of weeks? Abe said it would be fine, since his wife, Debbie, wasn't working. Besides, their daughter April, now 7 months old, would enjoy a playmate.

When Abe hung up, he, too, felt sorry for Stutzman. Leaving the Amish again. It would be tough.

"But I never understood why he went back in the first place," Abe Stutzman said later.

. . .

It was snowing when Abe picked Eli and Danny up at the bus station. Snowflakes stuck to the black fabric of their Amish clothes. It had been a long ride across the state to Greenville, which lay only ten miles from the Indiana border.

Immediately, Abe Stutzman decided that the towhead was the most mischievous and unmanageable little boy he'd ever seen—but only when Danny was around his father. Whenever Eli left the room the boy threw a small fit, but would calm down in a few minutes.

Stutzman stayed the night and told Abe and Debbie about his job training horses in Georgia, though he was going to take some vacation in Florida before his job started in March.

Abe asked why Stutzman didn't take the child to his parents?

The Amishman bristled. "I can't give him to them. They'll take Danny away from me and hide him so that I could never find him."

There was no reason to doubt his reply or even question him further. What he said seemed possible.

Before daylight the next morning, Stutzman and Abe left Danny asleep on the couch and drove back to the bus station.

"Get him a haircut and buy him some clothes. He's going to need them." Stutzman gave his cousin one hundred dollars.

A few snips of the scissors brought Danny Stutzman into the twentieth century. He now looked like a little *Englische* boy, but he wasn't really an *Englischer*, and no one knew that better than Debbie Stutzman. This little boy did not know English, and she certainly didn't know Deutsch.

While the little boy played in the house or outside in the snow, Debbie watched over him as if he were her own. In all the pictures she took of the child there was always one thing missing. The boy never smiled. In her mind, it was no wonder. His father never called to see how his son was doing.

On January 7, Stutzman mailed a letter to the Gingeriches from Hawkinsville, Georgia. He had written it as though Danny were with him.

> We arrived here yesterday noon . . . How is everyone? I and Danny are fine. Much to be thankful for. My and Danny's cold are much better. These people we are traveling with are good to us and are a great inspiration to Our Lord Jesus Christ. The one who died for our sins on the cross. Don't know what forwarding address to give besides home as I don't know how long we'll stay here.
>
> Only a son-in-law,
> Eli and Danny

Three weeks later, the Gingeriches received a postcard from Eli and, they believed Danny. At one point Stutzman had crossed out the word *I* and substituted *We're*—had he forgotten for a second that Danny was supposed to be with him?

> 1-27-79
> Hello,
>
> How do these lines find yours in the eyes of God? We're now in Fla. it is nice & warm most of the time. I am picking oranges part time. It rained last night & is cool this morning. It is about 45 degrees so we're just staying inside. I still have a sore and swelled mouth, but is improving.
>
> So long, Eli

Near the end of January, Stutzman convinced Abe and Debbie to come down to Florida to work and get some sunshine. He said he missed Danny. Stutzman said he would pay for the apartment and their way down there. In the midst of another frozen Ohio winter, the plan seemed justifiable.

When they arrived in Sarasota, Abe, Debbie, and April stayed for a couple of days with Debbie's grandmother while Eli and Danny checked into a motel. Stutzman looked completely different: his tanned face was now clean shaven, and his hair was cut short. He even wore cutoffs. He also had a brand-new car, a shiny blue Cutlass. He boasted that he had paid cash for it.

Stutzman found an apartment in Bradenton Beach—right across the street from the Gulf. Rent was a staggering five hundred dollars a month. Stutzman worked nights at the Holiday Inn as a busboy. Abe worked days at the motel.

One day Stutzman told Abe he was going to meet a girl at a shopping center and disappeared for most of the day. Stutzman seemed to have plenty of friends and was always going out, but he never brought them around to the apartment.

In March, both families returned to Ohio.

When Stutzman returned to Wayne County, he made several visits to friends and family. He spoke with his neighbors Wilma and Norman Moser, telling them what was only too obvious. He was no longer Amish. It was all for the best, he said. He gave them oranges he had picked in Florida.

He drove up to the Gingerich farm in Fredericksburg and boldly knocked on the door. He was happy now, he told them.

The Gingeriches felt sorry for Stutzman, but most of all they grieved for Danny. Now the little boy would be lost to them forever. They heard that Stutzman had gone to Bishop Yoder and *asked* to be excommunicated and put under the *bann*. Such a request was unprecedented. Now, whenever Stutzman came to dinner, he sat in the kitchen alone with Danny. No one could take food from him. He had to set it down first.

The changes on Moser Road were both dramatic and swift—Stutzman wasted no time in modernizing the farmhouse by installing a telephone and power. The Amish saw what was going on, but few dared to talk to him about it since he was under the *bann*.

Stutzman didn't seem to care. If anything, he seemed happy with the barrier between himself and the Order. He flaunted his freedom by buying and training more racehorses. New friends also began to show up, none of whom the neighbors recognized.

Norman and Wilma Moser and their daughter, Becky, had a front-row seat. The Mosers did what they could to help the widowed man and his sweet little boy. One time, Norman drove Stutzman out to see Ida's grave in Fredericksburg. Another time, he took Stutzman to see his psychiatrist. Moser watched from the hospital parking lot as several Amishmen pleaded with Stutzman.

Rumors circulated about their neighbor, and initially the Mosers thought little of such gossip, it was so outlandish. One rumor even had it that Stutzman had been engaged at the time of his wife's death. Another indicated that Stutzman had been involved with drugs and that his wife had been on her way to the bishop to tell him when she died in that mysterious barn fire.

The Mosers ignored the rumors. They looked after Danny, sometimes overnight while his father went away on what he said was horse business.

Wilma Moser took Danny to the local Head Start program—his stuttering was so bad that such early help seemed warranted. Soon Wilma found that she had become a mother figure to the boy. As such, she grew increasingly concerned, even alarmed, about what was going on at the farmhouse down the road, even though she couldn't put her finger on exactly what was happening there.

Amishwoman *Daisy Mast* came weekly to clean the Stutzman house, to do the mending, and to cook some meals. She was delighted when Danny helped her with the mopping, though he was only three. She noticed a lot of men coming and going, but she only met a few of them. Stutzman didn't include her in his life. He liked to keep things private. Mast noticed he always kept his wooden chest and desk locked tight.

Mast had known Stutzman for years, long enough to take most of what he said with a grain of salt. If others could forget what had happened at Marshallville and believe that he was totally "cured of his mental problems," she could not. After all, Stutzman was the same person before and after the stabbing incident. He hadn't changed.

One time he told her that he knew some people thought he was mentally disturbed.

"I know some Amish didn't like me taking Danny up to Ida's grave all the time, but I did anyway. I know some of them said I was crazy."

Stutzman's house had three small bedrooms upstairs. Though one was for Danny, the little boy seldom slept there. Instead, he slept in his father's room on the main floor. The master bedroom was unusual in that it had two doors, one opening onto the hall, by the stairwell, and the other into the family room.

In every way, from the wallpaper to the appliances, it was an *Englischer*'s house. The only thing hinting that it was the home of a former Amishman was the furniture that Amos Gingerich had made.

One thing certain visitors noticed, however, was that the master-bedroom doors locked from the inside. The lock over the door to the family room was unlike any seen before by some visitors. It was a large hook.

John and Lydia Yoder were among the many who stopped by to get a firsthand look at Stutzman's remodeled house. While they visited in the kitchen, the Yoders heard someone turn off the television, and a man's footsteps going up the stairs. Stutzman had made no mention of a house guest, and they didn't ask who it was, though they wondered.

Abe and Debbie Stutzman also came to see the changes

in the house. With Stutzman getting settled into the *Englische* world, Abe wondered if Daisy Mast would leave the Amish to marry him.

Since Stutzman's strange visit to Greenville, Chris Swartzentruber and his wife, Diane, had discussed the circumstances of Ida's death and shared some suspicions—though such feelings might have been tainted by bitterness. Swartzentruber felt Stutzman had "stolen" his brother's farm. Stutzman had pretended to go back to the Amish just to get a cheap farm, he thought.

The changes with the farm only confirmed Swartzentruber's suspicions. He went out to the new barn and saw for himself that what the Amish were saying was true. The barn they had built for the grieving Amishman was not an Amish barn. It was built for horses. Stutzman had decided to leave the Amish immediately after Ida died. What else could explain the barn's floor plan?

During the visit, Diane noticed that Danny was strangely quiet for a 3-year-old. The boy said nothing and paid little attention to the visitors. Diane, who had suffered a miscarriage, was drawn to the blue-eyed child.

The Swartzentrubers went upstairs to look at the rest of the house and found Danny in his bedroom, sitting silently on his bed. Next to the boy's bed was a pornographic publication with pictures of nude men and women.

All of a sudden, Danny's withdrawn behavior made sense. *He shows all the characteristics of being abused*, Diane thought.

On the way home Diane and Chris talked about the magazine and her suspicion that the boy might be a victim of sexual abuse.

"Eli seemed so soft-spoken that he couldn't hurt a fly. You know him, do you think he could be involved in something like that?"

Chris Swartzentruber said he didn't know.

"With all that has been said about Ida . . . Chris, I think something is going on. I think he's getting away with something." Then she said it. "I think he killed Ida, and I'm going to do what I can to find out about it."

Though she meant every word of it, and there were many times she picked up the phone to call the Wayne County Sheriff to inquire about Ida's death and investigation, she never dialed the number. Her husband had told her to mind her own business.

"With the Amish, what's done is done. They don't want any part of bringing all of this up. Ida is buried, and we don't have anything to go by. Forget it."

"But I can't. And *you* can't either."

What she would have given to have a little boy just like Danny.

Even before his wife's death, Stutzman had established himself as a first-rate horse trainer, and his reputation grew once he was free of the Amish and their yoke of rules.

Standardbred racehorses were brought from all across Ohio to the Amishman who could break any horse. Stutzman used gentleness and patience, they said.

Abner Petersheim, a quiet young Mennonite father who lived down the road from Stutzman, only saw his neighbor occasionally. After Stutzman had left the Order, their contact increased. Stutzman started going with Petersheim to the Mennonite church on South Kansas Road. Petersheim and his wife baby-sat Danny a few times, and though they liked the child, they felt he was a wild little boy. The Petersheims wondered why, if Stutzman was so good at taming horses, he couldn't control his boy.

On June 20, Stutzman said he had been feeling ill and needed bed rest. While Petersheim was over helping with chores, Stutzman asked if he and his wife Mary could take care of Danny while Stutzman rested. He also complained of problems with his kidneys.

Petersheim saw the poor man slumped in bed, weak and tired, and had no difficulty agreeing to the request. Stutzman had been a wreck ever since his wife had died two years before—everyone in the neighborhood knew it. To make matters worse, the Amish had ostracized him with the *bann*.

Who could live with all that?

Later in the evening Petersheim called to see how Stutzman was getting along. When there was no answer he became alarmed and summoned the Wayne County Sheriff's Department. He thought the worst, and wondered if his distraught neighbor had hung himself.

When the deputy arrived, they searched the yard and house—Petersheim looked up at tree limbs for a hanging body. Nothing was found. Stutzman, who had been on his deathbed, was missing.

While her husband and the sheriff's department were searching for Stutzman, Mary Petersheim stayed home with Danny and her children. She was frightened that Stutzman might come to their house. He had been acting so oddly, she didn't know what to expect of him.

The search continued the next morning.

Twenty-six hours after Abner Petersheim had seen Stutzman in bed, the sheepish former Amishman showed up at the Petersheim's to collect Danny. He apologized for being so late. He told them he had fallen asleep on a friend's couch—he'd had too much to drink.

For Petersheim, the story didn't ring true. The Eli Stutzman he had seen the day before had been far too sick to go anywhere—especially to a party. Unless, of course, he hadn't been sick at all.

CHAPTER ELEVEN

Late summer and fall found the fields of Thayer County changing from emerald to golden. Harvest came early in 1987, with mountains of corn, milo, and soybeans filling grain elevators from Bruning to Chester. Farm machinery clogged county roads. The mood was upbeat, a good ending to a prosperous year.

That fall, several communities celebrated centennials with bunting and banners. Locals lined up to sample food booths and to take a peek at the 4-H projects at the county fair in Deshler—the fair's seventy-fifth year. Still there was no answer to the riddle of Little Boy Blue.

Sheriff Young didn't know it at the time, but all of that was about to change. Events were in the works that finally were going to lead somewhere—fast.

Pleasantville, New York, is the headquarters of *Reader's Digest*, and no other publication could have a more suitably named hometown. Indeed, what the *Digest* does best are stories of the heart. The December 1987 issue, sent to subscribers just before Thanksgiving, featured an inspirational article typical of the magazine: "Little Boy Blue of Chester, Nebraska."

The *Digest* reaches more than 16 million homes and has a total readership of more than 50 million—no police department anywhere in the country could have achieved such widespread attention. And no department needed help more than Thayer County's.

November 30, 1987

A soft-spoken Abner Petersheim called from Ohio with information for Sheriff Young. He said he was reluctant to get involved, but saw some similarities between the boy described in *Reader's Digest* and a child he knew named Danny Stutzman. Danny's father was a man named Eli Stutzman.

"We knew them real well." Petersheim said in a halting voice. "My wife and I baby-sat the little boy until he and his father moved out west."

He gave the boy's date of birth as September 7, 1976. Danny was blond-haired and blue-eyed. He had freckles, just like Little Boy Blue. Danny had been staying with foster parents in Wyoming and his father had picked him up on the way to Ohio just before Christmas 1985.

"But he never got here. Several months later Eli told his parents the boy died in a car wreck somewhere out in Utah."

Young asked if Petersheim had any photographs of the Stutzmans.

The Mennonite man didn't think any existed.

"The boy and his father were from the Amish. They do not allow photographs."

Petersheim gave Young the names of the foster parents—*Dean* and *Margie Barlow*—and their phone number.

"I feel this is something that should be investigated," Petersheim said, "but please do not use my name."

For the first time in two years, Young had something he could investigate. This story sounded plausible—the boy's Amish background might explain a few things. Why no one had come forward, for example. Since the father had said the boy was dead in a car accident, it now made sense why no one had reported him missing.

He called the Wyoming number and spoke with the Barlows. Both were schoolteachers who had participated in various foster-parenting programs for a number of years. One child had been Danny Stutzman. They too had read the article and thought a connection might exist, though they doubted it.

"We don't think it is Danny, but it does kind of fit." They had little to say about Eli Stutzman.

Nevertheless, they had sent a letter to the Chester Police Department the preceding Saturday, with Danny's school photograph enclosed.

Since there was no Chester Police Department, Young figured the letter might still be down in Chester.

"Eli loved his boy very much, there is just no way that he could ever have harmed him," Dean Barlow insisted, his speech a jumble of nervousness. "My wife and I are absolutely certain about that."

Young thanked them and told them he might be getting back to them soon. First he needed a look at the photograph. The lead still seemed good, maybe even better after talking with the Barlows.

He dialed the Chester post office. The postmaster had no such letter. Young said he would try later.

The following day, Young learned that a misaddressed letter with a Wyoming postmark had arrived. Shortly afterward, he was staring at a school photograph. He didn't need to compare it with the morgue photos, so imprinted on his mind was the dead boy's likeness. His heart began to race. He read the typed letter, dated November 28, 1987.

> Gentlemen:
>
> I recently read the story "Little Boy Blue of Chester, Nebraska" in the December, 1987, *Reader's Digest*, relating the story of a dead child found along the roadside.
>
> On the remote possibility that there may be a positive identification, I'm enclosing a picture of a nine-year-old-boy Danny Stutzman who left our home in Wyoming December 20, 1985, heading

> for Ohio with his father. Since then neither his grandparents nor we have heard from him.

Margie Barlow had signed the letter. Young studied the photograph again. The kid was all smiles. If Little Boy Blue wasn't Danny Stutzman, Young reflected, beyond a doubt he was Danny's twin brother.

The teeth that had seemed so large and buck-toothed, were covered by his lip, a lip that field mice had gnawed off. No wonder the composite didn't work, he thought.

On the way back up 81, the sheriff cruised past the turn-off Chuck Kleveland had taken two years ago to go pheasant hunting, past Chester's cemetery, where hundreds had gathered for Matthew's service the Easter before last . . .

But that child wasn't really named Matthew. He had another name. Could it be Danny Stutzman?

He wondered about the man Lehman called Eli Stutzman. If he had done this to his boy, what had led him to it? Such thoughts were not new to the sheriff. He had long ago made up his mind about the individual who had left the child in a ditch, back when he had stood over the child's body in that bitterly cold cornfield.

Now, when there seemed a million things to know, Gary Young had reduced his questions to a solitary word: *Why?*

CHAPTER TWELVE

Dalton, Ohio, is a nice little town in the heart of Amish Country that for some lucky reason escaped the trappings of the Amish tourist trade. Restaurants catered to tourists, but that was about the extent of it. As it should be, not a single hex sign could be found in Dalton. The bright, stylized hex signs associated with Amish barns are purely a Pennsylvanian invention.

Yet, beneath the skin of that placid world, like a burrowing tick, something strange was happening at the Stutzman farm on Sand Hill. And whatever it was, the people who knew Eli Stutzman knew that the activity wasn't the kind of thing that made it into tourism brochures.

Norman Moser's mother, Luella, had a good view of the Stutzman farm—her rambling brick house sat up the hill above Stutzman's property. While she worked in her garden she could watch who came and went. In time, the plain-spoken old woman figured it out. She noticed that all the visitors were men.

"There were others who were waiting for Eli to remarry. I knew it wasn't going to happen. He wasn't the type to get married," she later said.

Larry Barlow lived in Akron, a homosexual trapped inside the body of a 40-year-old school administrator. Barlow wanted love and sex, though mostly the latter. Akron's only gay bar brought him a few contacts, and he found even more at the gay bathhouse in town.

Barlow was a gentle man who loved muscles. The house he shared with his mother was painted in Wedgewood-blue tones, a color he favored. If ever the clichéd adjective "flaming"—for a male homosexual—was appropriate, it fit the man with the pencil-sharp nose and jovial eyes.

"Come and stay with me," he told a friend. "I'll treat you like a king, as only a queen can!"

Yet Barlow had been married—that is, until his wife became suspicious about his trips to the library "to study." The truth was that Barlow had been at the college campus giving blow jobs, not reading books. It had been part of the repetitious pattern of his life that he half-hoped would change with marriage. It had started when he was a boy and invited other boys to his bedroom for a quick blow job.

Barlow, bored and looking for a little excitement, scanned the pages of *The Advocate*, a Los Angeles biweekly magazine devoted to gay sex, good times, and the accessories of the gay lifestyle. The biggest lure for readers was likely its large section of personal ads. Pages and pages set in minuscule type promoted men meeting men. The variety was astonishing, anything the lonely and horny gay man might want—including, of course, men looking for a date, maybe even a relationship. One ad in the 1979 editions stood out:

> Ohio W/m 140 lbs, 5'6", light brown hair, blue eyes. Am 28 years old & have a three-year-old son. I like male companion, cooking, horse racing, and country music, etc. Am tired of the bar scenes. I am a country guy and prefer country living. Hope to find someone to meet the gap. Call (216) 857-8099 and ask for Eli.

Barlow circled it, looked up the location of the prefix on the telephone number and checked an Ohio map for

Dalton. He didn't want to get involved with a man if he was too far away.

"I didn't want to drive three hours out of my way for a bum fuck," he said later.

Dalton was close enough. He dialed the number and talked with a shy man named Eli Stutzman.

Barlow's and Stutzman's first meeting took place in late November in the parking lot of a closed-for-the-season frozen-custard stand in Dalton. When the former Amishman arrived, he brought his son Danny.

Stutzman was everything Barlow wanted: masculine and handsome, and, especially appealing, he was Amish. Nearly every Saturday morning for the next two years, Barlow went to Dalton and spent the day doing what he called his "wifely chores"—cooking, cleaning, and taking care of Danny.

If Stutzman had one flaw, Barlow considered it to be his habit of spitting Wintergreen chewing tobacco into a Noxema jar he stowed under the front seat of his car.

The men did some sightseeing when time permitted. Stutzman showed Barlow Ida's grave in Fredericksburg, as well as the Cherry Ridge School and his parents' Apple Creek farm—though neither went inside to visit. Stutzman told him that since he had been under the *bann*, his minister father had refused all contact with him.

In December, Stutzman asked Barlow for $2,500, and Barlow was a little put off at the request since they barely knew each other. In the end, he gladly gave Stutzman the money. Stutzman said the loan was for business purposes.

Barlow's infatuation continued, though Stutzman did not return the affection. When Barlow purchased matching rings from the Akron Sears and gave one to Stutzman, his "husband," Stutzman thanked him but seldom, if ever, wore the ring. Indeed, their relationship never involved sex.

It wasn't that Barlow didn't try. One afternoon when they were in bed, Barlow pulled off his would-be lover's underwear and fondled his penis, but failed to arouse him.

"Eli slept through it—or at least he pretended to sleep," Barlow later said.

Because Stutzman seemed so uninterested, Barlow got the impression that he was naive about gay sex. Stutzman told Barlow that his first homosexual liaison was with another boy at a feed mill. The two went off in his buggy and had sex during their lunch break. He had several gay friends, including a gay couple from Wayne County, whom he saw regularly. But that was about the extent of it.

Barlow got the impression that the housemaid, Daisy Mast, was in love with Stutzman. He felt sorry for the girl. Mast didn't know it, but the hired boy had a much better chance with the boss than she did.

If Mast ever did catch a clue to what was going on it was the day Stutzman told her that he thought two men—frequent visitors to the house—were homosexual. Stutzman's tone was gossipy, and Mast later wondered if he had been just testing her reaction to the idea.

In the summer of 1979, Levi Swartzentruber, 19 years old and just having left the Amish, ran into Stutzman in a bar in Massillon. Though both were from the Swartzentruber Order, they did not know each other.

Stutzman hired Swartzentruber a week later, paying him $80 per month, plus room and board. Swartzentruber cleaned fence posts and painted the barn and the fence around it.

Within the next couple of months the rooms in the Stutzman farm were filled with boarders—two other former Amish boys came to live, though Swartzentruber never saw much of them, or of Stutzman for that matter. Stutzman had a wide circle of friends and seemed to go out every night. Swartzentruber saw Barlow a few times, but didn't get to know him well.

"Carloads of men used to come out to the farm," Swartzentruber recalled. "Some would come into the living room, some out to the barn for an hour or so. They kind of kept floating around, flipping in and out of the farm.

"Now it seems stupid I didn't know what was going on, but I really didn't. I blame it on the way I was raised with the Amish."

Eli, Danny, and Levi drove to Gladwin, Michigan, where the Swartzentruber Order had established a new colony. Amos Gingerich and his family had been among the first Amish to settle there. Levi Swartzentruber's brother, John, had married Ida's sister Lydia, and moved with the Gingeriches to the new settlement.

Danny seemed like a happy little boy, though the fact that he could barely speak Deutsch caused the Amish some sadness.

"We could see he was no longer Amish. We would have been happier if he had spoken some German," Amos Gingerich said.

The Gingeriches were left to wonder: things had changed so quickly for Stutzman. It seemed so convenient—the fire, the nervous breakdown.

"We were concerned Eli had not told us the truth," Gingerich said later.

After Stutzman, his son, and Levi returned to Moser Road, it became clear to the confused and somewhat sexually naive 19-year-old that living with Stutzman and the gay lifestyle was not for him.

"One time Eli insisted that I put on my old Amish clothes to go out to a club in the city. I did, and he ended taking me to a gay bar," Swartzentruber later recalled.

Another time Stutzman sent him to Barlow's to do chores—and to have sex with the school administrator. It didn't work out on both accounts.

Levi wanted to turn Stutzman in, but he was afraid to because of his own involvement in a lifestyle that would not sit well with the people of conservative Wayne County.

"I've got a new roommate coming, so you'll have to leave anyway," Stutzman told him.

Stutzman called his cousin Abe Stutzman, who now lived in Pennsylvania, and told him he had just returned from a trip to Oklahoma, where he had worked for a wealthy horse owner.

"This hotshot horse owner had a high-bloodline horse that he couldn't control. He heard about me and called me. He even sent me plane fare. I stayed for a month," Stutzman bragged.

The man wanted Stutzman to stay and train horses for a while, but Stutzman claimed he had suffered a broken rib in an accident on the track, when one horse had run over him while he was cooling off another.

When it came to gay men in Wayne County, Stutzman quickly became a celebrity. His farm with its barn parties had become a magnet, drawing gay men from miles around. In Wayne County's small and closeted gay community, everyone knew of him, and, for a time, they all wanted to meet him.

If Stutzman had been turned down when he offered money to give David Amstutz a blow job, he found plenty of other takers at home or in the gay bars he frequented. Visitors to his farm could count on action.

Ben Miller was one of the curious. Though he didn't consider himself homosexual, he had experimented some. It was the all-consuming lifestyle of some gays that turned him off.

Early in 1980, Miller heard that Stutzman and his friend *Henry Troyer* were taking a trip to Key West to visit a gay man who had lived with Troyer's parents on their Wayne County farm. Troyer, like Stutzman, had grown up Amish. And like Stutzman, he was gay.

Troyer couldn't drive because he was considered legally blind, and he felt the drive to Florida would be too much for Stutzman alone, so he asked Miller if he wanted to go. Though it seemed clear that Stutzman didn't want him along, Miller agreed anyway.

"I didn't really care that much for Eli, but I wanted to see Key West," Miller recalled.

When it came time to leave, Miller parked his car inside Stutzman's barn, and the three set out in Stutzman's pickup. Stutzman planned the itinerary. He indicated that he had traveled to Florida many times and had a lot of friends with whom they could stay along the way. He also knew the right rest stops or roadside parks along the interstate—such places were cruising spots where they could stop and have sex with a stranger.

Miller felt he had put a damper on Stutzman's little party. If he had been into the sexual stuff as much as Stutzman, perhaps they might have hit it off better.

Stutzman did little to endear himself to Miller. When the man wasn't being surly and reminiscing about his past, he seemed less than sincere. He was cool and detached when he talked about his wife's death. Miller thought he was lying.

"Why would a pregnant woman with a husband and a son risk her life in a milk house during a fire?" Miller later asked.

The first night they stayed at a horse farm outside of Atlanta, Stutzman having called ahead to let the man who lived there know they were coming. Miller gathered that the man and Stutzman were friends and that Stutzman had stayed there before—had maybe even worked there at one time.

The following morning the travelers stopped to fill the gas tank. Miller wanted a cup of coffee, so he went to a cafe across the road while Stutzman pumped gas. When Miller returned, he met an angry Stutzman.

"If you'd been here I would have got a free tank of gas!" Stutzman screamed.

He's mad because he had to pay for the gas . . . because I wasn't there so he could steal, Miller thought.

Miller apologized, but Stutzman wouldn't let up. Miller could do nothing right from that point on.

When they made it to Key West, Miller had had enough. The three of them stayed at their Ohio friend's place, a kind of rooming house next to the beach. Miller kept his distance during the day. At night, Stutzman and Troyer went out to party at the bars.

When it was time to leave, they discovered that the truck had started to leak oil. Stutzman blamed it on Miller.

"You caused this!" he yelled at Miller. "If you knew how to drive this wouldn't have happened!"

Miller took the abuse and even considered rerouting the trip up the coast to the place of a friend—a mechanic who could fix anything. He figured it would soothe Stutzman.

Nothing worked. Stutzman's haranguing continued.

In Kissimmee, Miller left the group and caught a Greyhound bus for Ohio. By then the man was stricken with fear. He wanted to make sure he got back to Moser Road before Eli Stutzman.

He couldn't shake the look he had seen in Eli Stutzman's cold blue eyes. It was as if the Amishman could have killed him in cold blood and not even blinked an eye.

Rick Adamson, 31, found a likely candidate for a date on page 28 in the April/May 1981 issue of *Stars*, a kinky gay correspondence publication known for the home sex photos of erect penises accompanying its ads—something the more conservative *Advocate* did not feature. It was true that some of the photographs in *Stars* were of young men with their clothes on, but those ads undoubtedly didn't pull as well as the more explicit ones. *Stars* was a gay man's cruising catalog.

The photo that caught Adamson's eye was of a nude, muscular young man posed in a stance that showed off his body. The background was the light-colored wood of a new barn.

> WELL-BUILT HORSEMAN—29, 5'6", 140, brown hair, blue eyes, with a hairy body, looking for same to share our lives together. Send photo and

phone number to: 2848 Moser Road, Rt. 1, Dalton, Ohio. See photo.

Though he knew the advertiser had kept his name out of the magazine on purpose and sought only written responses, Adamson simply used the address to get the phone number, and called Eli Stutzman.

A couple of days later, Stutzman came out to Adamson's apartment, and the two of them spent some time getting acquainted before they went to bed. Stutzman told Adamson his preference was for anal sex and, as Stutzman bent over, Adamson obliged—though it really wasn't what he was into. Stutzman ejaculated while Adamson was still inside him, and it was over. Stutzman didn't want to do anything else.

Adamson was a little disappointed, but not enough to pass up the opportunity to try again at Stutzman's farm a week or so later. After Stutzman had put Danny to bed, he and Adamson went into the master bedroom for sex. It was a replay of the time before—Stutzman climaxing while Adamson rammed him from behind.

Even though sex between them wasn't great, the two men became friends. Adamson even admired Stutzman.

"He was a real concerned father," Adamson later said. "He had arranged for Danny to get some speech training for his stutter. As far as gay activity, he didn't want his son to know any of it was going on. Anytime we messed around he made sure Danny was asleep first."

Adamson was a regular visitor to the farm that summer, visiting as many as two dozen times. Once, he came to Moser Road for a square-dance party in Stutzman's barn. It was a good turnout, with as many as thirty gay men attending. Adamson was amazed at the number of gay men Stutzman knew. As far as he could see, the parties were relatively harmless, a little bit of marijuana and a bunch of gay men looking for friendship and fun.

It was a conversation Adamson had with Jim Frost that

made him think twice about seeing much more of Eli Stutzman.

"Be careful about Eli Stutzman," Frost warned, "Though I couldn't prove it, I think Stutzman murdered his wife in that barn fire at his place."

With his dark hair and dark eyes, Timothy Brown might have considered a career as a model instead of a cop. At the time, he lived with his parents in Stark County and needed to establish thirty days' residency in Wayne County before he could join the sheriff's department as a deputy. A mutual friend—half of a gay couple who had been frequent visitors to Stutzman's farm—put him in touch with Stutzman, who was renting out rooms at his farm.

Brown moved in the first week of July 1981. *Matt Schwartz*, another Amish boy, had moved in also. Daisy Mast liked Brown, who, Stutzman had told her, was a friend from church.

Brown had been raised in rural Brewster, so he understood *Meidnung*. He also knew that sometimes the Amish break the rules. It happened at the Stutzman farm. At night, Stutzman would sometimes go out to the barn to talk with someone in a buggy who had come to visit.

While he lived on Moser Road, Brown learned that several businessmen from Kidron had loaned Stutzman money—it had something to do with the horses that kept coming and going at the farm.

Brown found Stutzman to be a good father, disciplining Danny with care and consistency.

More than once, Stutzman professed concern that the Amish would try to take Danny from him. He never said why he felt that way.

Danny, whose terrible stutter was exacerbated when he was excited, seemed afraid to sleep alone. He slept almost every night in his father's bed—not the bedroom upstairs next to Brown's.

Having Tim Brown's patrol car on the premises proved

too tempting for an Amish boy like Matt Schwartz. One time neighbors watched as Schwartz drove the car, flashers on, through one of Stutzman's fields. Stutzman and Brown were up in Cleveland at the time.

In March 1982, Stutzman left Brown a cryptic note—in effect, an eviction notice.

Brown didn't understand why Stutzman couldn't just tell him to leave the farm. It was a strange way to treat a friend. Brown had even loaned Stutzman a few hundred dollars with no questions asked. Stutzman referred to the cash as "advance rent payments."

The next thing Brown knew, Stutzman said that he and Danny were going to Colorado on vacation. Neither Brown nor Matt Schwartz knew what Stutzman had in mind. Later, it wouldn't faze them when they learned the truth.

Stutzman had struck a deal with *LaVon Kratzer* and sold his farm for $200,000—four times what he had paid Daniel Swartzentruber only five years before. The Amish wept at the news—they had lost more precious land to the *Englischers*.

Once they had taken possession, the Kratzers found something very strange. Why on earth, they wondered, had Eli Stutzman kept a stove and a couch inside the milk house?

PART TWO

Murder Out West

"Most people are alarmed and ask questions about a murder involving a friend. Eli Stutzman didn't ask one question."

—Travis County Sheriff's Detective Jerry Wiggins

CHAPTER THIRTEEN

May 1985

The first time he noticed the rancid smell, the sun hung low over the area known for the lump of earth called Pilot Knob, south of the commotion of metro Austin, Texas, and the noise of Bergstrom Air Force Base, in southwest Travis County. Raymond Kieke, his face as crinkly as buckskin left out in the rain and hung to dry again, scrunched his nose at the first whiff of the too familiar stench. White lines etched the corners of his eyes. The compact, trim man wore glasses, and kept a spare or two stuffed in his pockets so that they were there when he needed them.

Something was dead.

Pilot Knob rises 711 feet above crusty rangeland and fields of maize swirling over a craggy, arid landscape. The Knob is the remnant of a volcano that a millennium ago spewed forth in fury and then faded into extinction. It is the only visual break in an otherwise monotonous land. Farm kids head for the Knob as soon as they are old enough to ride. It's a destination in a place where there is little else outside of barns, irrigation ditches, and endless acres of cropland.

Austin is only twenty minutes away via the major north-south route of Highway 183, and Pilot Knob locals consider it a suitable place for the city folks—all noise and traffic. South Travis County is, after all, the country, a place where cowboy boots are second nature, not de rigueur. The area had been desert before irrigation, and the locals see beauty in the land. Two towns in the vicinity of Colton-Bluff Springs Road are Scenic Loop and Pleasant Valley.

Austinites would say neither place fits its name.

It was the evening of May 9 that Raymond Kieke first smelled the dead thing. The air was thick and hot, and the windows on his dusty pickup were rolled down: Kieke had assumed the position that leaves many farmers with a darker tan on their left forearm—he had propped his elbow on the window frame. The odor was strong, like that of a road kill that hadn't passed through the stage of stench to reach that of a dried, leathery mass. Kieke figured that a calf had wandered off or that maybe a coyote hadn't eaten all of its kill. It doesn't take too long in the Texas sun for fresh meat to become a stomach-turning, revolting mass that would gag a buzzard. He'd look into it later.

On the morning of Mother's Day, May 12, 1985, Kieke was checking on the cattle he grazed on the property he rented, just south of Colton-Bluff Springs Road. In part, he was there to check out the smell—it had reached the point where he could no longer avoid the inconvenience of investigation. He pulled to the side of the road and parked his truck. It was time to find the dead calf.

Kieke walked to a culvert on the south side of the road. The odor grew intense. New weeds edged the thicket of dead, winter brambles. He peered over the edge of the retaining wall built to halt erosion and looked into the ditch. The odor was overpowering and hideous. A body, black with death, was slumped with legs rigid and arms flailing. The body seemed to melt into the damp earth. Bright yellow sunflowers broke the somber pall enveloping the culvert.

Kieke had seen enough—more than enough, actually. He got back into his pickup and drove home. There, he called the Travis County Sheriff's Office. The dispatcher recorded the time of the call: 8:09 A.M. Kieke gave directions so that an officer could meet him on Colton-Bluff Springs Road, just off FM 1625—known to many as the road to the little town of Creedmoor, the farm road breaks off Highway 183 like a dried-up, brittle twig, jutting to the southeast across the rangeland. Returning to the culvert, Kieke waited downwind.

The dispatcher alerted Richard "Frito" Navarro, a deputy on patrol in the area. Dark-eyed Navarro, his black hair combed back over his head like a helmet, had seen his share of dead bodies. In fact, the remote area around Pilot Knob had been a popular site for the disposal of victims.

As one veteran cop later said, "If I had a body to dump I think it would be the first place I would go. There's no one out there, and it's still fairly close to town. Kind of convenient, I'd say."

Navarro followed Kieke's pickup truck to a point just beyond the culvert. The deputy didn't need Kieke to point out the site of the body. The stench was like a smelly rope pulling him toward the corpse. He immediately confirmed what Kieke had told him, and radioed for Homicide and the medical examiner—a body in a ditch, hidden behind the cover of weeds and grasses, didn't usually indicate death by natural causes. He secured the crime scene for the detectives and medical examiner—keeping his distance from the corpse.

If Navarro had looked up from the ditch, across the field, he would have seen the barn and pasture of Harry Reininger's farm. In the pasture was a beautiful stallion.

CHAPTER FOURTEEN

A monument marks the only spot in the country where the borders of four states converge: Utah, Colorado, Arizona, and New Mexico. Cottonwoods grow along ditches, sucking water from the bleak, juniper-studded landscape. Tumbleweeds are suspended forever, impaled on barbed-wire fences cordoning off rangeland. The jagged forms of the snow-covered La Plata range jut up from the desert.

The Four Corners' towns of Durango and Cortez, Colorado, and of Farmington and Aztec, New Mexico, show traces of the Hispanic, Indian, and Old West influences that mark the region: *pueblo, mesa*, and *wagon wheel* pop up in cafe names and design motifs. Breathtaking mountain and desert scenery draw in tourists from all points, to ride the Durango-Silverton Narrow Gauge Railroad, to wander the Anasazi ruins, or just to kick back and relax in Old West shops and restaurants. In winter, world-class skiing tops the itinerary.

As far as the gay scene of the early 1980s was concerned, locals confined themselves to the Diamond Belle Saloon, the bar in the red and white Gay Nineties Strater Hotel, and the Animas Riverside Lounge at the Durango Holiday Inn. Out-of-towners looking for gay sex also took in the Main Mall and the Narrow Gauge Train Station, both of which were listed in *Bob Damron's Address Book*, a pocket guide listing gay "cruisy" places.

When Stutzman connected with Colorado rancher *Terry Palmer*, the former Amishman made it clear that he wanted to get away from Ohio—more critically, away from the Swartzentruber Order.

The West was Stutzman's escape route, and, in the end, a death sentence for Danny.

Several years older than the Amishman from Ohio, Palmer was a trim man with smooth skin and fine features who had never before advertised in *The Advocate*. Yet, in the spring of 1982, following the suicide of his lover and adopted "son," he placed an ad answered by Eli Stutzman.

Stutzman's reply displayed a naïveté about the gay lifestyle that appealed to Palmer, who had a job requiring discretion, hence the ruse "the adopted son." Stutzman seemed a perfect candidate. In fact, the Amishman claimed he had never seen *The Advocate* until a Mennonite friend showed him the edition featuring Palmer's ad.

Stutzman wrote that he had been shunned by the Amish, and that it was causing his son some problems. He was looking for a new life, something wholesome for his little boy. He enclosed photographs of Danny.

Palmer, who was of Swiss stock and had been brought up on horror stories of the "weird" Amish, was moved by Stutzman's predicament. Palmer's grandmother had painted a sinister picture of the Amish.

"You have no idea how many Amish children never grow up," she had said.

"I was raised to believe that the Amish were strange, more or less that they worship the devil," he recalled. "I knew they had been thrown out of the Catholic Church in Europe. I wanted to help Eli get out of that situation."

Palmer flew to Cleveland and spent the Memorial Day weekend of 1982 at the Dalton farm. Stutzman played the shunned Amishman to the hilt, and Palmer bought it.

Stutzman said that when he was a young man he had been raped by an old Amishman in a feed mill.

"That's what made me gay," he said.

In June, Eli and Danny flew to Durango to look over

Palmer's ranch. Stutzman said the place wasn't large enough for what he had in mind, and left without making a deal.

In the summer he returned to Colorado, and, after a week with a real estate agent, Stutzman and Palmer put money down on a large ranch with a four-bedroom house, near Durango.

Palmer sold his small ranch, and Stutzman put up the down payment of $65,000. Palmer, who had fewer resources, agreed to make the monthly payments until their equity balanced. Palmer's chief asset outside of some farm equipment was a stallion valued at $15,000.

Though Stutzman had sold most of what he had in Ohio, he packed a buggy and the Amish furniture Amos Gingerich had built. Stutzman announced that he planned on introducing surrey racing to Colorado.

With Eli and Danny Stutzman gone from Ohio, Dalton neighbors worried about the boy.

"What would his life be like in Colorado?" Wilma Moser asked her husband. The Mosers could only assume the worst—the rumors about Stutzman's activities were no longer whispered. They were public knowledge.

On her way to work at Gerber's Feed Mill, Wilma Moser prayed that God would save Danny from the nightmare she felt certain he must be enduring.

On the surface, Danny Stutzman's life might have seemed idyllic given the magnificence of the Colorado ranch setting. Anyone seeing the 5-year-old likely would have believed him to be an average, happy child. He dressed in blue jeans, wore *Dukes of Hazzard* T-shirts, and had a ready smile.

But it was a facade. The truth was that Danny represented little more than a cover for his father's homosexuality. That had also been true in Ohio, but in Colorado, away from the Amish and the neighbors who had passed judgment on him, Stutzman felt free to ignore his son and cut loose. Terry Palmer provided the parenting role that Stutzman shirked.

Each morning, Palmer drove Danny to the county road to catch the bus for the fourteen-mile ride to the Ignacio Elementary School, where the boy had been assigned to kindergarten teacher Janet Green. Though drawn to the little boy, Green could barely understand him when he spoke, so severe was Danny's stutter.

His father was ready with an excuse. "Danny didn't speak much English until about a year or so ago," he offered as an explanation, when he enrolled the boy in November.

Danny, his hair now clipped so close to his head that he looked as if a Marine had shorn him, was assigned to a speech pathologist for twice-weekly therapy. Stutzman told the school that stuttering had been a family problem. "All seven of my brothers stuttered," he said. "All but my oldest brother talk fine now."

Almost immediately Danny began to relate more to Palmer than to his own father. The boy started directing his school activities to Palmer, who tried to avoid them, sensing that he was in the middle of a dangerous situation.

"Tell your dad. I don't want to hear it," Palmer would say, whenever Danny approached him with news from school.

While Danny was settling into a normal routine at school, things were happening at home suggesting renewed trouble with Stutzman's mental health. Of course, Palmer didn't know anything about Stutzman's previous breakdowns, other than what he volunteered.

In Ohio, Stutzman had been warm and communicative; in Colorado, he was often silent and moody. Palmer, who had expected both a partnership and a life with Stutzman, felt that the Amishman was slipping away. Once, when he asked Stutzman if he, Palmer, had done something wrong, the younger man snapped at him, "No. It's not you."

Another time, Stutzman became enraged after Palmer opened a box of Pennsylvania Dutch stickers he had purchased on the trip to Wayne County. "Throw them away! I don't ever want to see them around here again!" Stutzman screamed.

When Palmer spoke about his dead "son," Stutzman yelled at him to be quiet. "I don't ever want to hear about him again," he said.

"It was almost a Dr. Jekyll and Mr. Hyde kind of switch in personality. It was like he had a split personality," Palmer later said.

Strangely, there were times when Stutzman seemed like the caring man Palmer had met through *The Advocate*. Stutzman asked Palmer if he would be Danny's guardian should something happen to Stutzman. He had a lawyer draft up a document specifying the wish.

Palmer was flattered, but Stutzman's erratic behavior made him guarded.

"What about your relatives back east?" he asked.

"I don't want my boy with the Amish. Anyway, none of them would travel out west to get him."

If Palmer's relationship with Stutzman was faltering, the little boy continued to grow closer. Danny shadowed Palmer on the ranch. Since Stutzman had said he wanted Palmer to be close with the little boy, Palmer asked if he could take Danny to church.

"No! I've had enough of that in my life," Stutzman said.

Eli Stutzman had changed from the man Palmer had met in Ohio.

For a gay man who had initially professed disinterest in the gay lifestyle, Palmer noticed that Stutzman kept a sizeable collection of gay porno magazines and videotapes.

The number of Four Corners gays was small enough that when the gay and bisexual crowd got together everyone knew everyone. When Stutzman showed up in mid-October 1982, he was seen as new blood—"new meat," some joked—in a crowd that could use a little. Having sex with the same old bunch had become boring. Even drugs lacked the punch and excitement of a new sex partner.

Four Corners gays partied in two basic groups: Durango, Colorado, and Farmington, New Mexico. Though the Durango group included a doctor and a lawyer, most were average working-class gays, or ranchers like Eli Stutzman. Calendars were crammed with parties every Friday and Saturday night—and every holiday in-between. Hosts provided the gathering place, others brought drugs.

At 39, *Kenny Hankins* ran a successful business in one of the nondescript, dusty little towns around the Four Corners area. Hankins was closeted because of the small-town community. Yet he found action on the endless highways of the desert. His CB handle, "WW," stood for "Wienie Washer." Whenever he had the opportunity, Hankins climbed into the air-conditioned comfort of his Cadillac to prowl for men who wanted a blow job. He found a little bit of danger, and more than enough takers, among the truckers passing through.

Hankins met Eli Stutzman in the bar at the Holiday Inn in the late fall of 1982. As far as Hankins could see, Eli Stutzman was a gay sex symbol: a well-muscled body, blue eyes, and a neat mustache.

"He was a real hunk. He would get the attention at any bar he went into. Where in the hell did Mother Nature go wrong, because he's attractive, physically fit?" Hankins later asked.

Stutzman's biggest attraction—according to Hankins, anyway—was the size of his penis.

"Eli would always wear Levis, ironed, and was the type that he made damn sure of his pants. He was enormous. I would say he would make John Holmes look sick," he said.

At the time they met, Stutzman told Hankins that his lover and ranch partner Terry Palmer had threatened to harm him if he ever invited any friends out.

" 'Don't you ever bring anybody to this fuckin' house and don't you ever tell anybody that I play around cuz I'll beat your ass,' " Stutzman claimed Palmer had said.

When Hankins dropped Stutzman off at the ranch, the ex-Amishman said, "I'd invite you in, but you never know. I don't want Palmer to fly off the handle."

Stutzman, Hankins, and other gay men lived in a haze of marijuana and a white cloud of coke when they could get it. Stutzman also used "poppers." Amyl nitrate—or the similar formulas butyl nitrite or alkyl nitrate—were considered the drugs of choice for gays in the early 1980s. Inhaling the drugs heightened and prolonged the sensation of orgasm. Popular brands among Stutzman's crowd included Rush and Thrust.

As far as Hankins could see, Stutzman had been a user for some time.

October 13, 1982

On November 4, 1982, Wilma and Norman Moser received a tedious letter from Stutzman, who wrote endlessly about the ranch and Danny's progress in kindergarten. The real reason for the letter was buried in the trivia in the third paragraph. Stutzman complained that the Postal Service had mixed up his address and that he was getting X-rated mail he wasn't supposed to—it wasn't even addressed to him by name.

Stutzman had gotten wind of the stories about his X-rated mail and wanted to defuse them. He knew the Mosers would spread the word that gay letters sent to his old farm hadn't been meant for him.

For the kind of fun Stutzman must have been looking for, the Four Corners most likely proved a sexual playground with more new friends and variations than he could have hoped for in Dalton, Ohio.

Louise and *Mark Hanson* were what friends liked to call an "alternative couple." Mark, now in his middle years, had

had some gay experiences when he was a teen that he wanted to rekindle. Louise, an attractive woman who favored the New Age movement, went along for the ride. If some considered her a "Fag Hag," it was all right with her.

The summer of 1982 was her initiation into the gay world. By the time Eli Stutzman showed up in the fall, Louise Hanson might have thought she had seen it all.

She could not have been more wrong.

Eli Stutzman's name made it onto the guest list for Louise's impromptu birthday party. Stutzman brought Danny along. What Stutzman had his son do that night was both shocking and repugnant. Stutzman told his son to grab men's crotches.

"Danny must have been five at the time," Louise later remembered, still trying to shake the implausibility of it all. "Eli was encouraging Danny to grope men and swat them on the butt."

There was no doubt about the former Amishman's intentions.

"He was trying to teach him homosexual behavior," she said.

Danny did what his father wanted, willingly and innocently. *He had been told by his father to do it*. The boy giggled as he went from man to man, groping and petting.

"What are you doing, Eli?" Louise asked, cornering Stutzman at her party. *"He's just a little boy—let him be a little boy!"*

Stutzman was adamant. "I'm going to train him so he'll never have to deal with women."

Another who met Stutzman around the time he first arrived in the Four Corners was an artist/psychic/teenager from Farmington named *Michael Harris*. Harris noticed Stutzman at the early parties, always keeping to himself and being very discreet when he left with a trick.

"The first time I saw him in Amish clothes, I thought he was dressed up old-fashioned Western-style. When I asked him about it, he told me he was from that Amish religion. It blew me away."

You're kidding . . . and you're carrying on like this? he thought when he first met Stutzman.

It was obvious that living with Stutzman had been a mistake for Terry Palmer. The routine had become unbearable. After dinner, Stutzman usually went out or to his room to watch television alone, leaving Palmer to care for Danny and get him ready for bed. The strain was showing on Danny, too.

At night, the little boy frequently woke crying. He said he was afraid to sleep alone. He asked to sleep with Palmer, but the man told the boy he was too big. Danny's second choice was his father's bed, where he routinely slept. Palmer, trying to be helpful, approached Stutzman about the boy's sleep problems.

"It's none of your business!" Stutzman raged, before turning his back.

Stutzman frequently left the ranch, disappearing for several days at a time. He stayed a week in Reno, picking up tricks at the Gay Rodeo. He phoned from Albuquerque, where he said he was looking for construction work.

Palmer asked when he planned to return.

"I'll be home when I get there."

Yet, when it suited him and the circumstances required it, Stutzman continued to play his role as father. On December 10, 1982, he wrote to the Mosers that Danny had adjusted to his new surroundings and school just fine.

"It doesn't seem to bother him that 40 percent of the kids in his class are Indian and Mexican," he wrote.

In addition, he and Danny were planning on taking up skiing.

Over the course of the school year, schoolteacher Janet Green saw Eli Stutzman more than most other parents—five or six times. When Stutzman came to a school function for which the kids had made a big salad, he watched Danny to see what the boy ate.

"He was very concerned about his boy," she later said.

On New Year's Eve, Stutzman and a hundred or so gay men and women drifted in and out of a party held in a log cabin just off the highway outside of Durango. The Hansons also attended, as did Stutzman's ranch partner, Palmer.

Though the party was themed "favorite fantasies" and party-goers arrived in costume, no one outdid the host, who wore only a cape and a cock ring, a device used to encircle the penis and testicles in order to maintain an erection. The host repeatedly flashed his erect penis as party-goers milled around, drinking beer and smoking pot.

Among Stutzman's friends and lovers there that night was David Tyler, the stoned, groggy-looking owner of the Automatic Transmission Exchange, in Durango. Tyler had been busted in Utah for cultivating marijuana, and users in town knew they could count on him for coke and pot. For many, Tyler was seen as bad news, but for some reason he and Stutzman hit it off. Stutzman had partied with him at the Strater or Holiday Inn, and Palmer overheard Eli a number of times on the phone talking with Tyler from the ranch.

The gay hosts had installed a portable structure—similar to a mobile home—behind the log house. It was a large unit, built for sex, with several hot tubs and a sauna filling the floor. Condensation streaked the windows and temperatures soared to 100 degrees inside the adult playpen.

Louise Hanson would never forget what she saw and participated in. "The hot tubs were full of women and men doing anything you can imagine. Lesbian girls were licking each other. There were gays giving each other blow jobs, and there were different-sex couples having intercourse."

The biggest shock occurred when a Four Corners clergyman made a dramatic point of removing his wedding ring.

"Guess this doesn't cut it tonight!" the clergyman said, before stepping nude into the sexual soup.

Among the men licking and sucking at the all-night orgy was Stutzman, who paired off several times.

"He seemed to be really enjoying himself," Hanson later said.

At dawn a group of the tired and bleary-eyed party-goers were invited to Stutzman's ranch for brunch. The crowd was mixed and the talk centered on the fun of the night. But for the Hansons, the orgy in the mobile unit behind the log cabin had been too much.

"I'm not so sure we're like these people," Louise Hanson told her husband on the drive out to Stutzman's ranch.

During the brunch, David Tyler invited Stutzman and Palmer to a party at his home in Durango. Danny Stutzman showed off his train set. By afternoon the place had cleared out and Stutzman turned a cold shoulder to Terry Palmer.

"You clean up this place," he said.

After little more than two months together, Stutzman and Palmer's relationship was heading for the inevitable breakup—though, by Stutzman's standards, the relationship had been successful. After all, it had gotten him away from the Amish.

In mid-January *Ryan Bloom* moved onto the ranch. Bloom, a good-looking man a few years younger than Stutzman, knew immediately that he had walked into a mine field of emotions and betrayal in which Palmer and Stutzman were at odds. While Stutzman continued to display his anger at Palmer—the reason for which was still unclear—he was friendly with Bloom.

And so was Danny.

If Stutzman's plan was to have his son "learn the gay way," as he had stated at parties, it seemed to be working. Within the first two days of Bloom's arrival, Danny climbed onto his lap and tried to unbutton his clothes. The intent was overtly sexual. Horrified, Bloom pushed the boy away and went to Palmer.

"My God, Terry, Danny was trying to undress me!" he told Palmer. Palmer was not surprised. *Danny's father had taught him to do that.*

"He was trying to make a pass at me," Bloom later said. "I was shocked. I didn't know what was going on."

Bloom stayed behind one weekend when Palmer went to Denver for a workshop. Stutzman suggested they go to a party in the Grandview area, outside of Durango. Bloom, a father himself, was aghast when Stutzman took Danny along. When they arrived, Stutzman paired off with another man and began to make out. Other gay couples did the same.

"It was a gay group, a bunch of lesbians, and some college kids. Eli was on the floor kissing a guy and Danny was there, sitting there oblivious to it all. It was as though he had seen it a million times," Bloom recalled.

The scene was replayed later at a party at the ranch. This time Danny was the only child there as he watched his father writhe on the floor, his tongue inside another man's mouth.

Bloom knew that what was going on was wrong, but he copped out. It wasn't any of his business, he told himself.

He and Palmer, however, discussed the situation, and the older man considered reporting Stutzman to Social Services. In the end, he backed down. He didn't want anyone to know he was gay. Instead, he confronted Stutzman.

"I don't think you really should be taking Danny to gay parties," Palmer told him.

"Ryan's been blabbing to you," Stutzman shot back coldly. "You think you know a lot about kids, but you don't know shit."

Louise Hanson was another who considered notifying the authorities. For her, the impetus was a statement she heard someone make that Stutzman had been "messing" with his boy. But, like Palmer, she didn't report it. She *couldn't*. If she did, then she'd have to answer the question:

"Well, Louise, why were you at that party?"

She rationalized her silence later. "They'd probably just blow it off, thinking I was a busybody."

Later a gay man told the woman: "Eli said he was going to turn Danny over to his buddies for sexual favors." Louise Hanson found it hard to sleep that night.

But she did.

In January, Stutzman, apparently bored with Palmer and the Durango and Farmington gays, advertised again for sex through his old standby, *The Advocate*. This time he indicated he wanted a "topman," meaning he was a "bottom" and wanted to be on the receiving end of anal intercourse.

He also added an inch to his height.

> Hndsm masc hairy W/M early 30's, 5'7", 140#, into ranching, construction. Seeks topman with same interests. Write with photo to Box 185, Bayfield, CO 81122.

The response to Stutzman's ad must have been good. Each day in ritualistic fashion he brought the mail to the ranch and sorted it, setting aside Palmer's. One day, Palmer noticed a letter addressed to Box 185 and asked about it.

Eli grabbed the envelope. "It's not yours," he said, glaring before retreating to his bedroom.

Stutzman, however, continued to befriend Bloom and let him into his life—at least to the extent that he would talk with him. Much of what Eli said, of course, was a lie. One day he told Bloom that a man he was corresponding with had wanted a photograph.

"I'm certainly not going to send him a nude photo," Stutzman demurred, as though he couldn't conceive of such a thing. He apparently forgot about his nude photo in *Stars*.

If Palmer had ever thought even for a minute that things might improve with Stutzman, it was all thrown out the window when Danny started showing signs of being swept into the gay world. One night, while watching television, Danny reached into Palmer's robe and grabbed his penis.

"Danny!" Palmer said, standing up and brushing the boy away. "What are you doing?"

The little boy looked up, surprised that he had done something wrong. "I just wanted to see your body," he explained.

"Danny, I don't want to be touched there. It's not nice." For sometime, Palmer had noticed that Danny had a curiosity about the male anatomy. He colored pictures of phalluses.

For Palmer, it was time to get out.

"I couldn't live there, because I would suspect that something was going on with Danny. It tore me up, but the best thing was to get out of there," he later said.

The truth was, he was afraid that Danny Stutzman would do something or say something that would tip off people that Terry Palmer was gay.

Ted Truitt was 26, unhappily married, and living in a small midwestern town when he answered an *Advocate* ad Stutzman had placed. Truitt was looking for someone to help him out of the closet, and Stutzman, who was a dairy farmer like himself, might understand.

They corresponded and made plans to meet at the airport in Cleveland when Stutzman returned to Ohio after Christmas, 1982.

Though being with a man was what Truitt had wanted for so long, there was an emptiness after he and Stutzman had sex. If he had hoped before their first encounter that something serious might develop between them, it was clear Stutzman wasn't interested.

"Eli said he preferred men with hairier chests than mine," Truitt said later.

They drove out to Welty Road so that Stutzman could visit his parents, and Truitt stayed in the car an hour and a half, turning on the heater to keep warm.

On that trip, Stutzman showed up at the Kratzers and told them that the "strange mail" they had received wasn't meant for him.

"Those letters were for Tim Brown," Stutzman lied.

Stutzman told Truitt that his wife had had heart disease and died in a barn fire, smoke inhalation contributing to her death. "Eli told me he knew he was gay before he married," Truitt recalled. "He played around with some men a few times as an Amishman."

The Indiana man didn't ask why Stutzman had gotten married if he knew he was gay. Truitt already knew the answer. He had done the same thing himself.

The ranch house front door was locked, which was unusual. Though he had a key, Palmer, who had come home from work early to snowplow, figured Eli Stutzman didn't want to be disturbed, so he went on with the plowing. Later, three men piled into a car and drove erratically down the driveway. From the way they drove, Palmer thought they must have been drinking or on drugs. He wondered if Stutzman had been dealing drugs—it didn't seem like a sexual rendezvous.

"Who were those guys?" Palmer asked later.

"Some friends of mine." Stutzman's speech was clipped. "In the future, if you decide to come home from work early, please call."

In February, Palmer summoned the courage to break the ranch partnership. He was afraid Stutzman would be angry, maybe even violent.

"Fine. What do you want?" Stutzman was icy.

Palmer signed a quick claim deed, turning the property over to Stutzman for $5,000—Palmer's equity. Still strapped for cash, Palmer jumped at the chance when Stutzman offered to buy his tractor and some other farm equipment. Stutzman wrote out a check for another $5,000 as though it were pocket change. Palmer wondered just how much money Eli Stutzman had.

They also worked out a contract for Stutzman to care for the $15,000 stallion.

"He was so good with horses and he had the big ranch. It made sense that he could do a better job with the stallion," Palmer later said.

It was spring 1983 when Palmer and Bloom moved off the ranch, leaving Danny alone with his father.

Chuck Freeman drank too much and knew it, but whatever troubled him was so deep he couldn't stop. Yet, by all appearances, the man had it all. In his 50s, Freeman had amassed a considerable estate of ranch land, investment properties, and southwest Indian artwork. He had been married and was a father, but between drinking binges he lived on the fringe of the gay life. Freeman was sharp and knew a good time when he saw one. Eli Stutzman was a good time.

Stutzman wasn't particularly interested in the older man, at least sexually—though his money must have seemed appealing.

It wasn't that Freeman and Kenny Hankins, for that matter, were sexually inexperienced or naive about the gay world; it was more that Stutzman still had the kind of wild streak that the years in the closet had drained from them. Stutzman represented a last fling at outrageousness.

As he had repeatedly done with others, Stutzman continued to use horror stories about his father and the Amish to win sympathy. Freeman asked about Danny's mother, and Stutzman said that she had died in a tragic accident.

"We bought a secondhand car that we kept in a garage in town so that none of the Amish would know we had it. We were out driving and I rolled it, killing her. It was the first car I'd ever driven," he said.

At the ranch, later, he showed Freeman a snapshot of Danny and him wearing Amish clothes.

"That's the reason Danny stutters," he said, pointing at the black hats in the photograph. "It's the Amish. We weren't supposed to speak English for years, until school."

Stutzman typed a letter asking whether, if something should happen to him, Freeman would raise Danny. Again, as with Palmer, Eli's stated reason was his hatred for the Amish and the fear that they would take his boy away from him.

Freeman turned him down.

"Eli," Freeman said gently, "I'm just too damn old to raise any more kids."

It rained like hell the spring day that Stutzman invited ten gay men, including Freeman and Hankins, to a party at the ranch. Stutzman served an Amish-style chicken dinner.

Chuck Freeman marveled at his cooking.

"Eli was one hell of a cook. He could turn weeds into jam."

And he was a great father, too.

"When Danny tore his pajamas, his father told him he would make him a new pair the following day," Freeman added. "I was real impressed. He was going to *make* his boy new pajamas."

After the little boy went to bed, the men sacked out on the living room floor and watched gay porno videos.

CHAPTER FIFTEEN

Nobody could fault Glen Pritchett for not being a nice guy. Even after all the events that led him to Texas, he still would have given someone his last dime. If he'd had one. When he finally left Montana he had a sack of clothes and an impossible thirst that could only be slaked by beer—lots of it.

Though he was only five feet nine inches, his medium build and lean 152 pounds made him seem taller; a crown of wavy dark hair added to the illusion. His brown eyes were washed in the red that comes from too-little sleep and too much booze and pot.

In some tragic way, his life had been without hope. Like the old tattoo that drunken sailors would have etched onto beefy forearms, Glen Albert Pritchett was born to lose.

Born in 1961 to a Latter-day Saints family that had migrated from Logan, Utah, to Montana, Pritchett was the first son of Bob and Evelyn—a fifteen-year veteran of the Postal Service and his dry-cleaner wife. Glen Pritchett had a younger brother and two older sisters. None of the other Pritchett children had any trouble with the law—not brother Cecil or sisters Sharon and Nona.

When it came to trouble in the Pritchett family, Glen was always in the center of the storm.

It started early. Pritchett, who had never done well in school, began to rebel against the strictness of Mormon life.

He began to drink, skip school, smoke pot, and be a typical, out-of-control, hell-raising teenager.

"Incorrigible" was the word used by social workers who knew the boy.

For Pritchett's sister, Nona, the handwriting had been written on the wall in indelible ink for some time, maybe ever since her brother was born. The Glen she knew had been a runaway with a chip on his shoulder.

"Glen had always resented authority. He was constantly taking off," she recalled, years after his final flight from Montana. "Sometimes he would be gone for a week at a time—it tore my parents up. Nothing seemed to work. Nothing made him stay."

As a teen, Pritchett worried about not being popular—he had a fear of being rejected. Those who knew him later claimed that it was his insecurity that led him to seek refuge in the contents of a beer bottle.

When it got so bad that he could no longer be part of the family, his parents put him in a foster home up north in Cutbank, Montana. The family was LDS—as the Pritchetts wanted. The father was an FBI agent. The arrangement was fine for a couple of months, until a friend of Pritchett's sent him marijuana through the mail.

After a forty-five-day evaluation at the juvenile detention center of Pine Hills, in Miles City, Montana, Pritchett ended up in the home of Jo Lyn and Allan Kuser, in Helena. It was one of the best things to happen to him. The Kusers and their children—with whom Glen was gentle and caring—were the closest he had come to having a real family. They even took him on a vacation to California.

Pritchett tried to complete his education, but never got the knack of schoolwork and the attendance it required. His GPA was 0.53 when he withdrew from Helgate Senior High in the spring of 1978.

While in detention at the boys' home, he met a girl with the same kind of background as he had. *Sandy Turner* was a block away in Missoula's "Attention home," a short-term facility for troubled and defiant teenagers. Sandy's problem, she later said, was her mother, a well-meaning and controlling woman who had expectations of behavior her daughter could not meet. Sandy was wild. Sandy was incorrigible. Sandy was a runaway looking for trouble. All were designations offered by *Barbara Turner*.

But Sandy was none of those. She was a scared girl who, for some reason, got off on the wrong foot and couldn't come to grips with the way things should be—or at least the way her mother thought they should be.

Glen and Sandy, both 16, made their plans to run away at a Missoula Dairy Queen. A few weeks after they had hitched a ride to Billings, Montana, Sandy called her mother and told her she would come back on one condition: that she and Glen could wed. Mrs. Turner agreed.

On August 15, 1978, Sandy Turner and Glen Albert Pritchett were wed across the Montana border in Wallace, Idaho. The reception was held at the East Missoula Moose Lodge: cake, coffee, and punch were served. Sandy never left Glen's side, holding his hand with the devotion of the beautiful bride that she was. For a moment, those attending the party set aside prophecies of doom for the marriage. Just maybe these kids had something special after all.

The authorities at the Missoula boys' home suggested that it wouldn't set a good example for the other kids if they saw Sandy and Glen married and around town. They urged—"demanded," Sandy later said—that the couple leave. They packed up and got a place in Helena.

Then a miracle occurred—to Sandy and her parents it could have seemed nothing less. Pritchett pulled himself together and joined the Coast Guard. He was 17, with Pine Hills and minor scrapes with the law behind him. It was a chance at a future. He enlisted and was fingerprinted on February 6, 1979.

Friends told each other that Pritchett was going to get his life together, that he had the right idea—get into the military, learn to be an electrician, then come back to Montana and make a life for himself. It was neat and simple. Everyone was happy.

Everyone, of course, except Pritchett. He and Sandy left Montana, first for Reedsport, Oregon, then for Staten Island in New York. They hated Reedsport; it was dark, damp, and dingy.

"Even the beach was lousy," Sandy recalled.

The only thing good about Reedsport was the birth of a daughter.

New York wasn't much better. Pritchett had a grueling schedule, pulling duty every other day and on weekends. He relieved tension and boredom by continuing his love affair with the drunken state. He partied whenever he had the chance, leaving his wife at home with their baby girl.

Glen's sister Sharon got a call from him during which he complained about having to do things the Coast Guard's way. Sharon's advice was not exactly what Glen had been fishing for: "Why do you have to act that way? When they tell you to do something, just shut up and do it!"

In 1982 the Pritchetts' son was born in Montana, Sandy having flown back ahead of time. Glen returned from his ship in time to hold his son in the hospital. The following year, Pritchett was discharged from the Coast Guard and returned to Montana full time. He sat around the apartment drinking, using up most of the money from his unemployment checks while Sandy waitressed.

One time Barbara Turner took her daughter to Al-Anon, the support group for spouses of alcoholics. By then, however, the marriage was over.

September 6, 1983 was the culmination of the big slide for Glen Pritchett. At 10:00 P.M. his erratic driving caused a Montana Highway Patrol officer to pull him over under suspicion of drunk driving. When it was clear that he was too drunk to complete the alphabet and was swaying side to side during routine sobriety tests, Pritchett was arrested.

The 21-year-old told the officer that he had been on his way to see a friend in Helena and had consumed a six-pack of beer in the car on the way—that he hadn't eaten anything since the previous night.

Three days later, the young man was out of jail and in court. He was ordered to complete an alcohol-abuse program and was fined $505, with $225 suspended on the condition that the fine was paid and the program completed.

On September 8, 1983, Sandy filed for divorce. She was only 21, but she had been married for five years, and she had two children to raise. The court ordered Pritchett to pay $75 per month, per child.

Pritchett admitted himself to the hospital drug and alcohol program. He finished a day or two early and called Sandy to pick him up. In no time at all, though, he was shaking hands with a six-pack again.

The Missoula police were among the more frequent visitors to the Pritchett residence during the month of October 1983. They visited the apartment three times, each time finding a domestic dispute involving an angry young woman and a drunk man.

The Pritchetts' divorce was final on October 13, though they still saw each other and still entertained the hope that they could get back together someday.

Once Pritchett suggested that they leave the kids with Mrs. Turner and run away together, just as they had when they were teenagers. Sandy refused.

CHAPTER SIXTEEN

Eli Stutzman's Four Corners watering hole was a dingy bar that sat in a heap off Highway 550. Even today, it's a locals-only kind of place, despite its proximity to the main road through the desert. Though the logo is a martini glass, beer accounts for the lion's share of the bar's receipts. The men who sit inside and pass the day are as much a fixture as the beer taps they drain. Lonely small-town women go there to meet dates and, if they feel like it, take a ride with a handsome stranger to a motel or a deserted roadside.

Though the place never made it into *Bob Damron's Address Book*, men do all right there, too. At least Stutzman did.

The former Amishman surely must have stood out when he started coming in, first with Freeman, then on his own. Stutzman's appearance was neater than that of the regular cowboys and ranchers. His hair and mustache were perfectly trimmed, and his blue jeans showed the crease of a steam iron.

It took Freeman a little while to catch on to Stutzman's sexual modus operandi, and when he did he was amazed. Sitting at the bar, tipping back a beer, Stutzman effortlessly connected with men and disappeared into the bathroom or outside for a blow job.

Hankins, for one, thought he had Stutzman figured out: "Eli's deal is to smoke a joint, snort a popper, just get high, and as far as his sex drive and stuff, everybody that knows him says 'My God, the man is wilder than a peach-orchard boar!' "

Stutzman gave Freeman a copy of the guide to T-rooms or "trick rooms"—places men could go for sex. Stutzman had obviously studied the book and put it to good and frequent use.

"Eli Stutzman would have fucked a snake if he could have," Freeman later said.

Stutzman was unconcerned about AIDS. He once told Hankins he would never use a condom.

"I ain't fuckin' in no sock," he said.

One summer night at the bar, Stutzman met up with a construction worker from Bloomfield, and Freeman loaned him his car so the two men could trick. A while later, bored and impatient, Freeman went looking for them and found them just north of town. Stutzman, his pants down, was on top of the man, engaged in anal intercourse. Neither man paid much attention to Freeman—who even took a photograph for his collection.

Stutzman boasted about such conquests, and Freeman wondered what it would take to become one of the notches on Stutzman's leather belt. The closest he got was when Stutzman stayed over one night and they masturbated. Freeman finally saw what all the fuss was about.

It was the size of Stutzman's penis.

"I've showered with hundreds of men in the military, and Eli Stutzman was the biggest I've ever seen," Freeman said.

Stutzman appeared at Palmer and Bloom's new farm, saying that he planned to sue the Hjermstads—the people from whom the farm was purchased—because he had uncovered selenium in the soil—a harmful trace mineral found in high concentrations in parts of Colorado.

"But there isn't any out there. All of the places with

selenium have been mapped and recorded," Palmer answered.

"I don't care. I'm filing a suit against the Hjermstads for selling the place under false pretenses. I'm going to tell them I found selenium."

If Stutzman had wanted Palmer to be a party to the fraud, he had miscalculated. Palmer told him he was crazy.

Danny hugged Palmer's leg. "Could I live with you instead of my dad?" he asked.

Then Palmer grew angry when he found that Stutzman had taken the stallion for a trail ride in New Mexico—under the agreement, the horse couldn't leave Colorado without Palmer's consent. In response, Stutzman waged a hate campaign that would hit Palmer where it hurt the most—the secrecy of his sexual preference. Since Palmer believed no one in the community knew he was gay, to Stutzman, telling others could have been viewed as the ultimate revenge.

An old-timer who lived near the old ranch called Palmer one night.

"You the one that gives the blow jobs?"

"What?"

"I see there's a sign in the highway bathroom that says to call you."

"What are you talking about?"

"Better go look at it," the old man said.

Palmer grabbed a camera and drove out to the rest room, where he found written: *"If want a good blow job call Terry Palmer. He's over 50, but he's gut."*

The handwriting was Eli Stutzman's. Further, the second *good* had been spelled in German. Enraged, Palmer confronted Stutzman, but he denied he had done it.

While Stutzman was trying to get revenge on Palmer, new men like *Kevin Stansfield*, an army officer stationed in El Paso, Texas, came across one of Stutzman's advertisements. Stansfield, a Mormon, also shared a conservative religious background. Both preferred the country over the city, and, finally, both professed a love of children.

Stansfield drove up to Colorado for the weekend.

Like others, Stansfield initially saw Stutzman's good, gentle side.

"I watched Eli and Danny together as they fixed supper, and I thought, 'what a nice, wonderful relationship' they had. It was the ideal father and son relationship."

After the meal, Stutzman told Danny to put on his pajamas. A few minutes later, the boy came back to the kitchen wearing a blue blanket sleeper. He crawled on Stansfield's lap, and the officer read a bedtime story.

After Danny went to bed, the two men stayed up talking. Stansfield wanted to find out as much as he could about growing up as a gay Amishman.

Stutzman showed him a photograph of himself, posed in a buggy and dressed in his Amish clothes. He told Stansfield the photo was taken when he and some other Amish boys were racing buggies. From the way Stutzman described himself, in conversation at the ranch and in his letters, Stansfield assumed that Stutzman had left the Amish only recently—within the last year.

The friendly mood changed when Stutzman recounted the story of his wife's death in the fire. He said they had been sleeping, when she woke him and then left to save some animals, only to collapse in the milk house. The story was chilling.

"As he was telling me the story, the hair on my arms and the back of my neck stood up. All I could think was, *This man murdered his wife. He killed her to get away from the Amish community*. He didn't say it in so many words, but I knew it. I didn't *think* it. I *knew* it."

The sleeping arrangement that night also disturbed Stansfield. Eli's and Danny's bedrooms were connected by a bathroom, and Stutzman deliberately left the connecting doors open. Further, Stutzman's room was illuminated by a night-light.

"If we had sex and Danny got up, he would have seen us. He surely would have *heard* us."

Stansfield left the next day. He felt sorry for Stutzman and the sheltered Amish world he had been compelled to leave. Yet Stansfield couldn't forget the thought that Stutzman had killed his wife. He considered calling the police.

"What could the police do now?" he thought as he drove back to El Paso. "His wife was burned up and buried somewhere in Ohio. Calling the police was a silly idea. I didn't have anything to go on. It was all a suspicion."

In the end, he figured Stutzman's motive for killing his wife was to get his son out of the Amish community. He couldn't have just left Ohio and his wife—if he had the Amish would have taken his son.

"He must have loved his son an awful lot to do that," Haynes later said.

In spite of financial pressures, throughout the summer Stutzman continued his wild spree of pickups at the Strater and the Holiday Inn—even at the shopping mall in Farmington. He delighted in picking up the inexperienced married tourists or younger men—"chickens"—who came through the area. The parties turned into orgies, and summer 1983 drifted to fall.

Stutzman must have raced about the house, concealing any evidence of the gay life, when he learned his old friends Eli and Gail Byler were coming to see him while on a vacation trip to Ohio. The timing couldn't have been better. The Bylers arrived in time to celebrate Danny's birthday on September 9.

In the basement of the ranch house, the Bylers noticed all of the ribbons and trophies won by the stallion. Stutzman told them he had purchased the horse and intended to use it for stud. He made no mention of Terry Palmer.

Stutzman drove the Bylers around, showing off the spectacular Colorado landscape. His car was old, and he quickly apologized for its condition.

"A friend of mine borrowed my truck, because they were going to drive across country to New York and didn't think this one would make it," he explained.

The Bylers marveled at the size and beauty of the ranch, but Stutzman claimed that problems had just surfaced and that he might lose it.

"There's an Indian reservation near here, and the Indians are trying to get this land back," he told them. "Someday they might try to take the ranch from me. There's nothing I can do about it."

Stutzman said he and Danny had settled into a wonderful new life. They had both taken up skiing and were attending the Brethren Church in Durango.

Even better for the man who had suffered such tragedy when Ida had died, Stutzman said he now had a girlfriend. He even showed the Bylers a photograph of an attractive woman with long, dark-blond hair. When they left Colorado after a week with their old friend, the Bylers felt that Stutzman had finally found happiness and peace.

Of course, everything he'd said had been a lie.

In September, Palmer began to receive strange phone calls. Two or three times per week for several months, Palmer was awakened at 2:00 or 3:00 A.M. by the ringing of his telephone. When he picked up the receiver, he would hear the noise of someone hanging up—or worse, heavy breathing and gay sexual slurs. It didn't take him too long to figure out who the caller probably was—the biggest mistake of his life: Eli Stutzman.

While Palmer fretted about the horse, Stutzman continued to do as he pleased. On October 8, 1983, he threw a party with Michael Harris playing DJ. The small group of gay men and lesbian women danced and partied until 2:00 A.M.

As the party cooled down, Stutzman took Harris into his

bedroom and showed him some photographs of men he had met through *The Advocate*, and some shots of horses he said he owned.

"Eli was real proud of his place," Harris said later. "He told me that he wanted to make it into a gay dude ranch—if he could get the right backing."

Halloween in Durango is the town's Big Party. People fly in from Albuquerque and drive in from Salt Lake City to dress up and join in the unruly celebration—Colorado's answer to Mardi Gras. Though Stutzman told everyone he loathed the Amish, he wore his plain clothes as his costume. It was the ultimate put-down when he dropped his broadfall pants for sex with men.

Whatever happened between Wyoming teacher Dean Barlow and Eli Stutzman when they met in 1983 was something the Lyman, Wyoming, man deemed "kind of private" and refused to discuss with law enforcement officers when they knocked on his door years later. Married to a schoolteacher also from Lyman, Barlow, an excitable and nervous man, was given to odd and inappropriate bursts of laughter. Stutzman presented a smooth and controlled image, which he apparently found appealing.

Chuck Freeman also attended the party.

"One man showed up as a 'jolly green giant,' holding a can of corn and wearing only tennis shoes. Two ranchers wore only spurs and chaps, no shorts. Men paired off and went to the barn for sex. I think everyone in the country but the police department knew about the party," Freeman later said.

Barlow later told police investigators that he came down to the Four Corners to see his ill grandfather and a teacher friend. Yet somehow Dean Barlow ended up at a Four Corners gay party with Stutzman.

At the time, Stutzman told Barlow he was in the process of finding a buyer for the ranch. Barlow toyed with the idea of purchasing the place, though the $150,000 price was steep and his wife didn't seem interested. After the party, the two men went out to the mall to look at a costume contest. Stutzman, who said he could feel the beginnings of a cold coming on, gargled with whiskey in the parking lot.

"He didn't even drink it," Barlow later said, as if talking about some great character trait indicating abstinence from alcohol.

Barlow spent the night and the following day with Stutzman and Danny at the ranch, taking photographs of father and son. Stutzman presented his sweet, naive side, and Dean Barlow fell for it.

"Eli is a real religious person. I think he prays—it's a part of his daily practice," the Wyoming teacher later said.

Barlow encouraged Stutzman to look for work in Wyoming. "Our area is in a real boom," he explained.

In November Stutzman disappeared from the Four Corners, leaving without notice. Michael Harris, who had seen him in mid-October at a party, was amazed and sorry at the same time.

"David Tyler liked Eli so much that I wished I had gotten to know Eli better. None of us knew Eli was leaving. I thought he was trying to start the dude ranch."

CHAPTER SEVENTEEN

November 8, 1983

G*ertie Paton* wore her gray hair swept up off her face in the kind of minibouffant that required more hairspray than trouble. For more than forty years she had made her home in a tidy stucco house on the outskirts of downtown Austin, Texas. In the years since her husband's death, she had lived alone with her cat Missy.

Though she wore the kind of cat's-eye-shaped lenses favored by her generation, she missed nothing. And while her vision was not 20/20, she had no difficulty seeing the good in people. She put her "live and let live" philosophy into practice when she found out the "nice boys" across the street were more than just roommates.

Ray Watson and *Tom Agnello* were gay lovers, and though the Bible told her homosexuality was wrong, Paton set judgment aside. After all, they had been so kind, helping her with her yard work.

She was sorry to see them leave when they moved to San Antonio in 1981. The old neighbors kept in touch, and in 1983 Paton learned that Watson had had what Agnello called a heart attack, and died.

It was during the summer of that same year that Paton first heard of Eli and Danny Stutzman. Agnello brought over a batch of letters from Danny—including several school pictures. The boy had written to Agnello about his school in Colorado and signed them, "Love, Danny." Agnello was charmed by the boy's affectionate letters. He told Paton that he had found Stutzman through an advertisement and that, having corresponded, he planned to go to Colorado to get the Stutzmans. The three of them were going to live as a family.

Two weeks later, on the evening of November 8, a giant U-Haul truck pulled up in front of Gertie Paton's house, and Agnello knocked on the door. He asked if he and the Stutzmans could stay the night. The motel wouldn't take their U-Haul. Paton invited them in.

The following morning the two men started looking for a place to live, and Paton watched Danny. Even though looking for a house, Stutzman found time to rake twenty sacks of leaves in Paton's yard.

"I want to show my appreciation for what you've done for me and my son," he told her.

On Friday, Paton, who was expecting her son and grandson for the weekend, told Stutzman and Agnello that they absolutely had to get a place of their own that day. By noon they had found a place by the railroad tracks, at 3408 Banton Road. The stucco house had two bedrooms and a den. The yard was ratty, and the grimy interior could have used a scraping with a putty knife.

Oddly enough, although they finally had a place to live, trouble seemed to develop between the two gay men.

On the afternoon of November 14, Stutzman and Paton took Danny up to Maplewood Elementary for registration.

When they returned, Agnello blasted the old woman.

"You shouldn't have taken him! That's my job!"

That night, around suppertime, Agnello returned to Paton's and asked the old woman if she would mind watching Danny for the evening.

"Eli and I haven't had the chance to be alone yet," he explained.

Paton, who was tired, balked.

Agnello became angry again. "You're breaking up me and Eli!"

"No. I haven't got anything to do with that," Paton shot back, more in self-defense than anything else.

"Gertie, I'm never going to set foot in this house again," Agnello said as he left.

But the next morning, around eight, Agnello returned; he asked for Eli, who hadn't been home that night.

Paton didn't know what was going on. Later she learned that Stutzman and Agnello had had a big fight, and that during the night Stutzman and Danny had crawled through a window and walked to the Stop 'n Go convenience store on Thirty-eighth Street to wait for daylight.

The lovers who had met through the mail were finished before they had started.

The same thing had happened to Terry Palmer.

Stutzman's Ohio friends Eli and Gail Byler were stunned by the news about Eli's girlfriend, whom Stutzman said had followed him to Austin, where they had planned to marry.

"She took ill with cancer and died," Stutzman said.

Later the Bylers and Liz and Leroy Chupp discussed the tragedy.

"First his wife dies in a terrible fire and now his girlfriend. Eli seemed to have the most rotten luck in the world," Liz Chupp later said.

There was at least one bright spot in Stutzman's life. He told them he had been hired for a position teaching horsemanship at a college in Austin.

"Here he was with just an eighth-grade education, and teaching college. Can you beat that?" an amazed Eli Byler told a friend.

Full, leafy trees have a way of making even the most bleak of buildings look better than they really are, framing them with green. Oak trees line the street fronting Maplewood Elementary School, a big sandstone-colored brick school built in 1951 when the neighborhood was newer and safer.

As a decaying neighborhood, it draws those who can't afford to live anywhere else. A lot of the Anglos who live there are former counterculture types. Students from the University of Texas find cheap rentals with plenty of bedrooms suitable for lots of roommates. Poor blacks and illegal aliens also have found a home in the Northeast Austin area next to the airport.

Despite its diversity, the neighborhood is close-knit and tolerant. Gays have established an enclave in the area, and there is little violence directed toward them by straights.

The school itself is in the center of it all, abutted by railroad tracks and a creek bed that is a trickle most of the year. A hole in the fence running along the back of the school provides an invitation to transients.

At Maplewood, Danny was assigned to Janis Bradley, who quickly assessed the situation at the boy's home.

"Danny talked about all the men that lived there," she later said. " 'My dad's boyfriends' was the phrase he always used. I didn't judge it . . . this was the situation we've got to work with."

When Danny came to school one morning extremely tired, he told Bradley that his father had had a party, and that he hadn't gotten much sleep.

Terry Palmer, who had learned Stutzman had moved to Texas, sent a Christmas card to Danny. A week later it came back with "Refused. Return to Sender" scrawled on the envelope. The handwriting, Palmer said, was Stutzman's.

A few weeks before Christmas, Eli and Danny brought Gertie Paton a Christmas present—a piece of glass with a rose etched on it, and Paton hung it in her kitchen. Stutzman told her that he and his son were going on a trip.

"We're going to Wyoming. Friends sent us tickets, so we're going up to ski."

Stutzman and Danny flew into Salt Lake City during a snowstorm on Christmas Eve with little more than a couple of bags and some Christmas gifts for each other and their hosts, Dean and Margie Barlow.

One can only wonder what Margie Barlow made of all of this—particularly sending tickets to a man her husband supposedly met just once at a Halloween party.

The Barlows met Eli and Danny at the airport and snapped photos, for which Stutzman seemed grateful. He claimed to be worried that his grandfather was about to pass away, and said that he wanted to send photographs to him right away.

If Barlow had thought for a minute, it might have occurred to him that an old Swartzentruber Amishman like Stutzman's grandfather would be offended by photographs.

The Barlows drove east on Interstate 80, headed for their home in Lyman, in Uinta County.

The area might have reminded Danny Stutzman of the Four Corners ranch—rugged mountains and rocky enclaves. A few dormant oil wells dotted the landscape.

For Christmas, Stutzman gave his son a pair of roller skates.

Later, Barlow drove Stutzman out to the family ranch in Kemmerer, a town northwest of Lyman, in Lincoln County. While driving he asked Stutzman about the barn fire, and Stutzman explained that the Amish don't put lightning rods on rooftops—it tampers with God's will.

"What was it like to deal with your wife's death?" Barlow asked.

Stutzman, silent at first, grew angry.

"It was terrible," he said, refusing to elaborate.

When it came time to leave, Dean Barlow must have been hooked. He must have wanted the relationship more than Stutzman did. When Barlow phoned Stutzman later in 1984 and left a message on his answering machine, it got no response.

Around Valentine's Day 1984, Gertie Paton was invited to the Stutzmans' for dinner. Stutzman said he wanted to thank her for all she had done for him. Paton noticed the trophies and ribbons won by the stallion, and the Amish clothing Stutzman kept for Danny.

Stutzman increased his involvement in the local gay community, even serving as an officer for the Texas Gay Rodeo Association's Austin chapter. He spent evenings picking up tricks at the Round-up, which was at the time a gay western bar.

In the spring of 1984, Stutzman shocked local gays when he ran a classified ad in the *Austin American-Statesman*, saying that he was a country boy new to the city and looking for companionship. Stutzman told 34-year-old landscaper *Clint Skinner* that he had received more than two hundred responses to the ad. Stutzman invited Skinner to dinner and they had sex. Stutzman gave Skinner the impression that he was sexually naive and a homebody.

"He was a little too much country for my taste . . . he was raising chickens in the city!" Skinner recalled. "On the other hand, if I had known he was a 'bottom' things might have been different."

Skinner introduced Stutzman to a friend of his, *Jim Donovan*, an international banker and urbane opposite of most of the men Stutzman associated with. He liked Stutzman, who claimed he was looking for a permanent lover.

"I got the idea that Eli's opinion was, 'There's no shortage of finding someone to suck your cock, but a relationship, that's something else," Donovan remembered.

There were other ways to meet gay men, and Eli Stutzman tried them.

Compucopia was the gay world's answer to computer dating. Men input sexual vitals, likes, and dislikes and let the computer match them up with the perfect date.

San Francisco transplant *Willie Paynter* was member number 240. He was a six-foot-plus, blue-eyed man with a sexual appetite for uncircumcised—"uncut"—men. When he first landed in San Francisco he took a job as the office manager for a charitable foundation. Later he found his true calling as an electrician when a gay man taught him the trade.

Paynter had his first sexual encounters as a teen with men at bus stations in South Carolina, where he grew up as the scion of a fairly well-to-do family.

"My first time with a man," he later said, "was when I changed buses in Charlottesville and met a man in the restroom who took me to a near-deserted office building next door. I licked him off in a locked bathroom stall. I still remember his come on my wrist."

Paynter had met men through *The Advocate, RFD*—a rural gay men's magazine—and finally, through Compucopia. Like many gay men, Paynter saved every letter he received and copies of the photographs of the men who wanted to date him. He kept them all in a file box, and when the need arose—to fight a depression, or just to have the rush of a happy memory—he could review them.

On his application, he detailed what he was and what he wanted. Paynter was the active partner in anal sex, and he wanted to be on the receiving end of "rimming," the gay term for one man stimulating another anally with his tongue. The 36-year-old did not want a partner who was into sex toys, S&M, or "fisting"—shoving a fist inside a partner's rectum.

Tall and lean, Paynter was a straight-looking, educated man who loved the symphony, gourmet cooking, reading, and, more than anything, sex with men. His preference was a lumberjack type or a farmer, but years on the make had left him a little more realistic about what he'd turn up.

He wrote in his "personal statement" for Compucopia: "I am looking mostly for casual sex—*I'm a good fucker*—but would also like to find an uncut outdoorsman to move with to my family farm in the south someday. Also looking for a hiking/camping buddy."

Paynter paid his ten-dollar membership fee and sat back and waited for the perfect match.

On March 18, Eli Stutzman, also a member of the dating service, responded with a bare-chested photograph and a letter in which he described the size of his penis and explicitly noted his preferences for anal and oral sex.

Stutzman added that he was the father of a 7-year-old named Danny. A rubber-stamped image of a unicorn decorated the envelope and its Austin, Texas, return address.

On March 23, Paynter struggled with three different versions of his response to Stutzman's letter: he knew a good man when he saw one. He thanked Stutzman for the "very handsome picture," and noted that his own penis was seven inches, cut, and that his balls were on the small side—"particularly in Texas' cold weather." He reaffirmed his enjoyment of casual sex.

They talked on the phone, and Stutzman filled him in on Danny. Though Paynter wasn't particularly interested in meeting a man with children, he listened carefully. He wanted to know all he could in case he was to become the little boy's "stepfather."

On April 2, Stutzman wrote again, this time enclosing several more pictures of himself. One shot showed him clad in a bikini bottom and slung over Terry Palmer's horse. Stutzman wrote that it was late and that he'd had a hard day, signing off with, "Danny's in bed asleep and I should be, too."

Paynter caught a United Airlines flight to Austin on April 13. Stutzman had told him that he'd be working and that Paynter should walk to Banton Road—just a few blocks from the airport—and wait for Stutzman and Danny to return at the end of the day. Chickens in the backyard fueled fantasies that Stutzman might be the one to take back to South Carolina with him.

"I could envision that he would be a real good person to settle down with," he later said.

Danny, Paynter, and Stutzman had dinner at a Mexican restaurant, and the two men topped the evening off with sex. For Paynter it was as good as good got.

The following day, Paynter ran an electrical line to the clothes dryer. As the hours passed, it seemed that Stutzman was exactly what he had been looking for and Eli seemed to feel affectionate toward Paynter as well.

On Monday morning Stutzman and Danny dropped the love-struck man at the airport. Paynter cried all the way back to San Francisco.

Why do I have to go back to that horrible city? he thought. I could be here with this wonderful man in Texas, where it is warm and green and moist . . . and he's so well-hung.

In the spring of 1984, Stutzman told Austin banker Jim Donovan that he had met someone new. In fact, the new man—a porno star, no less—had moved into the Banton Road address with Eli and Danny.

"I'm not sure if he was a porno star or not, but from what I saw one night he could have been," Donovan later recalled. "If he made any movies, I doubt it was more than one."

Like all of Stutzman's other relationships, the one with the porno star didn't last long.

Three weeks after they met, Willie Paynter called Stutzman to let him know that Paynter was going to take a vacation. He planned to travel through Colorado and make a side trip to Austin.

"I have a new lover now," Stutzman said, his words crushing Paynter. "We have a monogamous relationship. It would be great for you to come, and you could stay with us, but we couldn't sleep together."

Paynter, who had been sure that Stutzman was Mr. Wonderful, fought back tears.

"Eli," he said, "I'm so attracted to you and I so much want to go to bed with you . . . it would hurt too much to see you. I won't come to Austin."

Stutzman said that he was sorry and that he hoped Paynter understood the situation. Then, even though he had just dumped the man, Stutzman still asked for a favor. He wondered if Paynter could stop by the Colorado ranch and check on a few things. Paynter, not wanting to shut the door on the relationship—after all, things might not work out with the new lover—agreed.

The harassing calls continued to frighten Terry Palmer, yet he refused to do anything about them.

Finally, Ryan Bloom answered a call one morning at 4:00 A.M. and asked the caller: "Where are you calling from?"

The crackly response Bloom thought he heard was *"Boston . . . We're having a hell of a party . . ."* He knew Eli Stutzman lived in Austin, and he became convinced that he had misheard—that the caller must have said *Austin*.

On May 3, Bloom went to the local sheriff, and the Austin police eventually notified him that the calls were indeed coming from Stutzman's address. Stutzman was told that such calls were a criminal offense, and the calls stopped.

"To this day, I can't figure out why he was harassing me," Palmer said later, still skirting the issue of their relationship.

Chuck Freeman and his foreman, Byron Larson, thought they knew, based on what Eli Stutzman had told them.

"Maybe Eli was jealous because Terry had taken a younger lover?" Freeman suggested, referring to Bloom's appearance on the Colorado ranch.

On May 28, Willie Paynter called Stutzman from Durango and reported that the ranch seemed fine.

During the last school conference, Stutzman told Janis Bradley that he wouldn't be able to be with his boy this summer and was looking for a summer camp.

"Do you know of any place I can take Danny?" he asked. She suggested seeing the counselor. Stutzman never did.

CHAPTER EIGHTEEN

W*anda Sawyer* was fed up with her husband. And who could blame her? *Mac Sawyer* drank too much, laughed too loud, and had a smile so gap-toothed a drunk driver could have parallel parked in the spaces between his teeth. He irritated her, and she wanted a divorce. Wanda Sawyer, who had left Michigan at 19 and had married an air force transportation airman in 1962, dared to want something new.

They had moved to Austin when Mac Sawyer was stationed at Bergstrom Air Force Base. After Austin, they had lived in Hawaii for twelve years. Wanda Sawyer had quickly become the kind of woman who could wear a floral-splattered muumuu without a trace of reservation. She reveled in it.

If one thing could be said of her, it was that she wasn't shy. She had a warm sense of humor that was frequently so bawdy as to make even a police detective blush.

Once she had cut loose from her unhappy marriage, she would stretch all boundaries to their limits.

Her hair was a halo of red, her eyes as wide apart as the towns on a map of southern Travis County. Best of all was her voice, which had a kind of cartoonish timbre that embued every word with personality and mischief. Wanda smoked like Mauna Kea, but never drank. Mac had done enough of that for both of them.

She returned to Austin, the town that held her best and

happiest memories, on June 27, 1984. She was sure her husband thought that if he bought her a house she would stay with him.

She left Honolulu planning to "kick Mac out on the street, right on his ass." The thought of it brought a smile to her face. Twenty-two and a half years and a kick out the door.

Before returning to Austin, Wanda stopped off in Iowa to visit her sister, *Susan Ruston*. The reunion was marred by her sister's problems with her son, *Denny*. Susan showed Wanda letters Denny had written while he had been away in the Marine Corps. The letters were disturbing. They may have come from the heart, but they were puffed-up, overblown sonnets to a woman—and the woman he directed the words of love to was Susan, his mother.

"They aren't letters a normal son would write to his mother. He wrote about love—mainly to his mother. He acted like—to me—like a husband would, writing these mushy letters to his mom," Wanda remembered.

Susan was very troubled. Something was bothering her son, and she didn't know what to do about it. Worse, there seemed to be evidence to back up her concern: Denny had recently and suddenly been discharged from the Marine Corps.

Wanda, the older of the two, tried to calm and counsel Susan.

"Well, you know, there's something wrong in it, the fact of him getting out of the service. No one goes into the Marines and gets out as early as Denny got out. Plus he was discharged on other than honorable conditions," she said.

The more Wanda talked to Susan, and the more they talked about Denny's letters, the more Wanda thought he was gay. She suggested that possibility to her sister.

"She didn't want no part of it. She could not believe her son could be like that. He was her only son, he was going to carry on the Ruston name," Wanda recalled.

• • •

Mac Sawyer, who came back to Austin on January 31, 1984, found a nice house at 5110 Ravensdale Lane. Sawyer still didn't know—Wanda would say "couldn't accept"—that she planned to dump him. The place needed a little work: new paint, the kitchen sink replaced, glass sliders repaired.

The Century 21 listing agent referred Eli Stutzman to them to make the much-needed repairs. Stutzman was quiet, friendly, and appeared to be a hard worker. A crew of several men accompanied him.

He came out in September.

Wanda's son, *Kyle*, went out front where the crew was working on painting the slightly run-down house. Kyle listened to a worker who was talking about being in a centerfold magazine, and Kyle's interest was piqued. Soon it became obvious that the magazines being discussed were gay publications. Kyle asked if the workers were gay, and was told, neither shyly nor militantly proud, that in fact they all were.

Later, Kyle went inside to talk with Wanda, who was working on the interior of the place. "You know, mom, I think they are all gays."

"No. Couldn't be." Wanda was surprised. They seemed so *normal*.

"I'm sure they are," Kyle insisted.

In the fall of 1984, an administrator at the Missoula, Montana, Youth Home got Glen Pritchett a job at 4Bs South Restaurant, and the troubled man moved out of Sandy's apartment.

"I always felt Glen left me and the kids because I wouldn't drink with him anymore," Sandy Turner recalled.

Though he was gone, there were still conflicts.

On September 21, 1984, Missoula police officer Gary Palmer, who was Jo Lyn Kuser's brother, answered a call at Sandy Turner's place at 326 Clay Street. Bill Mayberry had pinned Pritchett to the floor. Pritchett was angry that Mayberry was there with his wife.

"I'm not your wife, anymore!" Sandy told him.

Pritchett responded by hurling insults and smashing a window. Officer Palmer knew Glen Pritchett from his problems at the group home. A tearful and angry Sandy Turner told the officer that they had divorced and that this was her apartment. "I want him to leave," she told Palmer. "Get him out of here!"

By that time Sandy, who had earned her GED the previous year, was taking classes at the University of Montana. The morning after the police came, Pritchett asked for a ride to the edge of town. He said he was going to Helena for a while, though from there he seemed to have no plans. Pritchett left Missoula with nothing but a little bag of clothes. It was September 1984.

He was bitter and depressed about his marriage when he came to his sister Nona's place. He put one hundred percent of the blame on himself. It hurt that he was no longer with his son and daughter, and Nona had no doubt that Glen still loved Sandy.

"He knew his drinking had cost him everything," she said later.

Pritchett stayed at Nona's for three weeks, drinking and not doing much of anything. When he left he told his sister he was going to Missoula, then on to Idaho to see his younger brother Cecil, and, after that, to Reno, where his dad and uncle were living. Pritchett worked in Reno for a few weeks and then disappeared—with nearly one thousand dollars of his uncle's money.

"We didn't know where he went," Cecil Pritchett later said.

Two weeks after he left Helena, two of Pritchett's good friends were arrested on drug charges.

Later in the fall, Pritchett called his ex-wife from Austin. He had a job doing construction work and had moved into a house with a couple of gays.

Sandy was incredulous.

"Gays?" she asked.

"Yeah, faggots!" Pritchett laughed. "Can you get that?"

Sandy laughed, too. She couldn't imagine her husband—her ex-husband—living with some homosexuals in Texas. The Glen Pritchett she knew hated gays and would sooner punch one out than to move in with one.

After she hung up the phone, Sandy figured Glen had sunk lower than she had ever dreamed possible. If they had drugs and if there was plenty of drinking, maybe it was just plain convenience. Still, *gays?*

After Wanda Sawyer returned to Austin, one of her nephew Denny Ruston's ex-boyfriends got mad and told Susan Ruston that her son was gay. No matter how open-minded, no mother wants to hear that news. Susan took it hard. She even sobbed that "no one would be left to carry on the Ruston name." Wanda told her that the men working on her house were gay and that they seemed all right.

She decided to talk to Stutzman.

Wanda Sawyer is the type of woman who understands that if you want to know something—ask. Stutzman could have told her his sexuality was none of her business, but he didn't. He confirmed he was gay, and made her promise not to tell anyone. Wanda didn't care about his sexuality one way or another.

She asked Stutzman what kind of advice he could give Denny Ruston or his mother.

"The only thing I can tell you to tell your sister is, if Denny can't be himself, then it is going to be very hard on him if he knows he's gay. It's hard on the wife, it's hard when you have children, and it's hard on the marriage. Eventually, you really don't love that woman. You have no desire for her, yet you're forced, because this is the way society wants you to be," he told her.

Stutzman told her that he had been married at one time, but that his wife had died tragically in a barn fire. He said that he had known he had homosexual tendencies before he was married, but had been confused by them and unsure how to respond to them.

Knowing that he had been raised Amish, Wanda reasoned that such naïveté was not only possible, but likely.

One day, after working on the house, Stutzman asked Wanda if she'd like to go out, just friend-to-friend. Wanda, who had not gone out much since marrying and was a little stressed because of her upcoming divorce, was reluctant, but Stutzman persisted.

They stayed out late, going from bar to bar.

"Eli took me to a topless bar, and he was so embarrassed that he hadn't known it was one. I guess I didn't fully accept the fact that he was gay and couldn't relate to it. I could see the embarrassment. 'Let's just drink our drinks and go,' he said," Wanda recalled.

As their first night progressed, it became obvious Stutzman did not frequent these places. Not usually, anyway. Nobody knew him. And he seemed so uncomfortable.

Wanda chalked it up to his being out of his element. Stutzman wasn't used to straight bars.

Over the next several weeks, as Wanda and Eli became better friends, Stutzman took her to gay bars. Glen Pritchett, who now worked for Stutzman, often accompanied them.

Wanda began to accept the idea of men in drag, in dog collars, or entwined with studded strips of leather. It was weird, but the men seemed happy, and everyone was having a good time. It really could have been any bar, except, of course, that the couples were men.

She asked Stutzman if he would talk with Denny Ruston, maybe give him some support and encouragement. He said he would. Denny found Stutzman to be soft-spoken, yet possessing a sense of humor that he found appealing. Stutzman urged Denny to come down to Texas.

To pass the time and make a few dollars, Wanda took a job waitressing at the Pizza Hut on Reinli Street in South Austin. When she decided to file for her divorce, it was Stutzman who took her down to the county courthouse.

• • •

To hear Wanda tell it, her nephew Denny Ruston's short life was a sad saga of family betrayal, divorce, and whispers of sexual abuse—more than one topic suitable for producers of daytime talk shows, looking for juicy material.

Maybe Wanda exaggerated a tad. Indeed, if that was the case, that's all she did. Wanda Sawyer didn't like to stretch the truth. She didn't have to. She knew the truth was always more interesting than some silly story.

Denny's parents had split up when he was still a tow-headed toddler. His dad had fooled around with another woman and gotten her pregnant. Wanda and Susan's youngest sister had found out about it and was blackmailing Denny's father to keep her mouth shut. He paid her twenty dollars now and then and, if she pressed him, let her use the Rustons' car. Susan stood by idly, wondering what was going on and thinking it was all very strange.

As is often the case with divorce, a child forced the issue. Patty, Denny's sister, asked her mother one day: "Mommy, why does daddy sleep with Auntie?"

"Auntie" was the girl Susan had hired to baby-sit the children. Later, the baby-sitter got pregnant, and Susan left her husband.

Susan, Patty, and Denny tried to start over in Iowa, but, even though the court had decreed her ex was to pay the bills, he refused. Collectors garnished her wages. Susan, fed up, left for Michigan and moved in with her parents.

It was not the best place for the three of them. Pointing an accusing finger at her father, Wanda recalled: "It has never been proven, but it has been spoken of by the grandchildren that my dad sexually molested Denny (and three other children). My children were never left alone with him, except that one night (Wanda's son) stayed there—and after that he wouldn't stay no more."

When Wanda found out about what was going on at grandma's house, she tried to confront her mother with the issue, but the old woman refused to discuss it—or deny it.

Wanda, accepting and tolerant, later racked her brain to come up with the reason why Denny had turned out the way he had. She wondered if it was his home life, his toilet training, his mother, his father.

There were so many possible reasons, but no real answers. She wondered if she was merely looking for excuses for the way things had turned out.

Austin police officer Larry Oliver encountered Eli Stutzman and Glen Pritchett on December 20, 1984, in a parking lot off Handcock, in Austin. On patrol that night, the officer observed Stutzman's parked pickup, plus a couple of men standing around. When the officer and his partner passed by, the men got in the truck and drove to the other side of the lot, where Stutzman and Pritchett got out. Pritchett knelt on the pavement. When the men saw the patrol car approaching them, they again climbed inside the truck and started to leave.

Officer Oliver questioned Stutzman, who seemed evasive and would only state that he had stopped to let Pritchett stretch. Pritchett, who was drunk, didn't recall stopping, then added he had stopped to urinate.

The officer noticed a bloody scrape on the left side of the young man's forehead. At first Pritchett said the injury was the result of carelessness at a construction site.

Before leaving, Pritchett changed his story, telling the officers, "I got in a fight in a faggot bar."

On December 29, Eli, Danny, and Glen went to Wanda's daughter's wedding and reception. The three of them looked like a happy, albeit, makeshift family. Pritchett seemed closer to the Stutzmans than one would have thought possible in just the two months' time of their knowing each other.

Stutzman wore cowboy boots, a western shirt, and gray slacks that were an inch too short. Pritchett wore jeans, a jean jacket, and a chambray shirt. Danny was dressed just like his dad. As the reception wore on, Danny crawled into his father's lap and fell asleep. Pritchett slammed down scotch-and-waters, and Stutzman drank Budweisers.

Harry and Evelyn Reininger's inherited twenty-two-acre ranch was small compared to most of the spreads in the area south of the city, near the highway to Creedmoor, Texas. Since the place had a good barn and stables, the Reiningers decided to earn extra money by boarding horses.

Mrs. Reininger saw an advertisement in the *Weekly Bulletin*, placed by a man looking for a place to board his horse. She called the number and talked with Eli Stutzman, who told her he had a stallion that he was boarding at a stable near Onion Creek—not far from the Reiningers' ranch on Sassman Road. He was looking for a new place to take the animal. Stutzman agreed to the grandmotherly woman's price of forty dollars per month, and the deal was struck.

Stutzman came out with the horse he called "Chris," and made his first payment on January 1. He bragged about all the ribbons and trophies his son Danny had won showing the horse.

The Reiningers had no idea, of course, that Stutzman was lying and that it had been Terry Palmer's "son" who had won the ribbons.

Mrs. Reininger felt that Stutzman was a fairly successful young man. He had a good-looking pickup, and he introduced himself with a business card that read E. S. CONSTRUCTION.

Over the next few months, Stutzman came frequently to see the animal and to ride. At least twice he brought Danny along. One time he brought another man, whom Mrs. Reininger only saw from a distance. She thought it was a friend or an employee.

If Susan Ruston had a hard time accepting son Denny's sexuality, her third husband apparently found the situation intolerable. But it wasn't Ruston's parents who sent him packing for Texas. Everything came to a head when Ruston and his lover had an argument over where the younger man was going to spend New Year's. Denny was adamant that he would join his parents in Michigan; his lover said he would stay in Iowa.

"I finally figured I was old enough to make my own decisions and I'll do what I damn well wanted. So I packed up my shit and left," he said later.

He arrived in Austin on January 4, planning to live with his Aunt Wanda until she left for Hawaii at the end of the following month.

When he arrived at the Sawyers', Wanda, who continued to look for every excuse to get away from Mac, suggested they call Eli Stutzman. Stutzman came over, and the three of them went back to his place, where he introduced Denny to Glen Pritchett.

Denny made the assumption that Pritchett was gay, because he lived with Stutzman. He was later disappointed when he learned that Pritchett was as straight as the interstate to San Antonio.

Ruston's first night in the big city was one he would never forget, nor could the kid from Iowa have ever imagined it. Stutzman took Ruston and Pritchett out to a leather bar downtown. It was the Iowan's first encounter with the leather scene, and he later admitted he was a little shocked. Stutzman seemed to get some satisfaction from exposing the hardcore side of the gay world to the novice.

It was early morning when they stumbled back to Banton Road. Stutzman invited Ruston into his bedroom and shut the door. Pritchett flopped onto his bed and fell asleep in the other room. Danny was already asleep in his bedroom.

Ruston was nervous, but because Stutzman was such a good friend of his Aunt Wanda, and because they had talked on the phone a couple of times, he felt he knew him well enough to engage in anal intercourse.

Besides, the former Amishman wasn't bad looking.

"He had a nice chest, nice arms, a cute little round butt, a nice box—I wanted to see what the package looked like unwrapped."

Stutzman asked Ruston if he minded if Stutzman used a cock ring. Ruston had never seen one, but said it would be okay. Stutzman also said he thought it would be a good idea if he used a "butt plug" on Ruston. Ruston refused. He did not feel comfortable or that he knew Stutzman well enough to allow the insertion of the graduated latex cones into his rectum.

Stutzman satisfied himself and went to sleep.

After the first of the new year, Pritchett's phone calls to his ex-wife had moved beyond nuisance to the limits of harassment. Sandy Turner, whose roller-coaster life had left her shaky, viewed each call as a possible setback instigated by a man she needed to stay away from—father of her two kids or not. She coped with it her own way—with crying jags, cold beer, and an occasional scream back into the receiver.

Pritchett made four calls to her Missoula apartment in an eight hour period on January 25, 1985. The first call, at 6:31 P.M., lasted almost half an hour. The caller was the "sweet" Glen, caring and sober. Sandy told him she was getting married again.

"It's a mistake," he told her. "It's too soon. It's no good rushing into marriage."

"If it is a mistake, it's my mistake. It's my life," she shot back, saying good-bye to her ex-husband.

At 1:56 the following morning, Sandy's phone rang again. This time it was the obnoxious and drunken Glen—the man she had divorced in September. Nostalgia evaporated.

He was angry and insisted that she was throwing her life away and that the marriage would never last. He yelled and she slammed the receiver down in his ear.

Twenty-one minutes later, Pritchett called again. Sandy

listened to his tirade for only five minutes this time. Pritchett asked to speak with Sandy's fiancé, who Sandy had foolishly let slip was spending the night. This, of course, made Pritchett even angrier. Sandy hung up.

At 2:39 A.M., Sandy answered the phone and, at Pritchett's insistence, handed the receiver to her fiancé, who talked with the ex-husband for a minute or two. Sandy got back on the line, listened to a barrage of insults and doped-up reasoning, and hung up for the last time.

She changed her phone number the next day and never heard from Pritchett again.

One time, after work at the Pizza Hut, Ruston came over to the house and found Pritchett drunk and crying.

"He told me that he missed his 'wife.' He never once referred to her as his 'ex-wife.'

"Glen said he wanted to go back. It sounded very sincere. He missed her so much. I gave him my shoulder and he cried for a good twenty minutes," Denny later recalled.

Stutzman told Wanda Sawyer about the nightmare of being gay in the Amish, and gave that as the reason for his leaving the Order.

On another occasion he offered her the opportunity to wear one of Ida's dresses. She quickly declined, unable to bear the thought of wearing a dead woman's clothes.

While his father was running around Austin with sex on his mind, Danny seemed to be making progress in school.

Speech pathologist Ruth Davis had been seeing Danny twice a week for thirty-minute sessions in her office at Maplewood Elementary. She categorized the boy as a severe stutterer.

Danny told her that his mother had died in a fire. The way he talked about the incident made it sound as though it had just happened in Colorado.

Davis felt Stutzman was concerned about his child's progress, yet uncomfortable meeting with a teacher, as some parents were. Stutzman would sit quietly, his hands crossed and folded on the child-size desk. Yet it was Danny's behavior that struck her the most. When his father was in the room, the boy seemed unresponsive and didn't look at Stutzman as the man spoke.

One day Danny came to Maplewood with a black eye and bruises on his arms. Davis considered the possibility of child abuse and later recalled that the subject was discussed at a staff meeting, though no formal complaint was made.

CHAPTER NINETEEN

Wanda Sawyer had become like a mother hen to a most unlikely group of men, and it was hard on all of them when they learned she was finally going to leave for Hawaii at the end of February.

She was sad to be leaving Stutzman, whom she felt had been a true friend. She was even more disturbed about leaving Danny.

"Doesn't it ever bother you that your son is growing up in an atmosphere like this?" she once asked Stutzman as she drove home with him from the bars.

He didn't answer. It was dark in the truck, and Wanda couldn't even see his face to gauge his response.

Wanda even considered asking Stutzman if she could take the boy and raise him in Hawaii. She didn't ask, though, because she knew Eli would have been offended.

Yet, she did feel that he was a good father. It was just the environment that was all wrong for the boy.

On February 23, Glen, Denny, Danny, and Eli gave Wanda a going-away party. Stutzman gave her a plate of glass with a rose etched onto it, similar to the one he had given Gertie Paton. Wanda later added her own touch by painting it with red and green fingernail polish. She could have used purple or fluorescent yellow—other colors in her collection.

They also gave her a gigantic dildo.

She left four days later, after the divorce was final.

At first, Denny stayed over at Stutzman's place because it was easier than going home to Aunt Wanda's at 2:00 A.M. and waking everyone up. Eventually, Stutzman said he could move in.

Stutzman's house could scarcely accommodate two grown men and a child, and three men posed even greater problems. Stutzman had the back bedroom, his water bed nearly covering all the floor space. Danny's room was the small one in front, facing the street. Glen Pritchett slept on a sofa in the dining room, and Denny Ruston took Danny's bedroom. Danny slept with his father in the water bed. All of Danny's toys and clothes remained in his room.

When his father brought a lover home, Danny slept on the sofa in the living room.

As the weeks passed, Ruston learned more about Stutzman's life as an Amishman.

Stutzman confided that he had known he had homosexual tendencies even before his wife died.

"He told me he was cleaning the stables when he came across an Amishman masturbating in the barn. The man didn't know Eli was there at first, then the two of them 'engaged,' " Ruston recalled.

On another occasion, Stutzman told Ruston that a Wayne County businessman had given him a blow job, while he was still married to his Amish wife. Stutzman may have been referring to the time David Amstutz had turned him down. Or perhaps there was another time when someone else had agreed to a request for oral sex.

Once, when they were in the garage getting some tools for a job, Stutzman showed Ruston some clothes Ida had made. He had also kept her wedding dress, some of his work clothes, and Danny's first "dress." Everything was arranged neatly, and Stutzman knew exactly which drawer held which pieces of clothing before he opened it to show Ruston.

"Whatever happened to your wife?" Denny asked.

Stutzman told him about the night of the fire, a version that matched what he had told Wanda: Ida was feeding the baby when the fire broke out. Instead of coming and getting Eli, she went out and tried to fight the fire herself. Stutzman, still in bed, woke to find his wife missing, and later dead in the barn. He carried her across the road.

Ruston asked if he had a picture of Ida, and Stutzman shook his head.

"The Amish don't believe in photographs. It's robbing the soul."

Stutzman showed Denny a picture of a handsome man he called "Peter."

"He said he had met him in Colorado," Ruston recalled. "Before he and his lover bought the ranch. The photograph seemed to spark happy memories of his life in Colorado."

"Whatever happened to your lover?" Ruston asked.

"He died in a car wreck."

"Oh, really? What happened?"

"Faulty brakes," Stutzman said matter-of-factly.

Ruston wanted to know what had happened to the ranch. Stutzman told him that his deceased lover's parents had come in and taken everything that wasn't nailed down—and then some.

"They wiped me out. They came in and made me sell everything that was ours together and give them half. I sold most of the horses, but kept the one I brought to Texas. I lost everything."

As far as Denny Ruston could see, Eli Stutzman was a good father—at least when he spent time with his son. Stutzman once told Ruston that he was a member of a gay father's group, and that it was helpful for him to know that others were experiencing the same problems.

Sometimes it seemed as though anyone and everyone other than Stutzman spent time watching the boy. Pritchett, Wanda, neighbor Mark Taylor, and various gay friends baby-sat when Stutzman went out cruising, cock ring in tow.

Except for after school, before supper, Danny was never alone. Danny's routine was simple and everyone living at the Banton Road address was expected to ensure that it was maintained. The boy got up for school early—many times after his father had left for the day. He was to let himself in through the unlocked back door in the afternoon. Bedtime was 9:00 sharp.

The only time Ruston saw Stutzman raise a hand to the child was when he did not come directly home after school. The boy's bedtime was also critical. It was only after Danny was in bed that Stutzman could go out to the bars. "Danny knew that once he was tucked in, he stayed in bed until morning," Ruston said later.

On a few occasions the boy was left alone, but Stutzman didn't see it as a problem.

Ruston saw no signs of abuse. Stutzman's shower curtain was transparent plastic, so when the boy showered, there was little left to the imagination. If there were bruises on Danny, Ruston never saw them.

Ruston never brought any lovers home to Banton Road, out of respect for Danny and Eli. When he met someone he wanted to trick with he usually went to their place. Sometimes Ruston took care of business in the front seat of his '75 Chrysler Cordoba.

A rougher, more hardcore side to Stutzman came to light after Ruston moved in. The former Amishman seemed to drop his guard and made comments that indicated darker sexual desires.

"I'll slap you around and fuck your brains out," Stutzman told a man at a leather bar that catered to the crowd that dressed in harnesses, studded collars, and chaps. Stutzman, however, dressed more subtly. He wore a black leather arm band and vest.

The back door at the Banton Road house should have

been a revolving one, so many men came and went at all hours of the day and night. Stutzman, Ruston, and Pritchett partied every night.

One night Stutzman came up with something new.

"He said he had a trick in his bedroom and wondered if I wanted to join them in a threesome," Ruston recalled.

"Eli put handcuffs on the guy, behind his back, and used the butt plugs on him—going from finger-sized to almost fist-sized. I just watched. The guy was drunk. It was really strange—I had never seen anyone use handcuffs on someone else," Ruston said later.

Stutzman climaxed, got off the man, unhandcuffed him, and that was that. The man just lay on Stutzman's water bed in a stupor. There was no doubt the man had been brutalized. Ruston felt that if the man had not been so drunk, he would have begged to be released.

"He could not have enjoyed it," Ruston said later.

Danny, clad in Smurf pajamas, slept soundly through the incident.

Denny Ruston might have felt a little jealous over the whole thing. He later told people that he had found Stutzman to be a disappointing lover.

"To be perfectly honest, I found Eli to be somewhat boring in bed. He wanted to get himself off and didn't care about the other party. When it comes to out and out getting into it, I like to be satisfied, too. I never did get off, the first evening we were together."

Though he felt there truly was a friendship, Ruston was excluded from some of Stutzman's activities. Sometimes Stutzman would bring a man or two home and go into his bedroom and shut the door.

"I don't think I participated in that one occasion the way he wanted me to. I think he was a little bit hesitant about asking me to join in again. Still, I felt that he was into a different scene than I was—he was into toys and hardcore."

When Stutzman said he needed someone to clean his house, Ruston volunteered. The fact that it paid ten dollars was gravy. Stutzman's house was never very dirty.

One day, while he was cleaning the kitchen, Ruston wrote "I love you" on a scrap of paper, circling it with a big heart. He hung it on the old white Frigidaire.

That night, when Stutzman saw the note he crumpled it up.

"Denny, sit down," he said. "This kind of stuff cannot go on. You are a nice-looking young man. I like you a lot. But I don't want to sleep with you. I don't want to have a relationship with you. You are not my type."

Ruston was hurt, but didn't say anything. Stutzman did all the talking.

"What would have happened if somebody came in and saw this? I have a lot of people come in and out of this house. It wouldn't have been good for somebody straight to come in and see this kind of note."

After that, Stutzman and Ruston never slept together again. "I felt we were friends and that was it," Ruston said.

As far as Wanda Sawyer could tell from their phone conversations, her nephew was falling in love with Eli Stutzman. This both pleased and troubled her. It would make her feel more secure about Denny's future and safety if he were involved in a monogamous relationship. She was concerned, however, when she learned that Denny's feelings were not returned by Stutzman.

Ruston told her about the note on the refrigerator, and other gestures he had made to turn Stutzman into a lover. It is true that Denny had seen a lot in his young life, but his feelings were genuine. He couldn't understand what Stutzman's hang-up was. Why didn't Stutzman want him? There were times when it bothered him that Stutzman was going to bed with other men. He told Wanda about the threesome with the man in the handcuffs.

Later Stutzman assured her that he cared about Denny, but that it was only friendship he wanted. Denny was just plain too young.

"Wanda, I get so upset with Denny at times because he

doesn't want to keep it a secret. I can't afford for people I do business with to find out I'm like this," Stutzman said.

Wanda understood the problem, but she still felt sorry for her nephew. In the back of her mind she felt that Eli had led Denny on in order to get him to come down to Austin. But she couldn't figure out why.

Pot smoke filled the house on Banton Road. Almost every night the three men would kick back and smoke a 12-inch joint that Pritchett had rolled. If Danny walked in, Stutzman instructed the others to conceal the dope—although, considering what Stutzman had done with the boy in Colorado, such a gesture was more for the benefit of Ruston and Pritchett than for the little boy.

One of Pritchett's jobs was to roll twenty-five joints every night for Stutzman to take to work and sell during the day.

One time Ruston noticed a cache of marijuana in a trunk in Stutzman's bedroom, and he asked Stutzman about it. He wanted to know how much there was.

"A pound."

"A *whole* pound?"

"Yeah."

Ruston thought Stutzman was into heavier dealing than just selling joints to his employees.

"I'd seen him talking to a couple of people who came to the house in suits. Eli stayed outside in the front yard talking to them. Not really to visit, sort of a business meeting. They were in a Lincoln. Seemed really strange that Eli would be associating with people like that. I have a picture of people like that being with the mob," Ruston recalled.

Leona Weaver moved to Austin on March 12, 1984—the one-year anniversary of her husband's suicide. Weaver had grown up in the slums along the Sabine River in Orange,

Texas. She was overweight, had frizzy red hair and a history of activism, and loved mysteries.

She didn't know it then, but she had come to the right place.

Weaver met Denny Ruston at the Pizza Hut where she had taken a job. She liked him immediately. He was thin, gangly, and tried to be the center of attention. To Weaver, Denny Ruston was a big child who made a big show of flirting. He was playful, and in his overblown attempts to be liked, he was endearing.

Within a few days of their meeting, Ruston had become a frequent visitor to Weaver's apartment, across the street from the Pizza Hut. Weaver would feed him, listen to him, and, when she could get a word in, counsel him. Ruston seemed to trust her from day one. Weaver was used to that kind of quick bonding. Even strangers seemed willing to tell her their life stories.

When he finally told Weaver about his sexuality, she felt more relieved than shocked.

"Are you sure it doesn't bother you that I'm gay?" Ruston asked Weaver that first week.

Weaver shrugged. "It doesn't bother me that you're gay, as long as it doesn't bother you that I'm not."

Once the Big Secret was out, Denny Ruston started to talk about Eli Stutzman, whom he said was his lover. He told her that Stutzman had been Amish and that his wife had died in a fire. Stutzman owned a construction business, Ruston said, and had a little boy named Danny.

Stutzman could also get Weaver just about any drug she wanted, according to Ruston.

Pot was her drug of choice. It had been since she had grown up along the Sabine. Ruston had access to as much as she wanted.

"I used to get pot from Denny. He wasn't buying. I know that there was more than pot there, but I didn't do anything but smoke pot. I was going through Denny, who got it from Eli. He wasn't going through Eli to get it from somebody else."

It was late for a call to an early-rising Indiana dairy farmer like Ted Truitt. Eli Stutzman surely must have known that Truitt would have been in bed. It was after 11:00 P.M., April 21, 1985, when Truitt answered a call from his old friend and first male lover. The call lasted nineteen minutes. Stutzman said he was planning to leave Austin. There had been some trouble, and he needed to get away.

"Do you think you can put up with a visitor for a while?" he asked. His voice was that of the same old controlled, cool Eli. He even joked a little. He hoped he wouldn't be any trouble. If he had any reason to leave Texas other than to take a vacation from his busy remodeling business, Truitt was unaware of it.

Truitt, who had always liked Stutzman, was pleased at the prospect of a visit. "When are you coming?"

Stutzman seemed vague, but he said it would be soon.

Cal Hunter drove a cherry red '83 Dodge van with mag wheels and a running board, and spoke with the drawl of a native Texan, though the construction worker had grown up in the blue-collar east side of Indianapolis. In April, 1985, the 30-year-old Indianapolis man had found his way to Austin, where he was hired by Stutzman at the Texas Employment Commission (TEC).

As it turned out, Stutzman was looking for a new partner. He talked of big money.

"Eli said he made more than $60,000 in the first quarter of the year doing remodeling for out-of-town owners," recounted Hunter. "I didn't know what was happening at first, but later I learned how such things went. The real-estate management agent would send Stutzman on a job that would cost $10,000 to fix and charge the owner $30,000. They each got their extra piece.

"His other partner had gone back north to his family or something. He told me I could turn a real good profit working for him and eventually setting up a satellite operation."

Hunter did not know that Stutzman was gay until he had Hunter go to his post-office box by the Sears off I-35 to pick up mail.

"What I found shocked me," Hunter later said.

In among the stacks of letters and bills was a form letter or brochure of some kind from California.

"I thought it was a 'straight' sex brochure—it had something about deep throating, so I read it. But it was about fist fucking—how to put your hand up there safely. There was something else about bestiality, too. I thought I'd picked up the wrong mail—but it had Eli's name on it."

"I must admit I felt a little pity for Eli," Hunter said on another occasion. "My feeling was that if he had been raised differently he would have turned out straight. Austin was his first time out in the real world. He didn't want to be gay, but he just fell in with the wrong crowd."

Hunter figured something was amiss with Stutzman and his son when he saw the two of them together at the house or the job site.

"The relationship they had was almost like a master and servant," he recalled. "Danny followed his father around and wasn't allowed to say anything. He wasn't a son. He was a servant out of fear."

Like the second grader's speech pathologist, Ruth Davis, Hunter also saw bruises.

"Of course, I didn't see him naked or anything, but I saw bruises all over his arms," he said.

Dinner at Stutzman's place one night offered additional evidence that Danny was a victim of ongoing child abuse.

"We were sitting at the table, and Danny was just beginning to relax with me being a stranger and all. He started to talk, and he began to stutter. Eli hit him in the mouth so hard the boy fell off his chair.

"Danny got up on his chair and like a beaten little soldier

wiped the blood from his mouth and sat back at the table. He didn't say another word all night."

Hunter also wondered if the boy had been sexually abused.

"Eli used to pat and pinch his butt, more than just a father–son type of thing. It was the *way* he touched him. But none of that was my business. Construction work was my bread and butter, and I didn't want to mess it up.

"I know something wasn't right with Eli. There is an unnatural coldness in a man who would smack his boy across the mouth the way he did."

CHAPTER TWENTY

Churchgoers leaving for Sunday service in the vicinity of the Pilot Knob dump site noticed a considerable amount of activity on Colton-Bluff Springs Road the morning of May 12, 1985. A couple of patrol cars plus vehicles belonging to investigators and detectives had stirred up a cloud of dust as they parked in neat rows along both sides of the road.

In the space of one hour, quiet and kindly Mr. Raymond Kieke had been transformed from rancher to witness in a murder investigation. He gave his statement and told the investigators where he could be found—at home, just up the road.

Eight law-enforcement officers and investigators crowded together in the thick air around the culvert. Each of them could think of better ways to spend the morning, but a dead body draws gawkers and ghouls like flies, and the law-enforcement people were on hand to secure the crime scene as well as to investigate.

Travis County homicide detective *Jerry Wiggins* was one of the first to arrive. At 44, Wiggins was the quintessential veteran Texas cop; his haggard eyes never showed a trace of shock or surprise. Like other cops who lead lives wrought with long hours and temptation, Wiggins had a failed marriage. He knew it was his fault, and he regretted it, yet he was born to be a cop. He carried a gun the way most people carried a comb or a pack of gum.

Wiggins broke murders into two types: the smoking gun and the whodunit. This one was obviously one of the latter. The year, in fact, was shaping up to be a banner year in murders for the county—not the kind of record-breaking statistic that shows up on a chamber of commerce brochure. This was the fifth murder he'd worked, and it was only May. The year before there had been a total of seven.

Of course, he didn't handle all the investigations himself, but it was Wiggins's turn to work the weekend. His partner, Gary Cutler, was probably just getting out of bed. Lucky guy.

Juvenile Officer *Kelley Liesman* was there because she was the only officer from the sheriff's department who had volunteered to assist the two-person homicide team. She was just 24 and wanted to learn more about homicide investigations firsthand. *Harold Darby*, a detective terrified of bodies, also watched from the sidelines. For him, the smell was enough. He was working on not getting sick.

Travis County ID technician *David Weaver* and investigator Jim Hall of the medical examiner's office were also there to lend their expertise. Weaver, who had been with the county for four years, knew the Colton-Bluff Springs area well. He had been there at least ten times, most recently to investigate an attempted rape. A skilled composite artist, Weaver sometimes produced sketches rivaling a photograph in detail. Some cops thought they were more suitable for framing than for investigative work. Weaver and Hall looked for the "why" and "who." The official "how" would be determined at the autopsy by Medical Examiner *Roberto Bayardo*.

Jimmy Davenport, a patrol sergeant, heard the call and drove by. He stopped for a few minutes that morning, mostly just to get a look at what was going on.

Those who had a reason to be there went to work. Wiggins made some notes he would later incorporate into his report. A clump of dark hair was found on the victim's shoulder. Wiggins figured it had been torn from the scalp. Maggots covered the body. The eyes were gone, apparently from animal activity. Since the cutoffs were unsnapped, unzipped, and pushed down the victim's legs, Wiggins considered the possibility of a homosexual murder, though he knew most such murders involved some kind of torture. No evidence suggested that, but the body was so decomposed that it was tough to tell much.

Weaver grimaced at the sight of a couple of scorpions crawling on the corpse. He figured they had come to the corpse to feast on the maggots.

The ID technician recorded the scene with forty-plus color photographs before anyone could so much as move a maggot. In a crime-scene search, Weaver's standard procedure was to start at the body and work outward. Though the photos would be in focus, later when they were needed it would be difficult for some investigators to distinguish the body from the soil. Both were black. It was only the white—a writhing frosting of maggots—that seemed to form the shape of a dead man. The victim's limbs had a greenish cast. Blossoms of Queen Anne's lace framed each shot. Weaver also took wider shots of the area, including the farms and barns in the distance.

The victim wore no shoes, underwear, or shirt. There appeared to be a gunshot wound through the head.

A few of those present smoked cigars to mask the stench—a technique a number of investigators use during an autopsy or the discovery of a badly decomposed human body. Wiggins had another advantage: a bushy mustache that crowded his nostrils like a filter. Kelley Liesman breathed through her mouth and tried to get uphill as often as possible; she wished she had some Vicks or other mentholated salve with which to coat the inside of her nostrils and upper lip—another common technique. Meanwhile, investigators lifted the body onto a stretcher and hoisted it out of the ditch. Wearing jeans, cowboy boots, and a pearl-button shirt, Hall stood above the ditch like the Lone Ranger and gave orders.

Wearing rubber gloves, Wiggins and Liesman poked through the body-fluid-soaked earth with hands and fingers, searching for shell casings or other evidence. Wiggins explained a few things he had picked up in his years as an investigator, and Liesman listened carefully. The ghastly mire yielded no clues.

Near where the body had lain, however, a rusty shotgun shell was recovered from under a rock that had been resting next to the victim's head. Weaver studied the shell. "It's too old to be related."

"Collect it anyway," Wiggins said.

The investigators searched a quarter-mile radius and found nothing. Wiggins, Weaver, and Liesman scoured the length of the culvert. Nothing.

Measurements of the dump site's key features and its location were recorded. It was four feet ten inches from the level of the road to the body's location in the ditch. Wiggins noted that the body had been lying face up on an east-west axis, the head against the culvert, facing east. So fragile was the body that a good downpour could easily have washed the bones through the culvert and scattered the remains.

He wrote: "The odor was putrid, I recognized it as decaying flesh and body fluids."

Weaver, Wiggins, and the foul-smelling corpse, now in a body bag, rode in Jim Hall's county van to introduce Dr. Bayardo to his latest patient.

The Travis County Morgue is in the basement of Brackenridge Hospital, on the outskirts of downtown Austin's business district, only a few blocks from the beautiful, rosy-colored sandstone capitol building. Brackenridge is a run-down, borderline-condemned building with a leaky roof. It's an institution with an image problem, a reputation as the hospital for the poor and illiterate of Texas's capital city.

Medical Examiner Roberto Bayardo, 51, had been raised in Mexico, where he earned a medical degree at the Universidad de Guadalajara. The superior schools in the States and a fascination with forensics brought him across the border in 1967. Dr. Bayardo had been the county's chief medical examiner since June 1978, after coming to Austin by way of Harris County, Texas, where he had held the medical examiner's job. He had all of the right credentials: a medical degree, four years of training in pathology, and the stomach to handle what at times was an unsettling job.

Even his detractors conceded that the doctor never pointed fingers when someone made an innocent mistake. Dr. Bayardo had done thousands of autopsies, and he knew that the unexpected sometimes happened on the table.

The John Doe from out by Pilot Knob arrived around one in the afternoon and was numbered ME-85-466.

Autopsies are not a pretty sight, and, in spite of the medical jargon and protocol surrounding them, the doctor and his assistant are still hacking at a human body with saws and scalpels. None of that is lost on the investigators who observe such proceedings. In fact, Travis County sheriff's deputies and detectives call the assistant "Bayardo's ghoul." The ghoul's job is to saw open the head, do some of the meat-cutter's work for the doctor, and sew the body back up. One ghoul used a Swiss Army knife, which he kept in his pocket, to make the incisions. Most use a scalpel.

"That ghoul didn't last too long," Wiggins remembered. "He liked his job too much."

The easiest part of the autopsy is the first procedure, the external exam. Weaver, who assisted Bayardo with this part of the exam, took two series of photographs of the body. One, of course, would seem sufficient. But, in the game that must be played with defense attorneys, the second of the series was taken without the medical examiner's ID tag in each shot. This is done so that a defense lawyer can't say: "Is this exactly as the body was found? Was that little tag on the body when it was found?"

Every once in a while Weaver would respond to one of the doctor's motions to take another photograph.

Wiggins and Weaver listened carefully as Bayardo went through his routine—a routine so exact they figured he could do it in his sleep. Some, who had worked with the doctor many times, wondered if *they* could do it in *their* sleep. Wiggins's cigar smoke battled the odor from the dead man's body. The cigar didn't have a chance in the small and, in his opinion, poorly ventilated room.

Trace evidence—such as the carpet fibers that helped nail the Atlanta Child Killer, Wayne Williams—had emerged as a major advancement in forensics. Answers could be found under the lens of a microscope. Many medical examiners in the major cities now used special "clean suits" for the doctor and the assistant examiners. No particles or fibers could fall from these, as in the case of the old surgical scrubs. Bayardo, however, wore a disposable, white plastic apron over street clothes—things were not so progressive in Travis County. This office did things the old-fashioned way and looked only for the obvious.

Wiggins and Weaver knew they would be out of there before two. Dr. Bayardo's exams never lasted more than an hour.

Dr. Bayardo estimated that the victim had been in his early twenties. His ghoul weighed and measured the body. The victim was sixty-eight inches tall and weighed about 140 pounds. His hair was brown. The cutoff jeans were Bill Blass, with a waist size of 33. Wiggins studied the cutoffs for the marks or tag that might be left by a cleaner, but there were none.

Dr. Bayardo removed the cutoffs and placed them in an evidence bag. He noted that the victim's uncircumsised penis had not been mutilated.

The female greenfly doesn't wait long to deposit her eggs on a human corpse. As soon as the body is cool—after about twenty-four hours—females will light on a corpse and begin laying their eggs. Within seven days the larvae will grow to about a quarter of an inch in length. Though the maggots obscured much of the body, they were also of critical importance. Dr. Bayardo measured them—the largest were five-eighths of an inch long. To Dr. Bayardo, all of the evidence taken together indicated that the victim had been dead for about four weeks, maybe as long as six.

In some decomposition cases the fingertips are plumped up with a fluid injection. David Weaver would not use that technique on ME-85-466. Both hands and feet had slipped off like gloves and shoes. Weaver was forced to lay the loose skin from the victim's hand over his own to make the prints for identification purposes. The resulting prints were good, better than Weaver had hoped. Some fingers were intact and he was able to roll them on the FBI standard white card.

Every detail was documented on a form that Bayardo would have his secretary type on Monday morning.

A Y-shaped incision was made running from shoulder to shoulder then down the midline to the genitals. The precision of the doctor's scalpel was evident, but in the end observers would say the body had been cut open like a gutted bass. With the exception of the appendix, which Bayardo determined had been surgically removed, everything was autolyzed, but intact. The heart was normal, as were the liver and lungs.

Since no blood was in the body, a blood typing was not going to be a part of the examination. Given the mummified condition of the body, this was not unusual. Blood breaks down and separates shortly after death.

Weaver had to consider each of the doctor's words carefully. After the hundreds of autopsies he had seen Bayardo administer, he was fairly good at understanding Bayardo's heavily-accented English.

The head was saved for last. Saw cuts were made that revealed the gunshot wound—the victim had been shot through the left eye.

As was his procedure in his examination of bodies decomposed as badly as this one, Bayardo removed the jaws to have X rays and dental charts made.

Beneath the scalp, Bayardo hit possible crime-solving pay dirt and retrieved a distorted, mushroom-shaped .22-caliber lead projectile. Though it was badly damaged from its collision with the skull, the slug was a piece of evidence that could lead to some answers. In addition, Bayardo determined the path of the bullet: into the left eye and then the skull. The path was upward from the toes and into the head at about a thirty-five-degree angle, and from the right toward the left at about a thirty-degree angle.

Wiggins got up from the little built-in desk where he spent most of his time during the autopsy and looked at the wound. He figured that the victim had been shot by someone shorter than he was, or that he may have been shot while lying on his back.

Dr. Bayardo rinsed the bullet carefully, to avoid marring any of the delicate grooves that might later identify the murder weapon. No one really held much hope that the distorted, mushroom-shaped bullet would be very helpful, it was so badly damaged. But it was all they had. The medical examiner put it into a small manila envelope, which was labeled and notarized for evidentiary purposes. He handed it to Weaver. The chain of evidence was documented. It was 1:55 P.M.

They still didn't have a name for ME-85-466.

On May 13, 1985, the *Austin American-Statesman* buried an article on page B-5, headlined "Body Found Near FM 1624." Few beyond the victim's killer probably paid much attention to the article—such dumpings were common.

It was the middle of May, and the students in *Marilyn Martinez's* second-grade class could feel the heat of approaching summer the day Eli Stutzman showed up with paperwork from the school office to take Danny out early. Danny didn't know that he was leaving the school for good, but seemed glad to go with his dad. All of the kids wished him well and said good-bye.

Martinez wondered what the rush was and why the boy's father didn't wait two more weeks and let the boy finish the school year.

Stutzman said they were moving, though later she couldn't recall if he had said where.

"Danny was one of those little children you'd like to have more of in your class," she later said.

When Ruth Davis closed out her report on Danny Stutzman for 1985, it was with some disappointment regarding Danny's progress. She wrote on May 29, 1985: "No progress observed. Danny needs to . . . continue working . . . his monitoring skills have slipped during spontaneous speech."

What caused Danny Stutzman to "slip"?

CHAPTER TWENTY-ONE

Homicide investigator Gary Cutler was the flip side of partner Jerry Wiggins. Young, and as hip as a Texas cop can be, Cutler was the opposite of the grizzled, chain-smoking, Levis-are-all-right Wiggins. If Wiggins was detective as scientist, Cutler was action and show. For Cutler, being a cop was an ego boost.

Murder was their only link.

Over the years they had worked a number of intriguing cases, most notably the murders attributed to Henry Lee Lucas. Lucas had allegedly killed three in Austin, whose bodies were recovered just off the interstate. The murders had occurred in October 1979. Wiggins and Cutler had worked the case in 1983, when Lucas had started pointing out dump sites throughout Texas. The total number of murders ran up like a Las Vegas jackpot.

It was a great case, full of twists, innuendo, and even cannibalism. The national press covered the case. Cutler had thought it might be made into a movie, but it wasn't. Joseph Wambaugh, Wiggins's hero, talked about doing a book on it, but dropped out, reportedly because the story was too "difficult."

On Monday morning, Wiggins filled Cutler in on the body found out by Pilot Knob. Wiggins gave the details quietly and matter-of-factly. By the time Wiggins had painted the picture of the body and the autopsy, Cutler was glad he had been off on Sunday. Since the sheriff's office divided caseloads between north and south, the north being Wiggins's territory and the south belonging to his partner, the case would have been assigned directly to Cutler as lead investigator.

Wiggins had been the first to work the case, so he had entered his name in the case file.

Cutler took over and began the process of trying to find out who the victim was and, he hoped, to get some answers on how the victim happened to end up out in the middle of nowhere with a slug through his head. The victim had been dead for more than a month, and the trail was as cold as Bayardo's table-side manner.

The *Austin American-Statesman*, which the investigators liked to call the "American Misstatement," published a small article in that morning's edition. The text was only four inches, but it was enough to bring in a few calls from relatives and friends of missing persons, each caller sure that this might be his or her loved one.

Wiggins took a call from a Mrs. Dodson from Granger, Texas. She was sure the body was that of her son, Mike, who she said had a drug and alcohol problem. She had kicked him out of the house, and her heart still ached.

"What else could I do? I didn't know what to do," she kept saying. Wiggins listened and calmly took down the description. Mike had brown hair and a beard. His height was close to that of the victim.

He had not had an appendectomy, however.

"Ma'am, I'm sorry. The body we recovered had his appendix out," Wiggins said, trying to let the mother down easy.

"Well, he could have had it taken out in the last two months. Couldn't he?"

"It's possible."

Wiggins had learned that you don't argue with a killer or a mother. Both are always right.

Across the street at the medical examiner's office, Dr. Bayardo took down information from a caller who wished to remain anonymous. The caller believed the body to be that of a Michael Gordon. Bayardo gave the name to Cutler and Wiggins for follow-up.

Other calls came in. Notes were left on Wiggins's and Cutler's desks. Lots of people thought they knew who that body might belong to. A cousin. A brother. Always someone who was missing from somewhere.

Cutler had the victim's physical description entered in the Austin Police Department's missing persons computer. Nothing likely came up. Another option was to enter the details into a national computer, but because of the tremendous number of missing persons nationwide it was not done.

By afternoon it had become clear that identifying the body was not going to be easy. DPS notified Wiggins that it was unable to match the prints with any recorded in its Henry Fingerprint System, one of two standard national systems for comparing prints. Weaver had the little white cards with the dead man's prints forwarded to the FBI identification section in Washington. From there it would be a long wait.

And a long shot.

Weaver knew that only 20 percent of the population of the United States has been printed. If the John Doe had a criminal record or had been in the military, the FBI might get a hit. Otherwise, investigators would have to rely on phone calls and missing persons reports, and those were not promising.

Wiggins requested the thumb print from Michael Gordon's driver's-license application.

On June 3, a call came in from the FBI office in Washington. The prints submitted by Wiggins and Weaver had been matched, with fourteen points of identity, to Coast Guard prints belonging to Glen Albert Pritchett, a white male born

September 30, 1961. The victim had been born in Logan, Utah.

A teletype was sent to the Montana Driver's License Bureau and yielded additional information. Pritchett's last address had been in Missoula County. He had one arrest for driving under the influence.

Next, a call was placed to the Missoula County Sheriff's Office, and the dispatcher there indicated that the captain would call Cutler the following morning. The state police headquarters in Helena was also contacted.

At 10:00 P.M., the dispatcher from the state police reported that Pritchett had been arrested by the Helena police for driving under the influence, and booked into the county jail.

A step at a time, as many details as possible about Glen Albert Pritchett were pulled together. Each agency presented a new lead. A records check was requested of the Lewis and Clark County Sheriff's Office. Courtesy of that office, it became apparent that Glen Pritchett's life had seen plenty of rough spots. Pritchett had run away from home several times in the mid 1970s. He had been arrested September 3, 1984, for driving under the influence.

It seemed that Glen Pritchett had had nothing but bad luck.

The following morning Cutler received a call from Diana Duffield of the Montana State ID Bureau in Helena. She had some additional information about Pritchett. The bureau is the state repository for all criminal records—more than 90,000 Montanans have had scrapes with the law and earned a place in the files. Glen Pritchett's name was among them. Duffield had pulled up Pritchett's driver's license, and she informed Cutler that the victim's parents were a Robert Wesley and Evelyn Jean Pritchett. Additionally, she had learned that Robert had been employed as a maintenance man for the Postal Service. She didn't have an address.

Later that day, Cutler talked with the Missoula County Sheriff's Office, which agreed to send copies of the arrest record and a photograph of the deceased. At least now Travis County investigators would have a decent photograph of the victim.

Missoula County called again the next day with a phone number and a Council, Idaho, P.O. Box for the Pritchetts, who had moved to a town of less than a thousand, near Hell's Canyon, an hour and a half north of Boise. Cutler also learned about Sandy Turner—Pritchett's ex-wife—and his two children, their names, and their dates of birth.

Parents, a wife, two children. Jesus, Cutler thought, someone would have to notify them of the murder. Undoubtedly there would be tears, followed by questions. Who had dumped Pritchett out by Pilot Knob? Why had he been in Texas, anyway? Cutler dialed the number for the Adams County Sheriff's Office, in Council.

On June 7, Cutler contacted the Austin Police Department and requested a computer check on Pritchett. He learned that in December 1984 Pritchett had been questioned in a parking lot at Handcock Center. Pritchett had been drunk and in the company of a man named Eli Stutzman. Both men had said they lived at 3408 Banton Road.

The Banton address would seem to have been a good lead—an obvious lead—for the murder investigation. Later, Wiggins said that if he had been handling the case, he would have been there in a heartbeat. For some reason, however, Gary Cutler sat on it for more than a week.

His partner later suggested Cutler had waited because it was "just a fag murder."

CHAPTER TWENTY-TWO

May 26, 1985

It was a clear day under a blindingly bright sun—"beach weather," Stutzman called it—when an already remarried Wanda Sawyer stepped off the plane after an all-night flight from Honolulu. A lot had happened in the months since she had left the Texas capital. She had married a man who would scarcely understand and never condone her friendship with someone like Stutzman. She had come back to check on the spoils of her divorce and to watch her son graduate from high school. Stutzman invited her to stay at his place.

She was disappointed when she learned that Pritchett was gone.

"There was a family emergency up in Montana," Stutzman told her. "His son was injured in a car-tricycle accident."

Wanda found 18-year-old Sam Miller in Pritchett's place, a straight-from-the-farm Amish boy from Ohio whom Wanda felt personified the phrase "just fell off the turnip truck." Miller, from an Old Order Amish group in Newcomerstown, had come to Texas for work. A friend of Stutzman's had sent him.

Stutzman was in good spirits and seemed happy to see Wanda. Of course, Stutzman had a reason to be happy to see her—he needed money.

"Do you have two thousand dollars you can spare? I only need it for a little while," he said.

Not wanting to pry by asking why he needed the money, Wanda made the loan with the stipulation that she had to have the money back when she left for Hawaii in a couple of weeks. Stutzman agreed.

That afternoon, Stutzman, Danny, Denny Ruston, Wanda, and her daughter drove out to Hippy Hollow, a nude beach on the shores of Lake Travis. They stayed two or three hours. None of Stutzman's party went nude.

"One guy was over there beatin' his meat," Wanda recalled. "I said, 'Eli, if he's doing that for my benefit, he may as well give up and quit. It's not turning me on.' "

When they returned to Stutzman's place, Wanda apologized, but said she was so exhausted that she needed to get some sleep. Stutzman let her use his water bed.

When she awoke later that evening—around eight or nine—she went into the kitchen to get something to eat. The house was deserted. On the table stood a metal box larger than a cigar box. Inside, she saw a stash of what she instantly knew had to be marijuana. She didn't touch it. She didn't want anything to do with it.

The following morning Stutzman was sheepish when he approached Wanda to tell her they needed to have a talk.

"I know you saw what was on the table last night," he said.

She told him she had.

"That wasn't meant to be left there for you to see. I apologize."

"Eli, I'll tell you what," Wanda said, "if you want to do that kind of stuff, that's fine with me. But please don't put any on me and don't do any around me. And please don't let any of it get into my luggage. You do, and I'm dead meat. My husband told me that if I hung around with anyone who did this and got caught and it came between me and his job he'd choose the job. I've only been married two weeks!"

Later Wanda learned from Denny Ruston that Stutzman

usually kept his marijuana under his water bed. Still, she wasn't about to take any chances on getting busted at the airport. One time, she searched under Danny's bed, because it was the place she stowed her luggage. She also kept her suitcase locked. She didn't want someone to come by and drop some pot into her bags.

A pattern emerged nearly from the outset. Stutzman would take strange men into the bedroom and close the door. After a short while, the men would leave. The visitors were average guys, dressed in jeans and western shirts. It happened every day. Sometimes there would be two or three in a group.

Wanda didn't know what was going on. She felt that many of the visits were too brief for sex. She figured it was just Stutzman taking care of business.

A frequent visitor to the house she did come to know was Cal Hunter, Stutzman's foreman. Stutzman made it clear to Wanda that nothing should be said in front of Hunter that might cause him to pick up on Stutzman's homosexuality. He told Wanda that he was going to have Hunter handle most of his jobs so that he would be free to do some other work.

Whenever Stutzman did bring men home for sex, he usually made sure that Danny was in bed. As far as Wanda could tell, Danny didn't know who his father was sleeping with.

By then, the Denny Ruston–Eli Stutzman relationship had worn thin—at least as far as Stutzman was concerned. He told Wanda, "Denny is too possessive. He doesn't want me to go with other guys. If I have just one man—Denny—then others might pick up on me being gay."

Some things had changed between the time Wanda had left Austin and returned. There was something different about Stutzman. It was more than the fact that he wanted some independence from Ruston. His temper at home and at the construction sites was short. He didn't seem to have the patience he had once had. And he was forever leaving his work sites and running here and there.

Also, Wanda was left with Sam Miller more times than she cared to be. She thought Miller was a "dimwit."

Where did Eli rake this one up? she wondered.

It was just like Stutzman to take pity on someone down on his luck and bring him home and give him a job and maybe a meal. When Wanda told Stutzman she thought Sam Miller was an idiot, Stutzman was rather kind. "Well, at least he can do something."

"Eli would tell him to go unload the trailer," Wanda recalled. "Sam would say 'Now which way do I go?' "

At home, Sam Miller, the former Amish boy, was fascinated with television. Wanda and Denny Ruston felt as though it would have taken a crowbar to pry him away from the set.

"At night, Sam didn't want to go to bed because he wanted to stay up and watch TV," Wanda later said.

Occasionally all of the men would gather to watch the porno channel.

At night, if Ruston and Stutzman went to a party, they left Wanda with Miller and Danny.

Wanda wasn't concerned that Danny slept in Stutzman's bed.

"It didn't seem unnatural to me. I sleep with my children—even now. I raised my kids to think that when they see something like this it's not bad. My oldest was sixteen when he climbed into the shower with me one time. We got home from the beach, there was seven of us, and only two showers. I had my two youngest in, and my oldest said, 'Mom, I ain't got no place to take a shower, can I crawl in with you guys?' I told him, 'Sure.'

"I raised my kids to look at a naked body and see it was not dirty or nasty. Maybe that's the reason I can be broad-minded when it comes to homosexuals."

Sitting in the living room after work, shortly after she had returned to Austin, Wanda asked Stutzman about Pritchett.

"When is he coming back? I'd really like to see him," she said.

Stutzman told her Pritchett's son was still in critical condition and in the hospital. There was no way of telling when he would return, but he was definitely planning on coming back to Austin.

If Wanda had wanted to take Danny before she had left for Hawaii in February, she felt even more inclined to do so during her visit in the spring. Over the three weeks of her visit it became clear that, while Stutzman loved his son, he had little time for the boy.

Danny was under strict orders to come directly home from school and to wait in the house for the others to arrive. A few times, Stutzman would go pick up Danny at some woman's house a few blocks away. Wanda never saw the woman, but Stutzman told her she was a black lady who loved kids.

Wanda, who had raised her five kids with love and independence, felt that Danny was a little spoiled. He didn't have much in the way of toys and things—and he certainly didn't have new clothes—but he acted babyish at times. Wanda surmised it was because he didn't have the love of a mother.

Considering all their hard times, Wanda felt Stutzman had done as good a job of raising his son as could be expected. When Stutzman punished Danny, she didn't say a word.

"He never whipped him, but he smacked him. He slapped him in the face, when we were in the truck. Danny kept asking for something, he wouldn't leave it rest. Eli got very mad and slapped him."

On June 14, while Wanda was getting ready to go back to Hawaii, she again told Stutzman she was sorry that she hadn't gotten to see Pritchett this trip. Stutzman understood her disappointment and told her that he had just talked with Pritchett on the telephone.

"He told me complications have set in and the baby will

have to be put in traction," he said. "It sounds real bad to me."

Stutzman drove Wanda to the airport early the next morning.

She hoped Pritchett's son would be all right.

CHAPTER TWENTY-THREE

June 15, 1985

Wiggins and *Lawrence Salas*, a burglary detective whose name, like Wiggins's, "was in the barrel to work weekends," had a breakfast of *migas*—a green chili, cheese, and egg dish—at Taco Village, a cop hangout on Berkman Drive. Endless cups of coffee and a block-long chain of Camel straights topped off the meal as the two discussed cases, department gossip, and their plan to visit the Banton Road address.

It was Saturday morning, and most of Austin was asleep when the detectives took a table at Taco Village. The town was like that—hopping at night along Sixth Street and quiet and lazy in the morning as the party crowd slept it off. Streets were deserted. The University of Texas campus was still. It was the kind of quiet morning typical of Austin.

It was a good morning to get into the thick of the Pritchett murder investigation.

The two men were friends. At 40, Salas was not much younger than Wiggins, but called him the "old guy." It was a compliment. Whenever he had a case that was proving difficult or he needed advice, he went to see the veteran homicide investigator. Wiggins thought Salas was a good cop, conscientious and detail-oriented when putting an investigation together.

The Austin native had only one flaw, but it was a big

one. Salas couldn't write a decent report, even if his career depended on it. Maybe he didn't have the confidence. Maybe he was impatient, like Cutler. In police work, reports are a mundane exercise, a process during which the investigator synthesizes all he has learned at a crime scene or interrogation. He goes through notes and recollections and distills them into a report that, in the end, in court, is all that matters.

Some investigators' reports read like good novels, with clear narratives and a touch of drama. Wiggins's detailed reports were like that. The reports of Salas, on the other hand, were vague and frugal with details. And since his memory couldn't necessarily be trusted, if something didn't make it into his report, it was lost for good.

Salas didn't like to drive, so Wiggins took the wheel when the pair drove out toward the airport and Manor Road. Both were familiar with the area and considered it a high-crime neighborhood. A few of the older, established families tried to hang on as dwindling property values forced their neighbors to turn the tree-lined community into a community of renters, and a kind of combat zone.

The street address in the field report regarding Pritchett was 3408 Banton. Wiggins had no problem finding it. The address numbers were clear on the neatly painted white house—something bleary-eyed drug users looking for a score or cops looking for a suspect appreciate in a rundown neighborhood. The front yard, however, appeared well-maintained. The thick blades of buffalo grass were shorn and green. A 1978 green and silver Ford pickup with a trailer hitch was parked in the driveway. Like the yard and the house, the truck also stood apart from the other vehicles parked along Banton. Most of them were either old cars that had seen better days or jacked-up hot rods dripping oil onto the roadway.

The Texas plates on the pickup were noted: SJ943. It was Eli Stutzman's vehicle.

If Salas ever drew the connection, he later forgot it, and he definitely never made any written notes on it, but next door to the Stutzman address at 3405 Banton lived Mark Taylor. Salas had worked a successful vehicle-burglary case on Taylor a couple of months before. He didn't mention it to Wiggins.

Stutzman answered the door and identified himself. Wiggins told him that they were with the sheriff's office and that they were investigating the murder of Glen Pritchett. Records indicated that he lived at this address. Stutzman, dressed in blue jeans and a shirt, apparently ready to go to work, neither seemed surprised nor concerned about Pritchett's death.

He invited the cops in.

The house was spotless. A worn sofa adjacent to a TV dominated the living room, a raised area next to the entry. Stutzman told the investigators that Denny Ruston, Sam Miller, and Stutzman's son, Danny, lived there. Ruston was at the Pizza Hut already. Miller sat quietly, alternately dazed and lucid. He had never met Pritchett.

The detectives later maintained that Danny Stutzman wasn't at home that morning. In fact, Wiggins later said that he had never laid eyes on the child, and his notes back him up. But if the child wasn't there, where was he at nine o'clock on a Saturday morning?

Stutzman told the investigators that he hadn't seen Pritchett for several weeks.

"I put him on a bus for Montana in May."

Stutzman told Wiggins that he was a contractor specializing in remodeling, and the detective scanned the room for recent repairs—paint that didn't match, something that might indicate a patch job. Maybe a bullet hole had been filled in? It was obvious a carpenter wouldn't leave a bullet hole if he had half a brain and a bucket of spackle handy.

Stutzman said he had been letting Pritchett sleep on the couch, deducting fifty dollars a week from his paycheck. He had been expecting Pritchett to return to Austin after visiting his family in Missoula. He showed the investigators some blue jeans and shirts that belonged to Pritchett and that Stutzman had been keeping until he returned.

That Stutzman was pacing and seemed nervous was no indictment. Who wouldn't be uncomfortable or nervous with a homicide detective giving their house the once-over? While Salas interviewed Sam Miller in the living room, Wiggins looked through the rest of the house. The beds were made and the rooms were tidy. Nothing seemed out of the ordinary. He asked questions casually, and Stutzman responded, often volunteering more information than necessary.

"You have a horse?" Wiggins asked, indicating the ribbons and trophies Stutzman had displayed in his bedroom.

Stutzman nodded. "I keep him out in the county."

"Where abouts?"

"I had him out on a place on Onion Creek, but I moved him to a pasture off Sassman Road."

Close to the dump site, Wiggins thought. It was interesting, but it made Stutzman no more a suspect than Sam Miller or, really, anyone in Austin. But it was a link. Wiggins made a mental note of it.

Stutzman and Miller agreed to come down to the sheriff's office for a statement. Almost as an afterthought, Wiggins asked if Stutzman had any guns.

"Yeah, a .22 rifle and a 16-gauge shotgun. I keep them in my room. Do you want to see them?"

Wiggins watched Salas as he and Stutzman went to get the guns; .22 was the caliber of the murder weapon. Stutzman said that as far as he knew neither gun had been fired recently. He gave Salas a Marlin/Glenfield with a scope.

Sam Miller rode with the detectives, and Eli Stutzman followed in his pickup.

Wiggins moved Stutzman up a notch as a suspect. He had a truck that could easily have transported a body. He kept a horse out by the dump site. He not only had guns, he had a .22. But it was Stutzman's reaction to the news of his roommate's death that really made Wiggins suspicious. Stutzman hadn't seemed surprised by the news, he simply claimed to have believed his roommate was alive and well in Montana. Even more peculiar was the fact that he didn't even seem interested in Pritchett's murder.

"Most people are alarmed and ask questions about a murder involving a friend," Wiggins later said. "Eli Stutzman didn't ask one question."

The chain-smoking detective figured Sam Miller for a kid with a shoe size bigger than his IQ—he seemed naive and harmless. Conversation with Miller was futile, even though the detectives tried to get him to talk about himself, about Eli. In the end, they settled for small talk about the weather.

Stutzman was instructed to park along the strip on Eleventh Street, across from the north door of the courthouse. This was done to protect the chain of evidence—the detectives could see the truck from their office, inside the courthouse. It was merely procedure. In this case it hardly seemed critical. After all, it had been at least two months since the murder.

The L-shaped office was cluttered and smoky. Stutzman sat across from Wiggins in one end of the L. Out of view, at the other end of the office, Salas took Miller's brief statement.

Stutzman told Wiggins he had first met Pritchett in November 1984 at the Texas Employment Center, which was where he got most of his help. He said Pritchett didn't have a place to stay, so he had rented him a room.

"Anyone else living with you?"

"There was another man living there with us named Denny Ruston. Denny is a homosexual, but as far as I know Glen was not homosexual."

"Are you gay?" Wiggins asked, again thinking about the unzipped Bill Blass cutoffs the victim had been wearing.

Stutzman shook his head. "No. I'm bisexual."

The subject was uncomfortable for Stutzman, and Wiggins moved on to ask about Pritchett.

Stutzman described Pritchett as a nice, easygoing, and quiet type from Montana. He said he hadn't seen the man for two months.

"He kept talking about going back to Montana. About

two months ago he said he was going back to see his kids. He said his little boy had been hurt."

Stutzman couldn't remember the exact date that Pritchett, dressed in blue jeans and a short-sleeved shirt and wearing tennis shoes, had climbed on a bus headed for Montana. He hadn't seen Pritchett actually get on the bus. Regarding the date, he told the detective he could check Pritchett's time sheets.

"I dropped him off at the Greyhound bus station downtown and left. I had given him the money he was due, about six or seven hundred dollars. He said he would be back."

Stutzman told Wiggins he had spoken with Pritchett a couple of times after he had left Austin. Pritchett had called him from a pay telephone because, he said, his ex-wife's had been disconnected. It had been Stutzman's understanding that Pritchett would be returning to Austin any day.

Wiggins asked about Ruston, and Stutzman told him the basics. He was from Iowa. He liked to go to the gay bars on Red River and Ninth Street. Stutzman noted that Ruston had left for Iowa a couple of weeks before Pritchett had boarded the bus for Montana.

Wiggins wrote it all down on a yellow legal pad under Stutzman's watchful eye.

His statement concluded: "I don't know if Denny and Glen ever had sex or not but I wouldn't doubt it. I never had sex with Glen. Denny just likes to give blow jobs but is not into anything rough that I know of. I have no idea who would want to kill Glen."

Wiggins finished the interview by asking Stutzman if he would take a polygraph in order to clear himself of any suspicion.

Stutzman agreed and, in addition, volunteered to send Denny Ruston in for an interview that afternoon.

A typed version of Stutzman's statement was presented for his signature. In his haste, he neglected to correct a typo made by the central-records clerk. The typist had inadvertently changed Pritchett's name to Danny's in one sentence. It now read: "Danny smoked pot on occasion, and drank pretty heavily." The error was so glaring, it seemed strange that a father wouldn't correct it. But Stutzman apparently had other concerns.

One glaringly obvious omission from the interview was any questioning about Danny Stutzman.

Sam Miller couldn't believe it. He had just been questioned by the sheriff's office about a murder. It was enough to blow his mind.

In the pickup on the way back from the courthouse, an agitated Stutzman started to ramble, his words strung together with barely a gap between them. Miller heard Stutzman say one thing clearly: *"I killed him. He was getting in the way and I had to do something."*

Stutzman said it as though the excuse could justify the act.

Miller was too shocked to respond.

"I had to," Stutzman continued, "but don't worry, it will all blow over. If they question you again, just keep quiet. Don't say anything. You don't know anything."

Keep quiet. Miller took it as a threat. If Stutzman had killed Pritchett, his roommate—his friend—he just might kill again.

Miller sank low in the seat. Was knowing something like this as bad as participating? He listened as Stutzman went on, repeating, *"I had to, but don't worry."*

Miller didn't ask for details. He already knew more than he could handle.

When they got home, Miller grabbed a beer and turned on the TV. Then Eli and Danny joined him in the living room. Again, as unlikely as it seemed and as unnecessary as it was, Stutzman talked about the murder. This time he told Miller that he had been forced to move the body.

"I was afraid someone would find it," he said.

Again, Sam asked no questions.

According to Miller, Danny Stutzman also heard his father talk about committing the murder and hiding the body, but the boy had no real reaction to the information. It didn't seem to be news to him.

Stutzman said something about a funeral in Dallas–Fort Worth, and he left for the rest of the day. Danny went with his father.

Miller kept his mouth shut and didn't tell anyone what Stutzman had said. He didn't want to end up dumped in a ditch in the middle of nowhere.

He realized that coming to Austin had been the biggest mistake of his life.

It was the early lunch rush at Pizza Hut when Denny Ruston answered Eli Stutzman's frantic phone call. At first, Stutzman was firing off words too fast to make any sense. Ruston pressed his ear to the phone to shut out the noise of the restaurant.

"What did you say?" he asked.

"The police found Pritch's body."

Ruston felt the blood rush from his head. He was not composed enough to ask for additional information.

Stutzman rambled on anyway. "They took Sam and me in for questioning. They think I shot him and you helped. They want to talk to you. They want to question you."

Stutzman told Ruston to meet him in the parking lot of an Austin shopping mall. He said they had to talk it over before Ruston went to the sheriff for questioning.

Ruston agreed, hung up the phone, and, disoriented and shocked, drove to the meeting place. Later he wondered how he had made it there without wrecking his car.

When he arrived, Stutzman was already there, pulled over in a parking space. He motioned for Ruston to get inside the truck. Stutzman rattled off the same statements he had made on the phone: Pritchett was dead, the police had questioned Stutzman, they thought he had killed Pritchett and that Ruston had helped him do it. Stutzman's hands shook as he talked. Sweat beaded along his hairline.

"They accused me of murder," he said. "They think you helped me move the body."

Ruston wasn't one to handle stress well, and the pressure of the meeting in the parking lot was enough to cause him to retreat into a kind of fog.

"You have to go in, to talk to the detectives . . ." Stutzman insisted, giving Ruston a valium.

"Don't tell them that I met you here," Stutzman said.

Eli Stutzman was jittery, but Ruston was a nervous wreck. Stutzman hoped the valium would allow Ruston to at least give the sheriff a coherent statement, the statement he had told Ruston to give.

Ruston arrived at the sheriff's office at 2:00 P.M., looking every bit a Pizza Hut busboy on speed. Skinny, nervous, and disheveled, he talked fast as he gave Wiggins the basics and told the detective that he had met Stutzman in January, through his Aunt Wanda, and had lived with him at the Banton address. He had taken a vacation trip to Iowa on April 19.

"When I left, Glen Pritchett was still living with Eli. I got back to Eli's house on May seventh, a Tuesday. I asked Eli where Glen was and he said he had just left Sunday, May fifth, to go to Montana," Ruston stated.

Rancher Raymond Kieke had found the decomposed body on May 12, and Wiggins knew it was impossible for Pritchett to have been on a bus to Montana on May 5. Dr. Bayardo had determined that the victim had been dead four to six weeks. The murder had taken place in the middle of April, around the time Ruston said he had left for Iowa.

When he returned and found Pritchett gone, Ruston said, he had moved his things into Pritchett's room—and Danny had moved back into his bedroom. Later, when he thought about it, Ruston recalled that the drawers in which Pritchett had kept his clothes were empty.

With the affidavits he had taken earlier in the day in mind, Wiggins asked Denny Ruston about his relationship with Eli Stutzman.

Ruston answered quickly. "Eli and I are just friends," he said.

Just friends. It was the kind of remark a schoolgirl might make to convince her parents of her chastity. It rang with about as much truth.

"What about Pritchett?"

"I didn't know him very well." Again Ruston, smoke curling around his face, was emphatic.

He signed his legal name to the affidavit and, like Stutzman, agreed to a polygraph examination. Wiggins thanked Ruston for coming in and told him that an appointment would be set up. Ruston said he had nothing to hide.

After Ruston left, Wiggins noted the discrepancies in Stutzman's and Ruston's affidavits. How friendly were Eli and Denny? Denny and Glen? Ruston said he hadn't known Pritchett very well. Stutzman had said he wouldn't doubt that the two of them had had sexual relations. While the contradictory affidavits were a source of concern for Wiggins, what really bothered him were a couple of things that Stutzman had—or, really, hadn't—done: he hadn't asked *where* the victim's body had been found, and when he had been asked to take the polygraph, he had simply said yes. He hadn't asked, "Do you think I did it?"

Most innocent people do.

Back at Banton Road, Denny Ruston was tired and wound up so tight that the ticking of a clock could have made him jump. Stutzman gave him another valium, and Ruston went to his bedroom and smoked a joint before he fell asleep.

Between 1:00 and 3:00 A.M.—Ruston later recalled looking at his clock—Stutzman flipped on the light and woke him up.

Stutzman stood before him, fully dressed, wearing his work boots.

"Denny," he said, "I need some money. Do you have some you can loan me?"

Ruston had sixty dollars in his wallet, but he lied and said he was broke.

Stutzman asked if he could borrow Ruston's luggage.

"What's going on?" Ruston asked. "Are you going somewhere?"

"Yeah. My lawyer tells me to take a vacation and leave town until this whole thing blows over."

"Eli seemed real nervous, frantic, upset. Real worried. I'd never seen him like that," Ruston said later.

Ruston gave Stutzman three canvas tote bags, plus his marine duffel bag.

Stutzman grabbed the bags and began stuffing clothes and papers into them. He unloaded his dresser drawer and pulled some things out of his desk. He folded nothing—apparently there was no time.

"Where's Danny?" Ruston said from the doorway.

Stutzman didn't look up from his packing. "He's okay. He's with some friends."

Stutzman didn't say who, and Ruston didn't ask. Instead, he followed Stutzman around like a puppy as the frantic man packed.

One bag was stuffed so full that it took both men to zip it shut.

"Can you give me a ride?"

Ruston reluctantly said he would. "Eli, this doesn't look good. Are you sure your lawyer is right about this?"

Stutzman said it would only be for a little while.

Ruston followed Stutzman into his room and watched as his roommate started throwing things into his wastepaper basket. It was a collection of sex toys that Ruston had never seen in the months that he had lived with him. All Ruston had known about were the butt plugs and a single pair of handcuffs. That night Stutzman stashed a treasure trove of paraphernalia into the wastebasket: additional handcuffs, two vibrators, a pair of nipple clamps, various cock rings, and something called a ball stretcher, a device for encircling the testicles and stretching the scrotum.

Ruston was dumbfounded as he watched Stutzman load

it all up, pull the liner out of the wastebasket, and head for the door. When Eli Stutzman left that night, he only took what was important to him.

"Eli, it looks real stupid leaving like this."

"I know, but my lawyer said it would be better this way."

My lawyer. It was the second time he had mentioned his lawyer. In the previous six months, he had never mentioned having an attorney, or even knowing one. Even in his valium and marijuana fog, Ruston wondered what kind of lawyer would tell someone to leave town in the middle of a murder investigation.

They loaded the bags into Ruston's car, got in, and headed toward downtown, with Ruston driving. Stutzman directed him to a location off Interstate 35 and Fifty-first Street.

The place Stutzman had Ruston take him was a vacant parking lot between the city and a rural neighborhood, the kind of place where no one wanders that time of night. Across the empty parking lot, a bar called the Carousel Lounge was as dark and quiet as the Cameron Villa Rest Home, just across the way. An office-furniture store with a loading dock showed only a few security lights. Ruston dropped Stutzman off on the south side of the furniture store.

"I love you," he told Ruston.

"I love you, too." Ruston's answer was just words, a reflex response.

Stutzman got out of the car and, even though burdened by the full bags, walked quickly through the walkway between the store and another darkened building.

Ruston looked for Stutzman's truck. He didn't see it. There were no cars waiting to pick Stutzman up, either. Yet, he couldn't have been going very far—he couldn't have carried those bags much further on his own.

Ruston turned around and drove back to the freeway, then home.

The next morning he smoked a wake-me-up joint and

ran through the events of the night before. He checked the driveway to see if Stutzman's truck was still there—Ruston wore bifocals, didn't have the best night vision, and had been stoned, so it was conceivable that he simply hadn't seen the truck. Maybe Stutzman had left the truck in the lot, gotten a ride to the Banton Road address from someone else, and left Danny with them when he went inside to pack. That might explain why Stutzman's truck was no longer in the driveway, and why Danny hadn't been home last night. But if that was the case, why hadn't Stutzman had whoever it was wait for him while he packed?

Ruston also thought it strange that Stutzman never once went into Danny's room to pack any of his son's clothes. Had he already done that? Later, when Ruston checked, he found that Danny's clothes were where the boy had left them.

The next day, Mark Taylor, Stutzman's next-door neighbor, was at the Travis County courthouse checking in with parole officials in regard to the burglary charge Salas had busted him for, when he ran into Jerry Wiggins.

Taylor, 23, had seen the homicide investigator out at Stutzman's place two days before. He said he had some information about the case.

He gave the following statement to Wiggins.

"I knew Glen Pritchett, who lived with Eli. I have heard Glen and Eli argue before quite a bit. I heard them argue pretty seriously one time and I never did see Glen after that. I don't remember the date but it was some time in April. Eli started being real nervous and asking things like can they trace back to a gun from just a bullet. Eli has been acting real nervous since Glen disappeared. He asked me about the gun and bullet Saturday, right after the detectives left."

Was the statement true? Or was it the case of a young man in trouble with the law, and his hope that cooperation with the authorities might make it easier for him?

Later, Taylor elaborated on the argument between Stutzman and Pritchett.

"You're either gonna be screwing me or someone else!" Stutzman had yelled at Pritchett as they went toe-to-toe in the front yard of the house on Banton.

Screw? Was it sex? Or was it betrayal?

The night after he was questioned by the homicide investigators, Stutzman started packing his truck, Taylor later said.

"It was the last time I saw him."

Sam Miller called Cal Hunter with the news that Stutzman had fled Austin and left word that Hunter was to take over the construction business. Miller told Hunter to come to Banton Road the next morning and wait for Stutzman's call.

"Eli had a whole list of things he wanted me to do, mail to pick up, jobs to take care of," Hunter recalled.

"There's enough work to keep you busy," Stutzman told him, promising to pay him when he returned to Austin.

"After my trouble with the law blows over," he said.

Hunter reluctantly agreed.

"I didn't know it was murder he was involved with. I thought it had something to do with his little boy. Abuse or custody or something."

CHAPTER TWENTY-FOUR

When Denny Ruston showed up unexpectedly at Leona Weaver's apartment, he was a nervous wreck. It was all he could do to come inside and sit down before he began babbling about murder.

"They—*the sheriff*—just talked to me and Eli about Glen's murder . . . Glen was our roommate. They found him dead out in the county—near the pasture where Eli keeps his horse."

Ruston went on to explain to Weaver and her 20-year-old niece, Evelyn Martel, that after the investigators had questioned the two men, Stutzman had left town. *Fast*. In the middle of the night, no less. And he had taken his son with him.

Before either woman could ask, Ruston quickly insisted that neither he nor Stutzman had had anything to do with the murder.

"We didn't even know Glen Pritchett had died," he said.

"Why did he leave town if he didn't do it?" Weaver asked.

"I don't know. Maybe he did. Eli was scared, that's for sure."

When it finally set in that this wasn't a hoax that Denny Ruston was perpetrating, Weaver went to work trying to pry information from him.

"Well, do you know if Eli did it or not?"

Ruston said he didn't really know.

"Did you have anything to do with it?"

"No. I wasn't even here when it happened."

This statement troubled Weaver later. How did Denny Ruston know when the murder had happened? The most disturbing answers were the most obvious. Ruston had to have been there when it occurred—or else Eli Stutzman had told him about it.

"Who did it if Eli wasn't the one?" Weaver wondered aloud.

Ruston seemed ready for that question. He thought it was a former, disgruntled employee of Stutzman's named "Jay." He did not know his last name.

"I have a feeling he did it, and that Eli was only an accessory to the murder. It could be he was just there when it happened. Maybe he just helped move the body or something like that," Ruston said, adding that such a scenario might make some sense of the proximity of the dump site to the stable where Stutzman kept the horse.

"Maybe Jay *forced* Eli to help move the body!"

Weaver was skeptical. She kept thinking that Ruston knew more about the killing than he was letting on and that Stutzman had told him all about it when Ruston had returned from his vacation in Iowa. Ruston was keeping his mouth shut, she thought, because he was scared about something and, more important, because he loved Eli Stutzman.

June 17, 1985

Ruston returned to Weaver's apartment the next day, clutching a fist full of papers. He said he had proof that something funny was going on over on Banton Road.

Weaver and Martel studied the papers as Ruston chain-smoked and ran on about their significance.

They were time sheets for the weeks ending February 15, February 23, March 2, March 23, April 27, and May 4. Stutzman had made a notation on March 4, 1985, that he owed Glen $445, with entries made on March 5, 14, and

22. On May 4, the balance owed was $570, and a notation read: "Pd in full on 5/5/85."

"May 5 was the date Eli said he put Glen on the bus for Montana," Ruston said. "Look at the signature on May 4," he pointed out. "It doesn't look like Glen's writing, unless he was in a hurry or something."

The signatures on March 23 and April 27 were identical, and the time sheets dated February 15 and 23 and March 2 did not have any signatures at all.

It was the one dated May 4 that they all focused on as they pieced the story together. The forgery was blatant.

Weaver kept reviewing the date on which Stutzman said he had taken Glen to the bus (May 5), as well as the dates of the last time sheet (May 4), Ruston's departure for Iowa (April 19), and his return to Austin (May 7), and, finally, the date the body was found (May 12). She made a list in a notebook. She believed the time sheets were good evidence.

"The way it was all filled out, you could tell—there was no way this guy would have signed his name that way," she said later.

Martel suggested that the papers be photocopied before Ruston handed them over to the sheriff. She—and her aunt—had doubts whether Ruston could be trusted to do the right thing. Around midnight the three amateur sleuths found a photocopy machine at an all-night Safeway.

"Take the time sheets and give them to the sheriff," Weaver urged Ruston. Weaver didn't think Ruston had had anything to do with Pritchett's murder, she simply believed he had learned about the murder a whole lot sooner than he maintained.

If Jerry Wiggins thought Denny Ruston was a "trip" the first time he met him, the second time left no room for doubt. Ruston came in with six time sheets and a complete, detailed scenario of what they meant and how they were critical evidence against Eli Stutzman.

To Wiggins, Ruston seemed to be in the same nervous state Stutzman had exhibited during the investigation at the house and the interview at the courthouse office. And, like Stutzman, who had given Wiggins and Salas the rifle, Ruston was being overly helpful by handing over the time sheets and a theory to boot. Wiggins had seen his type plenty of times—sometimes these amateur cops were helpful, but mostly they got in the way when they fussed with the evidence.

Wiggins felt Ruston's motive was revenge.

"Denny turned vindictive. He was out to get Eli. I think Denny was pretty crazy about Eli as a person or as a meal ticket. He was mad that he had been left in this mess alone," he later said.

"He wanted to *prove* Eli Stutzman had done the killing."

The investigator felt there was enough evidence for a probable-cause warrant, which he hoped would lead to a confession. The DA's office, however disagreed. They wanted the detectives to come up with enough to land a grand-jury indictment against the ex-Amishman.

"Mark Taylor told us about the gun, Denny told us about the time sheets, and Eli lied about Pritchett's death when he told us he had put him on a bus for Montana, and then he left town in the middle of the night. He was our prime suspect—and then he was gone," Wiggins later said.

Leona Weaver rubbed the sleep from her eyes and did a double take at her alarm clock. It was 1:30 A.M. A visitor at that hour meant trouble. When she opened the front door she knew she was right. It was Ruston and another young guy, whom Ruston quickly introduced as his roommate Sam Miller.

Weaver had never heard Ruston mention Miller. She didn't know he had another roommate besides Stutzman.

"Something's going on at the house," Ruston said. "We keep hearing noises at the house, in the yard. Can we stay here for the night?"

She waved them inside.

The two of them seemed frightened beyond belief; their eyes were wide with fear. She thought they looked like a couple of little kids who had been frightened by a horror show. Ruston was even more jittery than he had been when he came over to tell Weaver about being questioned by Wiggins.

"What's the matter? What noises?" she said, after locking the door behind them.

"I think it's Jay. He's come back to kill us."

"Why would he kill you?"

"Well, maybe he thinks we know something."

Weaver thought they were overreacting, but in fact there was a murderer on the loose, so she listened and tried to calm them down.

Sam Miller said little. Weaver's heart went out to him—he seemed so out of place, so young. He seemed alternately lost and in a state of shock. He seemed more like a child than Ruston. He looked to be 14 or 15 years old, shy and nervous. Weaver offered him something to drink, and he politely declined.

Weaver couldn't imagine someone like Miller ending up in that house on Banton Road. He was out of his league with Ruston and Stutzman. Eli Stutzman, whom Weaver knew only by reputation and his sideline: dealing drugs.

Miller had his things in the car and said he would be taking the bus back to Ohio in the morning—as soon as he got the money being wired by a friend in Ohio. Stutzman owed him five hundred dollars, but Miller knew it was a lost cause. Besides, it would be worth that much to never lay eyes on the man again.

Weaver went to fix up the sofa bed, but Miller wouldn't let her. He didn't want her to think he was gay and planning to sleep with Denny Ruston that night. He insisted that he'd sleep on the floor. Weaver shrugged it off. It was too early in the morning to argue and try to win points as a hostess. At first, Miller even refused a blanket, but the frigid breeze from the air-conditioning got the best of him and he took one.

At daylight she tried to fix Ruston and Miller some breakfast, but Miller refused. He just wanted to get the hell out of Austin.

When Ruston returned from the bus station, he asked Weaver if he could stay with her until he finished the pay period and got his final check. Against her better judgment, she agreed.

On Thursday, June 20, Ruston and Weaver went out to Banton Road. When they arrived, they found an angry Cal Hunter. Hunter told them he planned to put a labor lien on Stutzman for back wages. It seemed a little odd to Weaver that Hunter had somehow decided that Stutzman had stiffed him and was never coming back to town. They listened to him rant for a moment before going inside.

Ruston showed Weaver the furniture that Stutzman said he had made back in Ohio. She was awestruck by its workmanship. She admired the dry sink, hutch, rocker, chest, and furniture in the living room.

The scene was strange. It was as if whoever owned the contents of the house had simply gotten up from one of the chairs and walked away.

Ruston took the television and an antique mantel clock that had belonged to Ida and Eli and put them in his car while Hunter started to close up the place.

"I'm not leaving this stuff here for someone to just walk in and take," Ruston told Weaver.

Weaver was glad to leave. She felt nervous, as though someone had been looking over her shoulder.

The next day Ruston and Weaver made a second trip to the house. Ruston was scared and refused to go without Weaver. Her sister loaned her a truck, and they went after the sofa Stutzman had told Ruston that Weaver could have, several weeks before.

The place had been ransacked and most of the furniture

was missing. Paper littered the floor like the remnants of a parade. It appeared that looters had come and helped themselves to whatever they pleased.

Weaver and her sister aimlessly wandered from room to room. In the dining room, the shelving running the length of the wall was still full of the glassware and crystal that they presumed had belonged to Stutzman's dead wife. In Danny's room, they discovered that someone had opened the trunk of Amish clothes.

Who did this? Weaver wondered. *What were they looking for?*

The Amish trunk had been placed up against the wall, with a toy chest sitting on top of it. Both had been moved with no regard for their contents.

Weaver knew Eli Stutzman wasn't coming back.

Each time Weaver came upon something of Ida's or Danny's she felt an incredible wave of sadness. Her sister felt it, too. Both of the women were repeatedly drawn to the boy's room, then to the dining room, and back again.

When she first saw the Amish clothes scattered in and out of the trunk, Weaver started to take them.

"I felt it was obscene to leave them there. I wanted to take them and take care of them. Her stuff. And the little boy's stuff. What was going on in that house was like raping her. I couldn't believe someone coming in there and taking her stuff," she later said.

She also felt sad about the little boy. His father was involved in a big mess, and he was dragging the child through the mud with him. It seemed cruel.

When it was time to leave, Ruston gave Weaver a houseplant from his collection.

A few days later, Weaver and Ruston went out to Banton for the last time. Stutzman had kept a few chickens in a coop in the back, and Ruston thought they should feed and water them. The chickens were gone.

Everything in the house, except the desk, the kitchen table and chairs, and the refrigerator, was gone. The crystal was gone. The Amish clothes were missing.

Personal papers, meaningless to the two of them, covered the floor. Weaver picked some up, but tossed them down again.

The place had been gutted.

Over the next couple of weeks, Weaver watched as Ruston grew even more irresponsible and erratic than she had initially believed possible. He hit the bars every night, picking up strangers one right after the other. He was edgy and anxious. The only thing that kept him in Austin was the fact that he was broke and that he had to wait for his check from Pizza Hut. Everything he had—except the clothes he was wearing—was packed in his car, ready to go when the paycheck came.

Just before Ruston left he told Weaver that he had VD. She threw her hands up and told him he should get to a clinic immediately. Ruston said that he didn't have time, that he'd take care of it in California once he got there.

"You're crazy," she told him. "That's what you get for going around picking up people you don't know. You don't know what you've got."

Weaver was relieved when Ruston finally left town. Even though this whole Eli Stutzman murder thing was intriguing and in a way had kept the summer interesting, she nonetheless hoped she'd heard the last of Eli Stutzman.

Leona Weaver was working at the back of the Pizza Hut, organizing and preparing the condiments for the salad bar, when the phone rang. The caller said he was Eli Stutzman. His voice, soft and tentative, filled her with so much fear that it surprised her.

"Do you know where I can find Denny?"

Weaver stammered and said that Ruston had left for California and that she didn't have a number for him yet.

"Well, I need to talk to him really bad. I've got to get hold of him," Stutzman said.

Weaver truly didn't know exactly where Ruston was, but damn well knew that if she had known, she wouldn't have given the information to Stutzman. Ruston had been emphatic when he left: "Don't tell Eli where I'm going. Don't tell him anything."

She asked for Stutzman's number—in case Ruston called her. Stutzman refused to leave one and said he'd call later.

Weaver went to her manager and told him, "It's him! What am I gonna do? He's gonna call me back!"

Her boss urged her to call the Travis County sheriff. With a little reluctance, she dialed their main number.

Detective Cutler, dressed in the "plain" clothes of a homicide investigator, yet looking every bit like a cop—Weaver figured it was his attitude that gave him away—came to the Pizza Hut and plunked himself down in a booth. Armed with his nice and easy Texas voice, Cutler was as casual as a sweatshirt. With a few pleasantries to break the ice and soften his potential informant, he hit Weaver with a proposition that stunned her.

"If you could get Stutzman to give you a phone number so that you can call him back, would you be interested in taping him? He might talk. Maybe he'll tell you something."

Say what? Weaver thought. *You want me to tape some probable killer's confession?*

Weaver's initial reaction was to say no, but for some reason—no doubt the would-be mystery writer and the detective in her—she agreed with one stipulation.

"As long as you keep my name out of it, I'll do it. I don't see how I could get hurt. I'll do it for you," she said.

Cutler smiled and told her he would be over to the Reinli Arms with the recorder and the tape in a day or so. Weaver smiled nervously and warned Cutler not to make too much of a show of being a cop when he came over.

"I have neighbors that wouldn't be too crazy about the law coming around, you know."

A day or so later, Stutzman made another call to Weaver at the Pizza Hut. Weaver was determined to get him to leave his telephone number this time.

"Listen, I can't talk to you on this phone," she told him in a half-whisper, hoping he would infer that the line had been bugged by the sheriff's office. "They've been coming around looking for Denny, and maybe we shouldn't talk on *this* phone."

Stutzman said he understood and gave her a number. The area code was 505—New Mexico.

Weaver called Cutler, and the following day he brought the recorder to her apartment to show her how the set worked—though they had to improvise, since Weaver couldn't afford a telephone of her own at the time.

As if Gary Cutler's presence had been broadcast via megaphone, word got around that the police were talking with some lady in the apartments. A few bikers even moved out of the Reinli Arms when they heard that a Travis County sheriff's detective was visiting Leona Weaver.

Cutler, who did not want to have the taped conversations blow up in his face later in court, was careful and did not offer Weaver any tips on how to get Stutzman to talk. He made no suggestions on what she should say. It was up to her. His only advice: "Keep him talking and get him to say something."

CHAPTER TWENTY-FIVE

June 27, 1985

After a first attempt yielded nothing but frazzled nerves, Weaver took Gary Cutler's mini tape recorder over to Evelyn Martel's apartment at Cameron Green. The women waited on the steps of the complex's laundry room for it to clear out. When it did, Weaver went inside and dialed the telephone number Stutzman had left at Pizza Hut.

So nervous she could scarcely breathe, Weaver started the conversation by saying that she had recently talked with Ruston, but that he wouldn't tell her where he was because he was scared.

Stutzman wanted to know why.

"I don't know," Weaver said. "I thought he was more or less off the hook because they confirmed that he was in Iowa the weekend Glen left."

"Tell him it's important that he calls me. And tell him to make sure and not to give out my phone number," he said.

The next few minutes were spent on the status of the Amish furniture. Stutzman wanted to know where it was, and Weaver offered little help. Her uncertainty seemed to annoy Stutzman. She did confirm, however, that she and Ruston had taken the clock, TV, and couch.

"What about the papers, ah, and stuff—the mail, papers, and stuff I had in my furniture?"

"I don't have any idea about that. I didn't see any of that," she said.

Stutzman thought the Travis County Sheriff's Department had taken his personal things. The idea was absurd, but Weaver played along with him to keep him talking.

"Well," said Stutzman, "everybody keeps telling me that they can't legally do that, but my attorney says, knowing Travis County Homicide, they'll do anything . . . they'll have to give it back once it's straightened out."

"What are you going to do, Eli? Are you gonna stay gone, are you gonna come back or what?"

"Well he keeps—my attorney—keeps telling me to hold off and wait. But, see, Cal had told me all of my furniture was gone. I'm getting to be confused."

Stutzman admitted he hadn't been able to reach Hunter for several days.

"I don't know," Weaver said, trying to keep the conversation on track. "It looks pretty bad to me. I mean, you know."

"Right."

"I mean your situation looks pretty bad to me."

"Talking about a mixed-up mess," Stutzman offered, as though none of what had transpired was his doing. He was a helpless victim.

"I'm telling you. I don't under—" Weaver stopped and tried again. "You know, Denny was real freaked out about it and everything, and so we talked a lot about it, and he's really . . . still freaked out."

She wanted Stutzman to think she knew everything, as if Ruston had told her the truth—whatever the truth was.

Stutzman indicated that Denny could have come with him to New Mexico and that "nobody would have known."

". . . That's what I told him earlier," he said. "But then he must have left the . . . but he did tell me the last time I talked to him, he can't stay in the house no more, he can't take it. . . . I said 'Well, I understand that.' But he didn't tell me he was leaving town."

How many times had Ruston talked with Stutzman after Eli left town? Weaver wondered.

"Yeah. Well you know he was real scared over there," she said. "He felt like he was being watched or something. Ah . . . he came over to my house, him and Sam both came to my house about one-thirty in the morning."

Stutzman brightened a bit. "Oh, really?"

"And they stayed over there. Yeah, they slept over there at my house."

"Golly," he said.

Stutzman said he didn't know why Ruston was frightened. ". . . I knew he was scared earlier, but I didn't think it was that bad, and I felt kind of odd. . . . I just kind of felt like I left him in the middle of the mess."

Weaver's hopes rose again. Maybe Stutzman would spill it now and tell her exactly what the mess was.

"And I wanted to talk to him," he continued, "but the main reason . . . was because of my little kid. Some of the stuff they asked him downtown was really obnoxious."

"What do you mean? You mean about being homosexual and stuff like that?" Weaver asked, straining to hear every word and hoping that the tape was recording every nuance.

"This was one scared dude on the phone," she later recalled.

"Yeah, that, and also about the whole murder case, the whole bit. And my attorney says, you know, they had no right questioning a kid that age."

If what Stutzman was saying was true, Weaver felt that he was damned right about it.

"And see," Stutzman said, "they tried to do that around my and Sam's backs. Sam was with me downtown too. They questioned him in the lobby—well I heard part of it, and Sam did too. So when this is all over they're gonna pay for it. And, ah, those guys from homicide are really crooked is the only thing I can tell, and they're gonna pay for it."

Stutzman's soft voice made Weaver's skin crawl.

"Well," she said, trying to get something definite out of him, "they obviously must have a case against you or they wouldn't be after you, huh? . . ."

In shrugging off her question, Stutzman dropped a bombshell. "They think they do. See, ah, it's pretty obvious that Glen, this guy, was murdered with my gun."

Now we're going somewhere, Weaver thought. *Come on, confess!*

"That doesn't say that I did it. Now, ah . . ."

"Maybe they're trying to get you for accessory or something," Weaver said. "Like maybe you knew about it or you tried to cover it up or something."

Stutzman hesitated, and Weaver tried to twist the blade deeper. She hoped he'd be frightened enough to say more.

"They can do that you know," she said.

"Well, that might be it, maybe that's what they are after, I don't know. But I and Sam both made that very clear, that we didn't even know he was missing."

Didn't know he was missing? Even Leona Weaver knew Stutzman's story about Glen Pritchett going up to Montana to take care of his injured son, and how he'd called down and talked with Stutzman on the phone.

"The first thing they jumped on us for, 'Was he reported missing?' " Stutzman recalled. "I said, 'I had no idea the guy was missing.' "

Weaver fumbled for the right words to get him to think she knew more than she really did. "Well, you know, Denny said they had some work orders, and they claimed they have some forged, that it's a forged signature on them. That's what Denny told me."

"Who had work orders?"

"The cops do."

"Then it must be time sheets."

"Yeah, time sheets."

"Uh . . . Forged time sheets?" Stutzman said, his voice full of surprise—not over the fact that the police had the doctored time sheets, but that they had any time sheets at all.

"Yeah. One with Glen's last signature. . . . You know, for that . . . ah . . . what's the date? I can't remember the date . . . April."

"They said it was forged?"

"No, this one wasn't," Weaver said. "April twenty-seventh. April twenty-seventh was the date on the one, I believe, and then on the next one, the next pay, the next time sheet was, oh, May fourth, but the signatures where he signed them was different."

"Huh," Stutzman said. "I didn't know about that."

"That's what Denny was telling me. That's what they told him."

"Huh, well that's a good one. So . . . so they do have the time sheets?"

"Yeah."

"I had told him to go ahead and give them to them if they want them because I said, you know, that's proof that he had worked."

The comment interested Weaver, because it indicated that Stutzman and Ruston had talked about the time sheets. Stutzman had told Ruston "to go ahead and give them to them." Denny Ruston had never told Wiggins or Cutler that he had seen or talked with Stutzman since being questioned by the sheriff's office.

"Well, what are you gonna do, Eli? You can't keep running forever."

"What am I gonna do?"

"I mean, obviously, you know, you're gonna have to do something about this."

"Well, my attorney has been telling me to blow it off. . . . See, he thinks it was Jay, another guy that had worked for me for a short period of time and I fired him. And I think so myself, because I don't know who else it would have been. Because he was the only person I know of that knew where my guns were at. That's the only other person, because Denny didn't know where they were at. Sam didn't know where they were at, and they confirmed that Denny had been with his parents that weekend when Glen left.

"But . . . then, also, my attorney keeps telling me there are two different fingerprints other than mine on the gun. Whose are the other fingerprints? I have no idea."

That was a new one.

"Well, see," he continued, "I didn't know that till a couple of days ago. The information keeps coming through real slow."

"Yeah," said Weaver. "They haven't talked to me yet or nothing. I don't think they even know anything about me except that Denny was staying at my house."

Again, Stutzman was surprised. "They do know that?"

"Yeah."

"Uh-huh, well if they come after you, make sure they don't get this phone number."

Weaver promised to keep it a secret.

Stutzman told her that Cal Hunter had taken some things out of the house on his behalf—before the furniture was taken. Stutzman asked that, if he came over to Weaver's place to pick up the television and the clock, would she let him have them. She agreed.

This would keep all the rest of his stuff away from the law, Stutzman implied.

"Whatever they don't already have. Uh, I'm not real sure what this is going to boil down to. If they keep going on . . . see, when I left I thought it was only going to be for two or three days," he said.

Stutzman said he had talked with his attorney twice in the last twenty-four hours.

"I may have to go back to Austin and face trial just to prove that I'm innocent."

"Yeah. You may have to. The longer you run the harder it's gonna be on you."

"Right. But . . ."

"It just . . . it really looks bad that you ran, you know."

"Right," he said softly.

"Not necessarily that you *did* it maybe, but you *knew* something about it," Weaver said, pushing again. All she wanted was one little confession, one little bit of information that would complete the puzzle.

"What I've done, I painted a real bad picture for them. But see, I didn't know all this stuff, and when I left it was supposed to be a matter of a couple of days. Well, it's gone totally out of proportion since then. But . . . what has happened is, I think, well, my attorney says, is that Travis County homicide had found out about Jay also, they weren't supposed to find out about him."

"Oh."

"They're not careful enough, and Jay knows that he is wanted. Therefore he's much harder to find. But if this keeps . . . going on, what I'm gonna do is, ah, put Danny, my son, give somebody else custody of him—temporary custody. So they can't get a hold of him and involve him anymore, just as they already have. And, ah, go back and do whatever it takes—just prove that I'm innocent. Because my attorney has said, you know, that he's got enough evidence to prove that I'm innocent. That's what he thinks, and he told me this morning to hold off a little bit longer to see if he can come up with Jay. And, ah, if they can, he's gonna, you know, have me come back and go to trial or whatever it takes just to prove that I'm innocent."

"Well," said Weaver, "I think that you should. I think you should come back and face it and get it over with. Because if you didn't do it, then you don't have nothing to be afraid of."

Stutzman indicated that the real reason he had fled Austin was because the police had harassed Danny.

"And I . . . I mean, it freaked me out with this thing, I mean, Christ, what's going on, I mean, this can't be. I said, harassing me is no problem, but my little kid is a different story. And my attorney says they had no . . . they should have never questioned him in the first place."

Weaver agreed. "I don't think they should have done that either."

Near the end of the call, Stutzman hit on the subject of his mail.

"And one of the biggest things is, you know, so much mail that had come in that I just told Denny and Glen to never leave it in the house. And if the desk was gone they probably took the mail too."

What could have been in the mail that was so important? Weaver wondered. What could have been worth more than the other things Stutzman had left behind?

He told Weaver that if Ruston called, to give him Stutzman's number and have Ruston call collect.

"I don't know what to tell you about calling me back," Stutzman said. "If I do call you, what I'll do is I'll just leave a brief message where . . . ah, I tell you what, I'll give you a code name."

A code name? It seemed weird, Weaver reflected, but under the circumstances what else could she expect?

"If you're not there, or you're busy," Stutzman said, "I'll tell them that you're supposed to call 'Junior.' I won't mention my name."

If Stutzman had known that his story was causing him more trouble than any physical evidence, he surely would have shut up. But there he was, running from Travis County, yet telling everyone that the gun used to kill Pritchett belonged to him.

Ballistics, however, had come back inconclusive. While it was confirmed that the bullet that killed Pritchett had been fired from a gun just like Stutzman's, the slug was so misshapen from impact that it was unclear whether his gun had in fact been the murder weapon.

In court, ballistics would amount to nothing.

Only the killer—or someone with direct knowledge of the crime—would know that it was the right gun.

Stupidly, Stutzman was concerned about his fingerprints being found on it. Since he had handed the gun to Wiggins, of course, his prints were naturally on the weapon.

None of this was lost on Cutler or Wiggins, but they needed more. No one was talking, and there wasn't enough to go on. This "Jay" to whom Stutzman kept referring didn't exist, as far as they knew. Throughout the investigation, the sheriff's office never questioned anyone with that name.

Cal Hunter had told investigators that he knew nothing.

By mid-July, the investigation had foundered, and Stutzman had vanished.

CHAPTER TWENTY-SIX

Stutzman and his son returned to the Four Corners area in late June. In Aztec, New Mexico, at the home of Stutzman's old buddy, Chuck Freeman, Stutzman confided to Freeman and Kenny Hankins that his roommate had been killed in Texas.

"My gun was involved," he said.

Freeman and Hankins hit the roof, but Stutzman assured them he hadn't killed anybody.

"My lawyer told me to get my ass out of Texas until this blows over," he said.

"That don't make sense, Eli," Hankins said. "You should go back. What kind of lawyer would tell you to get out of the state?"

"If I do go back they'll arrest me, and, when they do, they will pick up Danny and send him back to Ohio."

"To your folks?"

"Yeah. I'd much rather see Danny dead than have him live with the Amish."

Stutzman made a number of calls to his lawyer. Each time he got off the phone he announced some atrocity committed by the Travis County Sheriff's Office: they had taken his furniture, his money, his business.

Hankins asked who the attorney was, who was giving Stutzman all this bad advice—was he one of their lawyer friends from Durango?

"No, he's from Texas," Eli said, refusing to elaborate.

• • •

Danny Stutzman was showing signs of trauma. His stuttering had worsened dramatically.

"Danny could hardly spit a word out," Kenny Hankins recalled. "The kid was a mess. He couldn't do anything. He was like a baby. When he wanted to get a toy that was on the other side of the walkway, he just stood there and cried for his daddy to get it for him."

Stutzman said he was going to take Danny to stay with his friends Dean and Margie Barlow, in Wyoming. "They'll take care of Danny until I get situated and buy a house," he said.

The next day Stutzman and his son boarded a bus bound for Wyoming.

Leona Weaver and Evelyn Martel listened to the tape twice before Gary Cutler returned to pick it up. Each time the women listened, they heard the same thing: Eli Stutzman was a nervous, evasive man.

In all fairness, Weaver would concede that she came off little better than Stutzman. She cringed each time she stammered.

Weaver played the tape for Cutler, who sat stone-faced in her living room. When the tape was over, all he said about its content was, "You did good. Real good."

"He thinks it was the law who took his furniture and stuff. Did you take it?" Weaver asked.

Cutler shook his head. "What would we want with all of his stuff?"

Weaver also asked whether investigators had questioned Danny.

"We wouldn't do something like that," Cutler said.

Weaver didn't tell the detective about the drugs she knew Stutzman had sold—she figured they knew too much about her and her habits already.

"Shoot," she later said, "Cutler probably knew who I bought my little bit of pot from."

Her sister, however, told Weaver that she should have said something.

"They probably already know," Weaver replied. "If they're gonna find out about it, it ain't gonna be from me."

When Cutler left he wasn't sure what he really had. Stutzman had made one statement, though, that did seem to have some importance: that it was "pretty obvious" that Pritchett had been "murdered with my gun."

Who was the attorney Stutzman kept mentioning in his conversation with Weaver?

A couple days later, "Junior" called the Pizza Hut. He told Weaver that he was going to send Hunter over to pick up his TV and mantel clock. This terrified Weaver, who felt that things were getting out of control and that she was sinking deeper into this murder case than she wanted. *Send someone to my house!* Even having some killer's friend know where she lived was out of the question. She told all the workers at the Pizza Hut not to give out her address to anyone for any reason.

Every time Stutzman called, she had to sit down and drink a coke. She would shake all over. *What am I gonna do? He's gonna send someone to get that damn TV? How do I get out of this?*

The only answer was to lie.

"Listen, Eli," she finally said, "somebody came to my house. I was scared and I gave the TV to him."

"Who was it?" Stutzman asked.

"I don't know. The cops have been coming around too. I don't think you should call me again."

"You didn't give anybody this number?"

"No."

"Don't," he pleaded.

She hung up and never heard from Eli Stutzman again. When Weaver saw Cutler she told him that she hadn't heard from Stutzman since the call she had taped.

She figured it was safer reading and writing about murder than being involved in a case.

Sam Miller had hightailed it home to Ohio and enlisted in the navy. He kept his mouth shut about what Stutzman had told him in the truck on the way back to Banton Road.

He figured he'd live longer.

Stutzman made a call to Cal Hunter at his mother's house in San Antonio, wanting more help from his business partner.

"He wanted me to get some things out of his safe deposit box. I told him to forget it. I felt sorry for him, but I didn't want to get mixed up with the law. The police had told me they wanted Stutzman. Getting involved in murder was the last thing on my mind," Hunter said.

On July 5, 1985, Stutzman signed guardianship papers for Dean and Margie Barlow to administer medicine in case Danny became sick while he was away. He also signed two checks over to the Barlows to use for the boy's support. He told them that an employee of his had been murdered in Texas and that he knew who had done it and was going to track the killer himself.

After leaving Danny with the Barlows, Stutzman resurfaced at the Greyhound bus station in Fort Wayne, Indiana. Ted Truitt, the young dairy farmer who had lost his virginity to Stutzman in January 1983, was there to meet him. Stutzman was traveling light, carrying only the gym bags Denny Ruston had given him the night he fled from Austin.

Truitt had been looking forward to seeing his friend since the phone call in April.

"I'm going to be taking a little vacation," Stutzman had told him then, though he was vague about when it would be. Almost immediately Truitt knew this was going to be no ordinary visit.

Stutzman told Truitt he was involved in a murder investigation in Austin.

"One of my crew was murdered. The police questioned me about the murder. I told them I knew who did it—a guy who worked for me, but I fired him."

"Did the police get the guy?" Truitt asked.

"No. They didn't even try. I have to go get him myself. He's in Ohio," Stutzman said.

Truitt thought Stutzman was lying. It was obvious that he had left Austin with only what he could carry in his two arms. Even his gun rack and rocker and other furniture—things he had said he'd made himself—had been left behind. Stutzman had seemed so proud of his things that he would never abandon them.

Eli Stutzman had come to the little town outside of Fort Wayne to hide out, and Truitt didn't like it.

A lot of what Stutzman said seemed out of synch. He told Truitt that he had been driving up from Texas with a friend and that, when the police had pulled their car over to the side of the road, for some reason the friend had run away.

The story was disjointed and convoluted. Truitt didn't ask any follow-up questions. He didn't know where to begin.

Stutzman indicated that gay sex might have been involved in the crew member's murder, though he did not say if the man and he were lovers. He also said that he had been questioned by the police and singled out as a suspect, when, in fact, he'd had nothing to do with the murder. "But I know who the killer is," he repeated.

Stutzman later said that the victim had been working for him and that he was keeping his money in a savings account so that his ex-wife couldn't get her hands on it. He added that one night a friend had gone into Stutzman's house and been met by cops with drawn guns. The friend had been very scared when he called Eli.

It was as if Eli Stutzman were the writer, producer, and

director of a bad television show, with Truitt the captive audience.

Stutzman said his attorney had advised him to lay low for a while until the smoke cleared back in Texas. Truitt figured Eli should have turned himself in to the police, especially if he was innocent. *I have a killer in the house*, he thought.

"Eli had changed. Something about his eyes wasn't the same—there was a coldness, a distance. His eyes were mad looking," Truitt later said.

Stutzman also looked sick. Red blotches mottled his body. He complained that the rash was itchy, even painful. At first, Truitt thought it was scabies, but Stutzman said it couldn't be. Truitt took him to his doctor.

Later, when Truitt snooped around Stutzman's things, he discovered that the medication Stutzman had been prescribed was indeed for scabies.

Several times through the summer, Truitt went down to the farm to call a friend of his in Newcomerstown, Ohio. Truitt was convinced that Stutzman was a killer, and the friend concurred. The word among the Amish was that Sam Miller had stumbled on a murder in Texas.

Truitt told his friend that Eli Stutzman had said the killer was now in Ohio, and that he was headed there to find him. The prospect was not a good one.

"Whatever you do," the man told Truitt, "keep him away from here. I don't want to run into him in Newcomerstown."

Truitt said he would do his best. The problem was, he wanted Stutzman to leave Indiana—even the fugitive's phone calls were getting to him.

Once, when he answered the phone, the caller, a woman, asked for "Junior."

"There's no Junior here—" Truitt began, but Stutzman cut in.

"Oh, that call's for me. *I'm* Junior," he said, taking the phone.

That was news to Truitt, who had never known anyone

to call Stutzman by that nickname. Stutzman offered no explanation, and Truitt didn't want to know about it anyway. He felt as if he already knew too much.

"I felt that at any moment the police were going to bust in and cause a scene. It was the last thing I needed," he later said.

Another caller, this time a man, asked for "Junior." Stutzman was weeding the garden when Truitt answered the call.

"Look," Truitt told the man, "this guy's name is not Junior. He's wanted for murder, and if you are looking for a time and place to meet him I suggest you give it up."

The caller was surprised, but didn't believe Truitt.

"I still want to talk to him."

Truitt couldn't believe it. *What is with these people anyway?*

Truitt noticed that Stutzman always knew when the mail carrier was coming and that many times there were things for him; more often, he had mail that needed to be sent out.

He must be looking to meet more tricks, Truitt thought.

One time Stutzman had Truitt drive him over to the Western Union office in Auburn, Indiana, to pick up some money he'd had wired to him.

"It's money from the ranch in Colorado," Stutzman said.

The news about the murder in Texas reached the Gingeriches in the Beaverton, Michigan, settlement. They wrote to Stutzman the first week in July, but their letter was returned. The Gingeriches were beside themselves with concern for Danny, so on August 21, 1985, Amos wrote to the Austin Police Department.

> . . . we would very much like to come in contact with our grandson Danny which is Eli's son. We hear rumors that Eli is in trouble with the law . . .

A week later, Sergeant Al Herson of the Austin Police Department's missing persons section sent back the following reply:

> It is true your son-in-law is in some trouble with the law. Your grandson is with his father and I am not able to divulge his whereabouts at this time. He is no longer in the state of Texas. My information indicates Danny is okay and he is with his father . . .

Herson was technically correct that he couldn't divulge Stutzman's whereabouts due to privacy laws. In fact, however, no one in either Austin or Travis County law enforcement knew where Eli Stutzman was—they had lost track of him in July.

Meanwhile, Stutzman had taken a break from Truitt's farm, a great relief to the Indiana man, and gone into Ohio, where he signed up for a new driver's license and fabricated a new middle initial and birth date.

Stutzman returned to Aztec, with his scabies cleared up, a new social security card, a new name. *A new man.* Yet he still had the same old problem—Danny. He planned to leave the boy in Wyoming until he had gotten back on his feet again and put Pritchett's murder behind him once and for all.

Eli moved into the trailer house on Chuck Freeman's six-hundred-acre ranch near Dutchman's Hill, in Aztec, New Mexico. He worked on the so-called Breakaday Ranch—"Either we start at the break of day or we break something everyday"—for five dollars an hour, painting, pouring cement, and putting up rails.

Whenever he called Danny, it was from the back bedroom. On September 7, two days before Danny turned nine, he spoke with someone at the Barlows' number for thirty-one minutes.

The next day, Stutzman dispatched a letter to the Gingeriches. He and Danny, he said, had returned from a two-month vacation—having moved back to New Mexico on June 15. He claimed that Danny had spent July and August in a children's summer camp—"He chose to go to this camp instead of traveling."

The truth was that Danny had been abandoned by his father.

> Danny said he enjoys school here more than in Texas. School started Sept. 3. He is getting tall, hard to keep in clothes. He had his 9th birthday yesterday.

In desperation Amos Gingerich wrote to the Austin police again. *Would they help find Danny now?*

CHAPTER TWENTY-SEVEN

Just before Halloween, Dean Barlow and another man—a live-in friend, as he later described the man to police—dropped Danny off at Breakaday Ranch on the way to the American Poultry Show in Albuquerque. Barlow had packed the boy's belongings in a box, believing the stay was going to be permanent.

Stutzman, naturally, had other plans.

Danny played on the farm, and Stutzman had him take pictures of him for his ads, including a shot of his Levi's-clad backside. It wasn't likely that taking such a photo mattered much to the boy. Neither was it likely that the boy didn't know why his father wanted a "butt shot." By 9 years of age, Danny had seen it all. Those who saw him a month before his death felt that the boy was showing signs of emotional wear and tear. Danny, according to the ranch foreman, Byron Larson, was "in his own little world."

Freeman saw different behavior.

"That kid couldn't sit still. He was always trashing things, cutting up the garbage cans and breaking eggs in the henhouse."

When Barlow returned from the chicken show, Stutzman told him to take Danny back to Wyoming.

"My roommate is an alcoholic—this isn't a good place for the boy to be," Stutzman said.

Later, Barlow told police, "Danny cried all the way to Mesa Verde. He really missed his dad."

Stutzman's excuse was lame, if indeed that had been the excuse he gave to the Wyoming man. It was true that his roommate drank some, but he hardly posed a threat to the child's safety. Further, Danny had been in and out of situations far more unsettling ever since his father had left the Amish.

Perhaps Stutzman didn't want the boy around because he got in the way of his fun—though even that hadn't been a problem in the past. Regardless of the truth, however, Stutzman still projected the image of the model father.

On November 4, he mailed a letter to the Gingeriches. An obvious forgery, the letter was a deliberate attempt to mislead the Amish about Danny's whereabouts. Stutzman double-spaced on notebook paper and made a couple of errors with letter spacing to make the writing look childlike. He even misspelled *week* as *weed*.

> Dear Susie
>
> How are you? Dad and I are fine. The weather here is not very cold. I like school. I play soccer in school. My team won second place. I got my report card this weed. I got good grades. I am in third grade.
>
> Love, Danny

The Gingeriches wondered if "Danny's" letter had been in answer to their contact with the Austin police. But if Stutzman had sent the letter to stop them from looking for their grandson, he had miscalculated.

The Eli Stutzman they knew had forged notes before—at Stoll Farms in Marshallville and at Keim's farm in Apple Creek. They didn't know that Stutzman had been lying when he claimed that Danny was with him in Georgia when he had actually left the little boy with cousin Abe Stutzman.

With the Texas murder on his mind, Stutzman became increasingly irritable—he was no longer the easygoing man he had been before the trouble in Austin. He still went to parties, however, wearing his Amish clothes if a costume was needed. Friends knew that no matter what preoccupied him, Stutzman would always have time for sex and dope.

Late one cold, fall night Kenny Hankins and Eli Stutzman were among a group partying at the Diamond Belle Saloon, at the Strater Hotel in Durango. Stutzman bristled when David Tyler approached their table.

"Get the fuck out of here," Stutzman told Tyler, who immediately left for the hotel bathroom.

Before Stutzman followed, he told Hankins, "If Tyler would pay me what he owes me, I'd never have to work again."

Hankins didn't know what Stutzman was talking about, though he did think it might have something to do with drugs.

"That was the last time I saw David," Hankins said.

On November 7, Chuck Freeman and ranch foreman Byron Larson had had enough of Eli Stutzman.

"Byron called me and told me to get rid of the son of a bitch," Freeman recalled later.

If seeing Stutzman canning pears in the nude hadn't been enough to cause a rift in the trailer house on Breakaday Ranch, there was the run-in Larson and Stutzman had after Dean Barlow dropped Danny off.

Larson, going to the freezer next to Stutzman's bedroom window, saw Stutzman, again nude, doing something he didn't like. "I don't know what he was doing. I think he had been exercising, laying on the floor naked. He pulled the curtains right quick."

What Larson saw was something he later refused to repeat—except to his boss.

Chuck Freeman filled in the blanks: "Eli was jacking off and Danny was in bed with him when Byron came by the deep freeze.

"That's about the time he called me and said for me to get Stutzman the hell out of there!"

Freeman asked Stutzman why he'd pulled the curtains on Larson.

"Well," Stutzman sniffed, "he was looking in the window."

Larson shot back: "I was getting something out of the deep freeze and you were by the window stark-ass naked. You didn't really impress me—I'm built the same way, you know."

"Eli, we can't have this. We live in a Baptist community—even though we aren't Baptists!" Freeman told his friend when he gave him the boot.

Stutzman packed up his toolbox and moved into a trailer on *Kevin Whitten*'s property, sharing the place with one of Whitten's friends, *Ray Peters*.

"Eli and I shared a lot," Peters said in a 1988 interview. "We had late-night talks about religion, his family, his relationship with his father.

"Eli thought the Amish religion was a dumb religion, a joke, because they kept changing all the rules."

Peters also said Stutzman laughed at the tradition of bundling. "Everyone was having sex," he said.

Kenny Hankins stopped by Whitten's place to pick up Stutzman before going into Durango to party. Stutzman smoked a joint and told Hankins that he and Whitten were having some problems over his roommate at the trailer, Ray Peters.

"Ray and I were down by the river barbecuing and messing around."

Stutzman implied that the messing around was sex—whether it was true or not didn't matter. He knew it would impress Hankins.

"Kevin came and caught us. He got real mad, real jealous."

• • •

If AIDS hadn't put a damper on the gay scene in Durango, what happened in November did.

A tourist saw the body from a passenger's window on the Narrow Gauge Railroad the morning of November 11. The woman told her husband, but he dismissed it as a bum sleeping it off in an old military trailer behind the Automatic Transmission Exchange. When the train returned, the woman saw that the bum in jeans and suede jacket still hadn't stirred. She and her husband notified the police.

The tourist had discovered the battered, blood-soaked body of 36-year-old David Tyler. Tyler had been bludgeoned to death.

"His head had been smashed like a hard-boiled egg," said a Durango police investigator who attended the autopsy.

The murder, a crime nearly unheard of in the bustling tourist town, was a mystery. No suspects emerged, in part because of the closeted nature of many who knew Tyler. Sketchy details finally came to light. On November 8, a bunch of gay men had partied at the Holiday Inn, in room 167 overlooking the Animas River.

Tyler's 1971 Suburban was found parked at the motel.

November 29, 1985

To Stutzman, the car must have seemed like a junker, and the price of nine hundred dollars a bit steep. He had complained to Freeman and others that the attorney in Texas had taken most of his money and that he was only making five dollars an hour at Whitten's place.

But on November 29, Stutzman put three hundred dollars down on a 1975 AMC Gremlin at Neil's Auto Plaza in Farmington. A week later he paid another three hundred dollars and took the car from the Auto Plaza's lot.

Dennis Slaeter, whom friends considered a "gentle giant," was only 24 when he was murdered in a storage room at Junction Creek Liquors in Durango. The Fort Lewis College student from Missouri had been shot in the back of the head. Cash from the store was missing.

There was no evidence of a struggle, though two possibilities easily explain that. Slaeter could have been forced into the basement storage room at gunpoint. Or he could have known the killer.

For jolted Four Corners' gays, it increased their paranoia. Slaeter had known David Tyler, had used drugs Tyler provided, and had been to his house. Some thought the college student might have been gay also.

Someone out there is killing gay men, Louise Hanson thought.

It had been more than three years since a murder was last committed in Durango. Now, in the space of less than a month, two men were dead—two men who had known each other.

Around that time Kevin Whitten noticed that a Uberti rifle and a Colt Sauer were missing from his ranch, though how he could possibly notice *anything* missing would be beyond anyone who knew the man. Like the NRA's worst nightmare, Whitten kept his guns scattered throughout his place. Easy access was one thing, but a gun in every other room was, even he admitted, careless.

He confronted Stutzman, who said he hadn't taken the guns. He said he thought Ray Peters had them.

Whitten asked Peters about the guns, but Peters denied having them. Whitten figured it had to be Peters who was lying. The Eli Stutzman he knew was a study in honesty and good Amish values. What he didn't know was that Stutzman had become skilled at implicating others: he had said that Abe Stutzman was involved with drugs and that that was why he left Greenville, Ohio; that Ed Stoll had stolen parts from a store and that that was why he left Stoll Farms; that "Jay" had killed Pritchett . . . it was always someone else.

• • •

Before leaving the Four Corners for Lyman, Stutzman made arrangements with Kenny Hankins to take care of some boxes he needed stored.

"There isn't much room in the back of the Gremlin," he said, indicating that he wanted to save room for Danny's things.

Hankins also agreed to take care of Stutzman's mail, holding it until he got to where he was going.

On December 10, Stutzman pawned Whitten's missing Uberti and Colt at King's Pawn in Durango. It netted him $210.

He needed all the money he could get.

Stutzman stopped in at the Farmington K-Mart and purchased a blue sleeper and mailed a letter and a Christmas card to *Al Jorgensen*, a Missouri farmer who had "met" Stutzman through an *Advocate* personal ad and had been corresponding with him for a couple of months. Though Stutzman dated the letter December 11, he did not mail it until two days later—the day he left the Four Corners to pick up Danny from the Barlows. In the letter, he said that Danny might not be with him when he came east—that the boy would rather spend Christmas with the friends he was staying with; that he didn't, after all, relate well with Stutzman's family. . . .

Jorgensen received the letter on December 16. By then, of course, Danny Stutzman wasn't going anywhere. Ever.

CHAPTER TWENTY-EIGHT

December 15, 1985

Just to the right of the center-fold in an atlas where the rectangular state of Kansas is usually cut into two squares is Salina, Kansas. Salina is at the crossroads of U.S. 81, which turns into U.S. 135 en route south to Wichita, and the state's main east-west route, U.S. 70. From Salina, it's less than one hundred miles north on 81 to Chester, Nebraska.

Salina is the hub of Saline County, so named for the Saline River, which joins the Smoky Hill River at the point where the town was founded in the 1850s. Local folklorists tell visitors that Salina is an Indian word meaning "Where two rivers meet."

In all directions outside of Salina lie the small towns that look with neither envy nor scorn at *the* city—at least, that's how their inhabitants view Salina, with its population of 45,000. It is a place, a necessity, for shopping, and it is a place to go for services that cannot be supported in towns less than a tenth its size. The bigger cities—Topeka and Wichita—are far enough away that they are reserved for special trips.

The small towns that pockmark the smooth fields of wheat blanketing Saline County are blessed with names that nicely fit their founders' heritage or their plentiful natural resources. Holland and Bavaria, and Gypsum and Wells, are a few.

It had been snowing heavily off and on during the days before December 15—the day Stutzman found his way to the little town *John Yost* called home. A 30-year-old school-teacher, Yost had also met Eli Stutzman through an *Advocate* personal ad.

Yost had not yet found holiday cheer, though he planned to decorate his place and put up a tree when Eli and Danny Stutzman came to stay, though he didn't know exactly when the Stutzmans would arrive. The weather, of course, was always a factor for car travel. Further, Stutzman had been vague about his plans when he last spoke to Yost. He had said he would be driving up from the Four Corners to Wyoming to pick up Danny at the foster parents' home.

"My mother's sick. She might be dying," he had said, before leaving for Wyoming. "It might be the last time Danny and I get to see her. She's been asking for him."

It was just after daylight, about 7:00 A.M. Sunday, when Yost answered the front door to find Stutzman standing before him, backlit by the early morning light. Stutzman seemed smaller than Yost had imagined, but that was fine. He told himself not to make a snap judgment based on physical appearance. Stutzman was also shy, almost a little sheepish, as he stood in the doorway. He even hung his head slightly.

Of course, his son had been dumped in a ditch in Thayer County, Nebraska, only hours before.

Yost was surprised the little boy was not with his father. Stutzman had talked often about how much he had missed his son during the months they had been separated.

Stutzman explained that he had called ahead before leaving for Wyoming and that Danny had seemed so happy, looking forward to Christmas with the Barlows, that he had let him stay with them.

"Danny was so excited. There were presents under the tree for him. He didn't want to leave."

Yost didn't think to ask about Stutzman's mother and how she was doing, even though she was supposedly the reason Danny and his father were going to Ohio in the first place. In fact, the Kansas man's judgment was a little clouded by stress. All Yost could focus on was how nervous he was about meeting this Amishman. He had built his expectations higher than the tallest poplar in Saline County.

Yet Stutzman didn't look too good, at least not as he did in the photographs he had sent with his letters. In those shots, Stutzman's face seemed fuller, almost youthful. Yost rationalized that Stutzman's haggard appearance was the result of too many hours behind the wheel. Considering Stutzman's arrival time, Yost calculated that he must have been driving all night. Understandably, he looked exhausted.

Yost had no way of including in his calculations what had happened a few hours prior to Stutzman's arrival. He didn't know that only hours before Danny Stutzman had been abandoned in a remote ditch just across the state line.

The day was spent visiting Yost's parents and sister—on the off-chance that the two gay men became a serious couple—and eating a hearty meal at a local truckstop. Yost even drove the Gremlin that Stutzman boasted having paid only nine hundred dollars for.

"Don't you think I got a great deal on it?" he asked.

After the men had sex, two things would always stand out in Yost's mind—the foremost one being the size of Stutzman's genitals. Yost had never seen anything like them before—Stutzman's penis and testicles seemed abnormally large. Yost asked him about it, and Stutzman confided that he was not the only one in the family who had been so endowed. Three of his brothers were that way also.

The other thing Yost noticed was the way Eli Stutzman's

body felt. His muscles were incredibly tense; they felt like steel.

"I thought his body would clank when I touched him—he was so stiff, so hard. I chalked it up to being a ranch hand or construction worker. Or maybe he was as nervous as I was," Yost later said.

Yost didn't worry about AIDS. After all, he had been negative on his AIDS test, and Stutzman had reported the same on a test he claimed he'd had performed in Durango. And if Stutzman hadn't wanted to use a condom, Yost could understand. He didn't want to use one either.

Stutzman seemed distracted and a little put off as Yost took him from place to place showing him the town, the countryside, and his family. He later described Stutzman as "not exactly a barrel of laughs, but I assumed that it was because he was Amish. He was so reserved."

The situation brightened, however, and Yost was genuinely touched when Stutzman bought some ornaments and the two of them decorated the Christmas tree.

After a time, Stutzman opened up and told Yost about his life as an Amishman, his first homosexual encounters, and his wife Ida. He neither mocked nor ridiculed his Amish background; he just knew that the quaint ways of Swartzentrubers were not for him.

"The Amish believe marriage partners are brought together by angels," he said. "You might notice a girl seems a little more special than the others, and that's because angels are guiding you."

While there was an apparent sweetness about Eli Stutzman—Christmas ornaments, the talk of angels, and a love for a son who was spending the holidays away from him—a darker, disturbing side also became evident.

Stutzman confided in Yost about the murder in Austin. He said little about the victim himself, beyond the fact that he was his roommate and employee. His attorney was taking care of the situation, and if he had been a possible suspect in the case that was now in the past. Further, Yost did not get the impression that Pritchett was Stutzman's lover—just an employee who happened to room with him.

Stutzman said Pritchett's murder was unquestionably "drug-related." It wasn't clear from that whether Pritchett had been buying or selling, or exactly what kinds of drugs were involved, and Yost didn't ask.

Stutzman's life had been riddled with untimely deaths. Yost was not so stupid as to dismiss the coincidences. He was simply infatuated enough to let them slide past his better judgment.

If Yost was falling for Stutzman, Eli Stutzman was simply arranging the next date, the next man.

Al Jorgensen heard from Stutzman on December 19, when Stutzman called collect from John Yost's place. Stutzman confirmed the story from his letter the week before: Danny wanted to remain with the Barlows. Stutzman planned on arriving the following day, Friday, around noon.

When it came time for Stutzman to leave, Yost was feeling closer than had seemed possible only five days before. They had gone from pen pals to lovers. In spite of his connection to so many deaths, Stutzman seemed gentle and caring. Yost did not want to lose him.

"I want you to leave something here so you'll have to stop by on your way back west," Yost said, as Stutzman prepared to pack for his trip to Ohio.

Stutzman grinned and handed over Danny's Christmas present, a soccer ball.

"Until I get back," he said.

Yost knew how much Stutzman's son meant to him, and there could be no doubting now that Stutzman must have felt something for John Yost. Why else would he leave the soccer ball? Yost just knew Eli Stutzman would return after Christmas.

The Gremlin pulled out of sight, down the snowy street, toward the main highway. Stutzman slipped out of town as quietly as he came.

CHAPTER TWENTY-NINE

December 20, 1985

It was about 4:30 P.M. when Stutzman's Gremlin turned off the County Road and drove up the lane to Al Jorgensen's farm. The Missouri man figured icy road conditions must have slowed Stutzman down on U.S. 70 to Kansas City, the route he had said he would be taking.

The bare-chested photograph Stutzman had sent hadn't prepared Jorgensen for how good-looking the man was in person. His eyes were a deeper blue than chips of glacial ice, and his form rippled with more bulk than Jorgensen thought the man's small frame could support. Stutzman was taller than his host by an inch or so, and Jorgensen hoped Eli would not be disappointed with him physically. It was true Jorgensen was older, but he was in fairly good shape.

"From hard work," he liked to say.

Jorgensen was nervous. Eli Stutzman was the first gay man he had ever had in his home. He asked how Danny was—he expected when they began corresponding that he would meet the boy whenever his father came through Kansas City. Stutzman had written and told him on the telephone how close they were.

"They were inseparable since his wife died," Jorgensen later recalled.

Stutzman repeated the line he had practiced for a week: "Danny wanted to stay in Wyoming with his friends."

The friends, Stutzman said, were an unconventional family of two men and a woman. One of the men, a schoolteacher, was married to the woman, also a teacher. Stutzman said the husband had been his lover.

Jorgensen's fantasy was that sex with Stutzman was going to be wonderful, a joyous experience. *Ecstasy at last.* He could hardly wait. But he was also afraid, aware of the taboos, aware that he had been raised to believe that what he wanted to do with Stutzman was considered immoral.

Yet, in the end, none of that mattered much. Sex with Eli Stutzman was joyless. The naked men jacked off and went to sleep. It was over in a sudden, quiet flash.

Jorgensen later likened the experience to that of a prostitute and a john. Not that Eli Stutzman was paid for his services, but there was an emptiness about the act. It might have been Stutzman's style, but it wasn't what Jorgensen was after.

"It was obvious he didn't care about it," Jorgensen later recalled. "It was like he just did it to pay the motel bill."

He thought that Stutzman might be preoccupied with his mother's illness and his son spending the holidays without him. It wasn't as though he didn't have a lot on his mind. Christmas was less than a week away, and Eli Stutzman must face the holiday alone, without his loved ones.

Jorgensen felt sorry for him.

Stutzman's Gremlin had been packed to near capacity. Bags of clothes, tools, and even work boots filled the backseat and the majority of the area beneath the hatchback. From his letters and phone conversations, Jorgensen had gathered that Stutzman was a transient type, going wherever there was work. Stutzman indicated he might be in Ohio for a while, maybe getting a job doing construction.

Stutzman said he had been having difficulty with his antifreeze—the car had been running hot since he had left

Colorado—and the two men worked on it Saturday morning. It was a chance to get to know each other as friends. After the previous night, sex was out.

Among his bags of clothing was one filled with Amish clothes: shirt, coat, broadfall trousers, and black felt hat. It was Stutzman, in fact, who pointed them out.

"My cousin is getting married, and I'm going to his Amish wedding when I get back to Ohio," Stutzman explained. "Since I was shunned I haven't had the chance to see too many of my relatives and old Amish friends."

"Are they going to allow you to come to the wedding?"

Stutzman smiled and nodded. "An Amish wedding is a happy gathering. They will be a little more likely to welcome me to this than to any other Amish gathering."

Jorgensen again felt sorry for Stutzman. Being shunned by the whole community must have been a horrible ordeal. As a gay man, he could relate to it.

Chuck Freeman was doubled over in hysterics. A letter Stutzman had written to a potential lover in Alamosa, Colorado, had been returned to the ranch because of an insufficient address. Freeman had gotten his hands on it and ripped it open, and now he howled as he read Stutzman's description.

". . . I've got a big dick—11 inches—and low hanging balls . . ."

He showed it to Byron Larson, who had thought Stutzman was a weirdo of the first order anyway. The letter only confirmed his opinion.

"It's bad enough to tell something like that to your girlfriend, let alone your boyfriend," Larson said.

Stutzman claimed he had lost his horse ranch in Colorado when his lover died in a car wreck. Since his lover's family did not recognize the gay men's relationship, they had kicked him off the ranch. He was now odd-jobbing it.

As the next couple of days passed, it became increasingly evident to Jorgensen that Stutzman had become adept at playing on people's sympathies. Like other gays, Jorgensen felt, Stutzman had perfected crying when he had been required to deal with his family while denying his sexual feelings.

He could turn it on when he needed it.

Stutzman talked about his late wife Ida and the tragedy of the barn fire. According to him, his wife's funeral was a disturbing and painful ordeal of its own. "A lot of Amish came—close to two hundred. They seemed more concerned with watching me and judging my reaction than . . . with her death," Stutzman remembered.

When Stutzman drove away on December 23, neither man had any real visions of being lovers. Yet, Jorgensen still kept after Stutzman.

"He was hot on the griddle," he said later, "and I wanted to see what would happen with us."

Stutzman had said nothing of Texas. Al Jorgensen never even knew he'd lived there.

Christmas Eve 1985

It was late Tuesday afternoon, the time of a winter's day between daylight and the chilly edge of evening, as Eli Byler walked between outbuildings on his North Canton, Ohio, farm. Snow had powdered the ground like talcum powder, and the crackling of a fire left no doubt it was Christmas Eve.

The Gremlin with New Mexico plates pulled up the lane, with Eli Stutzman behind the wheel. He hadn't called or written that he was coming. In fact, Eli Byler hadn't communicated with him since the fall when Stutzman had been in Ohio putting up some siding at Dr. Bissell's. The Christmas Eve visit was unexpected.

"Where's Danny?" Byler asked, when he noticed that Stutzman was alone in the car.

"Danny's in Wyoming skiing. You know how much he loves to ski! I couldn't take him away from that and the foster family—he's gotten close to the kids." In fact, Danny's reality was that of a frozen corpse, laid out on an embalming table in Lon Adams's funeral home in Hebron, Nebraska.

Stutzman grinned, shrugging his shoulders. "You know kids . . ."

Byler wondered what kind of a father would let his son stay in Wyoming while he returned to Ohio for Christmas. It didn't seem right. Danny idolized his father and wanted to spend every minute he could with him. All they had was each other. On the other hand, Byler could understand that Danny, being an only child, probably missed the companionship of other kids.

Stutzman said he had spent a couple of days with Danny in Wyoming skiing and had originally planned to bring Danny along with him. But the 9-year-old had wanted to stay.

Byler figured his own children might choose to play with friends instead of going to see grandma. But what parent would give a child that age the power to make his own decisions?

Stutzman seemed tired. He made a few phone calls, then visited with the Bylers, who insisted he stay with them as long as he was in Ohio. They also invited him to Christmas Eve dinner with Gail's parents.

When they unloaded the car, Byler noticed a big toolbox and a sleeping bag in the hatchback area. The door on the driver's side was broken and couldn't be opened from the inside. To get out, Stutzman had to crawl across to the passenger door.

"I borrowed the car from a friend. My truck broke down," he said.

On Christmas morning, Stutzman excused himself from the living room, where the family had gathered to open presents. Stutzman said he was going to call Danny in Wyoming to wish him a Merry Christmas.

It must be hard to be around someone else's children on Christmas when your child is so far away, Byler thought.

Stutzman went into the den and dialed. No one could hear his conversation with his son and no one tried to listen. Nearly an hour later he emerged.

"How's Danny?" Byler asked.

"He's doing fine. He got a lot of nice things for Christmas. He seems real happy, but he misses me."

Stutzman had a sheepish look on his face and wasn't forthcoming with details about what his boy had received for presents. Byler didn't think much about it at the moment, but later he figured Eli must have felt guilty about not being with his son.

"I would have felt guilty, too, if I wasn't with my boy on Christmas," Byler said later.

At 8:40 A.M., Christmas Day, Stutzman called Al Jorgensen and talked for nine minutes. Stutzman let him know that he had seen his mother and was now staying with friends.

"It was just a friend checking in," Jorgensen later said of the call.

Stutzman called John Yost next. He told his Kansas lover that his mother had taken a turn for the worse and was likely to pass away any day now.

"I'm going to stay a little longer than I planned," he said.

Stutzman shared Christmas dinner with friends in Canton. He told them the same story: his boy was skiing in Wyoming. The next day he told Byler that the hostess had chided him for not bringing his son with him for Christmas.

Eli Byler could scarcely argue with the woman's sentiments.

"A boy's place is with his father," he said.

"Danny doesn't need these anymore," Stutzman told the Bylers, giving them a pair of brown paper bags filled with clothes: Pants, shirts, socks, even underwear, all folded, all clean and very neat. The Bylers appreciated the clothes—it was nearly impossible keeping growing boys dressed. In Colorado, he had also given them some of Danny's clothing that he had outgrown.

Yet the clothing in the paper bags were not castoffs. They had been packed carefully. The bags contained enough clothing to outfit a child for weeks. In addition, Stutzman gave the Bylers a coat he said Danny had outgrown.

The vinyl coat was too large for their son Josh. But they didn't think anything of it; they hadn't seen Danny since they had vacationed at Stutzman's Colorado ranch.

The coat stayed in Josh's closet for a year, until he had grown large enough for it to fit properly.

Later, Gail Byler would be sickened when she learned that the coat had been worn by Danny the day he died.

Stutzman gave the Bylers' daughter a book on horses, and the little girl was thrilled. She loved horses as much as Danny had. He also gave her a beaded Indian purse.

Byler had never been one to pry, but there were a few things he wanted to ask Stutzman, and since Eli was there at Byler's doorstep, it seemed as though the conversation was meant to be. As he sifted through his questions, he discarded the most personal. He didn't want to know about his friend's sexuality—though he had heard the rumors. The answer might be more than he could handle, and might change a decade-long friendship.

He'd heard that the Kratzers had received pornography in the mail. He figured Stutzman might look at it just for kicks. At least maybe the old Eli Stutzman he knew might.

That left him with Texas. The rumors had circulated all summer that Stutzman had been involved in a murder in Texas. None of his friends had been able to corner him and ask him about it.

"Eli, let's talk about what happened in Texas."

The question was asked, and now Byler would get an

answer and could put the nonsense, all of the innuendo, to rest. Eli Byler wanted the information firsthand.

But just then the phone rang, and Byler went to answer it. When he returned, the moment had been ruined, and Stutzman never answered his question.

On Sunday, Eli went to church with the Byler family. He seemed so much better, so much more relaxed than he had been in September. Byler felt that whatever had been troubling him back then must be gone by now. Byler was glad to see his friend happy.

Stutzman came and went during the couple of weeks he stayed at Byler's place. Whenever he left he told them he was going down to Apple Creek to see his mother, who he said was still very ill.

Stutzman returned to the Bylers' one day visibly upset. He said his father had met him on the porch and told him not to come there again. Old One-Hand Eli didn't want to see him anymore. His father was as mad as Stutzman had ever seen him.

Stutzman said that later he had managed to sneak a visit with his mother.

At the midpoint of his stay in Ohio, Stutzman went down to Benton to visit friends, and, later, to house-sit while they were away. He never said who they were or how he met them.

Al Jorgensen wrote Stutzman in care of Eli Byler's address. He wanted to know how things were going with his mother's health, and had he had a good time at his cousin's wedding?

Stutzman wrote back on December 31 that he was staying at the trailer belonging to the gay man he had traveled to Key West with. The man and his lover had moved to Texas and needed someone to watch their place. Stutzman had agreed to.

It was closer to his parents' farm than the Bylers' place, so he could more easily see his mother.

> It was shocking at first to see the condition of my mother. I don't believe at all she realizes who people are. My sister doesn't think so either. I haven't been able to see change either way since I've been here. I wish they would put her in the hospital, but dad doesn't think it's necessary. So far I've managed to see her every day for awhile. Dad hasn't said too much so far to me about being around, surprisingly.

Stutzman indicated he had made it to the Amish wedding and had a good time.

> There were some that looked at me out of the corner of their eyes, but most of them were pretty good.

He wouldn't be planning any ski trips—not until his mother's condition improved.

Jorgensen wondered when the Amish were going to leave Stutzman alone and accept him for the nice guy that he was? Staring at him with accusing looks—it was so unfair.

No wonder the guy has a hard time communicating feelings—he's afraid, Jorgensen thought.

January 11, 1986
The Bylers took Stutzman down to see Liz and Leroy Chupp, now farming in Kentucky. Stutzman again repeated that Danny was skiing in Wyoming.

"He's in ski competition now. He has gotten real good," Stutzman said, adding that the boy had won some races.

"We talked about it for some time," Liz Chupp later recalled. "The Amish don't ski, so we were real interested in learning about Danny. Eli seemed so proud."

Stutzman left the Bylers on January 17, saying he was going back to New Mexico to return the borrowed Gremlin. Before leaving he paid for his phone charges.

"I can't believe it that I didn't notice that there were no calls to Wyoming," Byler said later.

As January gave way to February, the unbearable winter chill of the snow-powdered Kansas prairie only made John Yost feel more lonely. He wondered if Eli Stutzman felt the same.

The weeks apart had erased any of the concerns he'd had about his new lover. The murder in Texas, the dead wife, the dead lover from Colorado—none of it mattered. Too many things about Stutzman were just right.

He found Stutzman's phone number in New Mexico and dialed it—it was the number to the trailer house on Chuck Freeman's Aztec ranch. The number, however, had been disconnected. Maybe Eli was still there? Maybe he just couldn't afford to pay his bill? Yost searched again, this time pulling up the number of a friend of Stutzman's who lived near the ranch.

The man who answered the phone said Stutzman had moved to Texas. He didn't have a phone number, but the man provided an address in Azle, Texas.

Yost mailed a valentine and waited. He didn't want to be pushy; he just wanted Stutzman to know how much he cared and how much he wanted to see him again. No strings. No pressure. He would wait.

Stutzman, meanwhile, mailed his last car payment—$176—to Neil's Auto Plaza on February 8. One can only wonder why he told Eli Byler that the car had been borrowed, yet bragged to John Yost about the great deal he'd gotten on it. . . .

Yost received an answer of sorts from Eli Stutzman on Valentine's Day.

There was no return address on the small white envelope postmarked Fort Worth, Texas. Inside, Yost found the three photographs he had given to Stutzman when they first met through the ad. There was no explanation or good-bye. As far as Yost was concerned, Stutzman had sent him a "Dear John" letter.

But why? Yost's first reaction was to find Stutzman and talk with him. Maybe Stutzman needed help? Maybe he was in some kind of trouble?

Weeks passed. Maybe a month or two. Later, when he tried to put it together, Yost could never be sure. All he knew was that he was not going to let Eli Stutzman slip out of his life forever. He got his telephone number from Stutzman's friend in Ohio. The number was to a place in Azle, Texas.

Stutzman was cool and abrupt when he answered Yost's call.

"I don't want you contacting me anymore. You took a big chance sending me that card. If my boyfriend saw it he would get angry at me. Don't call me. Don't write to me at all."

Stutzman was adamant, but Yost didn't want the conversation to end at that. He wanted to know who Stutzman was involved with and what the circumstances of the relationship were.

"I've fallen in love with one of my sisters' husbands and we've dropped out of sight."

"Your brother-in-law?" Yost didn't know what to make of that.

"Yeah. That's why we're hiding out down here. We don't want her to find us. He'll have to pay alimony. That's why we came out here. We're just laying low until it blows over."

Stutzman said he and his brother-in-law/lover were running a successful vending-machine business in the Fort Worth area.

"We had to hide out. We didn't want to leave a trail." Stutzman emphasized his words with sincerity and urgency.

When Yost thought about it later, the story seemed outlandish. Yet, Stutzman had talked so fast and given so much information, there seemed little room or need for questions or details. How had his family taken all of this? First, losing Stutzman to the modern world, then losing a son-in-law to Stutzman? It was a regular Amish *Peyton Place* with Eli Stutzman as the lead character.

Stutzman was so anxious to end the conversation that Yost didn't ask about Danny.

A little sadly, Yost put away the soccer ball. Stutzman wouldn't be coming back for it after all.

Stutzman stopped in at Kenny Hankins's new trailer house in April to pick up a few things, spend the night, and test some bad news. He stunned Hankins with the news.

"I've just come from Danny's funeral. He died in a terrible traffic accident in Salt Lake City," Stutzman said.

Hankins thought something was wrong, something other than Danny's death.

"He had no emotion about it whatsoever. A man who just lost his kid, I thought he would have broke down and bawled, but he showed no emotion, just he's gone, that's it," Hankins later said.

Stutzman's blue eyes were cold and distant.

"The Barlows' Bronco was going onto the freeway on-ramp when a truck hit it broadside," Stutzman said. "Danny suffered massive head injuries—his head swelled up like a balloon."

Hankins was shocked, yet Stutzman remained oddly controlled.

Stutzman said he had flown up from Texas to go to the funeral.

"How come you have a car then?" Hankins asked, trying to pin Stutzman down.

"I had a car up there already."

Stutzman stayed the night in Hankins's mobile home.

"I got a sheet and draped the whole thing, because that

way the sun wouldn't be shining in and exposing him to my neighbors. Whether he slept nude I don't know. He was dressed when I got up the next morning," Hankins recalled.

They loaded up the boxes that he had left. Now he had room in his car for the stuff.

Stutzman gave Hankins a couple of sheepskins as a thank you.

"I told him they were nice, because he had a couple in the box, along with a straw hat and several other things. Pictures, knickknacks and stuff, and two cock rings. They were bull rings! *Solid chrome rings*. He had two, one bigger than the other, and I shook my head when I saw them," Hankins said.

Stutzman left without seeing Chuck Freeman. Hankins did notice, however, that he placed a call to Kevin Whitten.

The Gingeriches received a letter from Stutzman, postmarked Farmington, New Mexico, April 14, 1986. Stutzman apologized for being so late, but their letter, dated February 26, had just reached him.

"It had no zip code on it," he wrote.

Again he played up the charade that Danny was with him and enjoying school and involved in the soccer program.

"He finally has all of his new teeth which make him look quite different," Stutzman wrote, "He had some trouble with a couple teeth. Had to take him to the dentist twice."

Stutzman hinted that he and his son would be taking a trip in the summer to see the family.

He directed some comments to Susie, who had expressed concern over Ida's Amish clothes and other belongings: "All of Danny's Amish clothes and Ida's clothes, are all packed in the chest with mothball, and I plan on keeping them till Danny is grown and give them to him."

The letter was sent the same week *People* came out with the story of the unknown boy from Chester.

. . .

Stutzman called Hankins to say he was settled into a place in a small town near Fort Worth—a nice big house on Toronto Road in Azle, Texas.

Stutzman called again and asked Hankins to send some of the things from the boxes stored at his house. He said he'd had a falling out with the man he was living with, and was moving across the street.

"He wanted some sealed envelopes and the pictures of Danny and of his wife," Hankins said later.

Hankins couldn't help but notice a newspaper clipping about the barn fire that had taken Ida's life. It surprised him, and he told Chuck Freeman about it.

Stutzman had told them his wife had died in a car wreck. "*We secretly owned a car . . .*"

Of course, the photographs of the woman were not of Ida Gingerich. She was Amish, and they didn't pose for photos. Maybe one of them was the same photo Stutzman had used as his "girlfriend" when Eli Byler and his family came out to Colorado on vacation in 1983.

Into the summer of 1986, Hankins continued to forward letters for Stutzman, who occasionally sent him twenty dollars to cover postage.

Weeks after Stutzman had told him that Danny had died in a car wreck, a letter arrived at Hankins's addressed to "Eli Stutzman and son Danny."

The return address was that of a Stutzman in Ohio. Hankins figured it was Stutzman's father.

This is one hell of a note, Hankins thought. If Stutzman's dad knew the kid was dead, why was he writing? Hankins had understood that when Danny died Stutzman had told his folks. They hadn't come out because they don't fly.

So now what was Stutzman up to?

PART THREE

Judgment Day

"I wanted to leave Danny where God could find him."

—Eli Stutzman

CHAPTER THIRTY

Amos Gingerich was working in his generator-powered carpentry shop building picnic benches for the *Englischers* when the death letter came. It was postmarked Fort Worth, July 30, 1986. His son Dan opened it and read it aloud.

> 7/29/86
> Dear Folks,
>
> Greetings in his name, who shed his blood for us.
>
> This is Tuesday morning 10:30 A.M., the Temp. is 104 degrees already. Hope yours are all well. With some things have not all been well recently. But I'm sure our good Heavenly Father knows best. He gives to be taken.
>
> I just found out this morning that the message I sent yours last week was returned instead of delivered. It was a Mail-A-Gram (Tel-A-Gram). The post office's reason was because there was no ph. # included for destination's party.
>
> The sad news is about Danny. He was in a car accident near Salt Lake city on Monday of last week (July 21st) around 10 A.M. & died at the hospital in Salt Lake City Utah, on Tuesday night 11:30 P.M. (July 22nd) due to head injuries.
>
> Grave side services were held on Thursday

> (July 24th) for Danny in Kemmerer, Wyoming where Danny is buried at the [Barlow] Family cemetery.
>
> I'm sorry you did not get my message. But I tried. When I had the message sent I was assured that the message will be delivered to yours personally by someone for your local post office no later than Wed. 10 A.M. July 23rd your time.
>
> Danny has been at this children's camp at Lyman, Wyoming since June 1st. (Same place as last summer) Which is run by the [Barlow] Family & was being taken to the airport by [Dean Barlow] to Salt Lake City, where they were hit by a semi truck. He was going to fly here to Dallas–Forth Worth Airport, where I was going to pick him up. I received word of the accident at noon Monday just as I was getting ready to go pick him up. So I went to Salt Lake City Monday afternoon, and got back here yesterday.
>
> Am finishing up a project here I started earlier, will probably be here about 2 more weeks & will return to N. Mexico.
>
> So long for now,
> Eli.

The stationery featured pictures of running horses and upbeat mottos: "There is only one success . . . to be able to spend your life in your own way."

Stutzman had obviously found *his* way. Without Danny.

For the Gingeriches, relief followed the immediate shock of the death message. Amos later told his family, "If only this could be true. It would be an answer to our prayers. God did not want the boy to suffer anymore."

Still, parts of the letter were puzzling. There was no way the Gingeriches would have missed the boy's funeral if Stutzman had truly tried to get hold of them. It would not have been difficult to call an *Englischer* in the Beaverton, Michigan, community to get a death message delivered.

"We would have gone by bus or rented a car and driver," Gingerich said years later, still unable to make sense of his son-in-law's motives.

In Apple Creek, Eli and Susan Stutzman received a similar letter.

Word spread about the boy's tragic death.

Liz Chupp called Stutzman to offer her condolences. Stutzman had been so kind to her and Leroy when their five-year-old daughter died in a farm accident in Kentucky.

Now both of the old friends had lost a child.

Stutzman sobbed as he recounted the accident that took his boy's life.

"I was so thankful for the time we had in the hospital," he said. "Danny drifted in and out of consciousness, and we were able to talk before he died. It was a very precious time for me," Stutzman said.

"He told me what a great father I was . . . and I told him how much I loved him. I can't believe he is gone. Danny is my last bond to my dear Ida."

Later, Chupp figured Stutzman had told her only what he thought she wanted to hear.

In August, Stutzman returned to Ohio to see old friends and rekindle happier memories. He made it to the gay bar in Akron, where he ran into Rick Adamson, the man who first met Stutzman when the former Amishman's nude photo and convenient address had caught his eye in *Stars*.

"Danny died in a car wreck in Utah . . ."

Amos Gingerich wrote his suspicions to his old neighbor in Fredericksburg, *David Yoder*, an Amishman who had done considerable traveling.

"Amos was troubled and wanted to get to the bottom of Eli's story," Yoder said.

The Amishmen agreed that a little detective work was needed—a trip to the Barlow family cemetery in Lyman, Wyoming, would be a good place to start. If that led nowhere, they wanted to find the hospital where Danny had died.

Gingerich wrote ahead to the police, but since there was no police department in Kemmerer, the letter didn't reach the authorities in Lyman until later. "We are looking for the Barlow family cemetery," the letter said.

Amos, his daughter, Susie, and son-in-law Andy Miller joined Yoder at the Chicago bus terminal, and arrived in Lyman on Wednesday, November 12, a little after 6:00 A.M.

At the police station, they were told to wait at a café while Dean and Margie Barlow were notified. The police had never heard of a Barlow cemetery, and they didn't have any records indicating an accident involving Danny Stutzman and Dean Barlow.

"We were having breakfast, and they called for us to come down, and we hurried to meet this Dean Barlow," Gingerich recalled.

At the station, Gingerich gave a nervous and confused Dean Barlow the letter from Stutzman recounting Danny's death. The Barlows had brought a photo of Danny, just in case the Amish had confused him with another Amish boy.

"It's Eli's stationery, his handwriting," Barlow said, sinking into a chair as he read the letter. "But none of this is true . . ."

Margie Barlow sat like a lump, looking as though she had been shot.

"We had the boy until December of 1985. We haven't seen him since," Barlow said.

The Barlows showed a copy of the July 5 agreement they had made with Stutzman to care for Danny.

Around nine o'clock, the Barlows took the Amish up to the house and introduced their children.

"They liked Danny, he was a good boy, an intelligent boy, they said. He was good on their computer," Yoder recalled.

The Barlows hoped the news of Danny's death was a terrible mistake. They said Stutzman had been working at a cabinet shop in Benton, Ohio, and Danny had been attending a Mennonite school. They had talked with Stutzman a couple of times after he had left with Danny, but each time they had asked to speak with the boy, they had been told he was either asleep or outside playing.

"He took Danny to see his ailing grandmother once a week," Barlow said.

Margie Barlow served cookies and gave Amos a photograph of Danny and Eli taken in front of their Christmas tree on December 14, 1985—no one knew it then, of course, but it was Danny's last photograph.

The Amish wondered how Barlow and Stutzman had become friends. Barlow said it was through a thoroughbred-horse deal. As a story, it was possible. After all, nearby Evanston did have Wyoming Downs.

Still, there was something about the Barlows that made the Amish wonder if they were being completely truthful.

When the Amish indicated that Stutzman had had a bad temper or some emotional problems in the past, they were met with disbelief. That was not the *Eli* they knew, they said.

Dean Barlow said that when Stutzman ran into trouble over the murder of his employee in Texas, he and his wife had agreed to take Danny in.

"Eli had a wood-working business, and had a few fellows working for him that did not get along the best, so one fellow took Eli's gun and shot the other. Eli's fingerprints were on the gun, but the other fellow's were on top of Eli's," Yoder later recalled the Barlows saying.

When he came to pick up Danny in December, Stutzman said that he had been cleared of the Texas charges.

Dean Barlow bought the Amish soda pop and drove them the hundred miles to Salt Lake City. It was no trouble, he insisted. His father had cancer and he was going to visit him anyway.

Barlow told Amos Gingerich, "Eli has some questions he needs to answer."

The Wyoming man wanted the Amish to know how wrong he thought the *bann* was, how much it had hurt Eli

Stutzman. Maybe his hurt had contributed to all of the lies.

Amos tried to explain. "It is not a boycott, we do it so they repent."

The next day the Amish caught a train for Denver's bus station, though they had considered going to Durango to see what they could turn up. The trip had been the furthest west Amos and Susie Gingerich and Andy Miller had traveled.

After returning to Michigan, Amos Gingerich received a letter from Margie Barlow. The Barlows had written to Stutzman again and there had been no response. "We thought for sure Eli would have called or written us by now, so we are a little worried," she wrote.

In Ohio, David Yoder continued the role of detective, but nothing panned out. At the Benton Mennonite school, no one had heard of Danny Stutzman.

Chris and Diane Swartzentruber were on a buggy ride with their friend Amos Slabaugh, who lived south of Kidron, when Eli Stutzman's name came up. The Amishman said he had heard that Danny had died in a car accident and that some Amish had gone looking for the child's grave, but that they couldn't find it.

"Right when this was said, I'm not a real religious person, I don't attend church, but I do believe in God. Something went through me. Chills," Diane later recalled. "I knew something else had happened to Danny."

The talk went to Ida's death.

Diane spoke up and said she and Chris had always thought Stutzman had murdered his wife.

"Her neck had choke marks on it and the tongue had been bitten in half," Slabaugh said.

They wondered why something hadn't been done.

When the Swartzentrubers got home, Diana told her husband that she knew Stutzman had killed Danny, too.

"Chris knew it too. We just *knew* that he did. But we didn't know where he was. Nobody did."

David Yoder went to a sawmill near his home and called the Barlows when the *Reader's Digest* article came out about Little Boy Blue. He and others were convinced that Danny Stutzman was the boy who had been buried in the Chester cemetery.

Margie Barlow said she would come forward and contact the authorities. She had also read the article and wondered if it could be Danny.

She sent a letter to Amos Gingerich.

> Dear Amos,
>
> David Yoder called me yesterday regarding the *Reader's Digest* article "Little Boy Blue of Chester, Nebraska." I, too, have been haunted by the story of "Little Boy Blue" ever since I read it, but have been busy with the speech team and my classes, so have not acted upon it. Also I thought maybe I was just grasping at straws and being emotional. David's call made me realize that maybe I wasn't the only one receiving gut level feelings about the story.
>
> After David's call, Dean and I discussed the situation and decided to contact the Chester, Nebraska, Police Department directly instead of going through our police department. We feel this route will bring faster answers. I am enclosing a copy of our letter to them. I will let you know what they answer.
>
> A couple of details leave room for doubt. Unless Eli bought him one, Danny did not have a blue blanket sleeper. I'm not sure he had perfect teeth. I thought at one time I had to take him to the dentist, but may have been confused with my own children's appointments. If I'm remembering

> correctly, Eli left with Danny December 20. He should have been in Ohio by December 23. If he followed I-80, he wouldn't have been close to Chester, Nebraska. I checked this out in our atlas. Danny was in good health when he left us although he had had a cold and the doctor had prescribed some antibiotics which he was taking.
>
> But, then I wonder why Danny never wrote us . . .

Amos Gingerich, for one, felt that Danny was dead. But he knew it hadn't been a car wreck.

"Sometimes we feel that maybe Danny got killed some other way," he wrote back to the Barlows.

CHAPTER THIRTY-ONE

December 1, 1987

Once Gary Young and Jack Wyant had a name, the information flow became a deluge. They learned that Stutzman had two middle initials and two social security numbers. His wife had died in a fire in 1977. He had moved to Colorado in 1982 and finally on to Texas, where his roommate had been shot and dumped in a rural ditch in 1985.

Dumped in a ditch? The scenario was familiar. And, even though the autopsies and pathologists' reports hadn't fixed a cause of death, the case was still a murder as far as the Nebraskan investigators were concerned.

It had to be. Everything about the case, and the suspect, suggested foul play.

Young requested school photos and records from the elementary school Danny had attended, after the Barlows did some digging and said they doubted they had anything with the boy's fingerprints still on it. Later, they sent a copy of *The Velveteen Rabbit*, which Danny had read.

Young spoke with Stutzman's Mennonite neighbor Abner Petersheim again, this time seeking information on the whereabouts of Danny Stutzman's grandparents. Lehman referred the sheriff to David Yoder, the well-traveled Amishman who had gone out to Lyman with Amos Gingerich.

Yoder told him about the letter Stutzman had sent his

in-laws with the story of the fatal car accident. He gave Young the phone number of an *Englischer* near the Gingerich's Michigan farm. Later that same day, Gingerich called Young, telling him that Stutzman was supposedly in England working at a stable.

"His parents have a letter from there," Gingerich said.

Holmes County, Ohio, sheriff's investigators went to Welty Road and got a copy of the letter:

> 11-15-87
> Dear Mother,
>
> Greetings from above, in His name. How are you all? I am fine. Much to be thankful for. I received your letter 2 weeks ago, by way of N. M. I guess that's why it took so long. The weather is cool & foggie here this time of year, earlier it was much nicer.
>
> I'm keep'in busy with my work. And am working with horses, which I spend a lot of time on.
>
> Wish you all well, in good health & all. Would be sorry to hear other wise.
>
> So long for now.
> Eli

The envelope carried a foreign stamp, but was without a postmark. The return address was 92 A North End Road, Kensington West, London W, 14, England. On the envelope Stutzman repeated the date, 11-27-87.

Later, when Wyant gave the address to Interpol, the news that came back was of no help—there wasn't any such address in England.

The fact that it hadn't been postmarked was also checked out. Postal authorities conceded some stamps slip through the system without being canceled. On the other hand, it was possible that Stutzman—or someone helping him—had put that letter in Eli H. Stutzman's mailbox as a red herring.

As more was uncovered about Stutzman, such a subterfuge seemed increasingly likely.

Included inside a package from Danny Stutzman's elementary school were his last school portrait and his report card envelopes. The envelopes were packaged for the crime lab in Lincoln. Young was disheartened—the report cards themselves were missing. They would have been an even better source of fingerprints.

From his office in Thayer County, Young dispatched a letter to Jack Wyant.

> Take a good look at the largest photo. Compare it with the morgue photo. You will see a couple larger freckles in the same places on both photos. Also the shape of the ear is the same. I am sure we have a name for our December '85 victim.

Margie Barlow called Sheriff Young with further confirmation. The Barlow family was certain that the morgue photo was Danny.

Through the La Plata County, Colorado, Sheriff's Office, Young got hold of the man who had sold Stutzman and Palmer the ranch. Young learned that Stutzman couldn't make the payments after he and Palmer dissolved their partnership. The man said he had foreclosed on Stutzman in November 1984, but had been ordered to pay the former Amishman $7,500. He had held off on payments until June 1987.

June through November the man had mailed monthly checks to 400 Toronto Road, Azle, Texas. Oddly, four of the checks appeared to have been endorsed by someone other than Stutzman.

In a letter postmarked Dallas, in September, Stutzman had written saying that money was tight and that he had needed cash earlier. The September check endorsement was one of the only two matching Stutzman's signature.

. . .

Diane Swartzentruber sat straight up in bed as a sketchy report came over the 11:00 P.M. TV news.

"They flashed across the screen that a Wayne County man was being sought in connection with his son's death—they didn't say his name. I got goose bumps on me. It was so weird," she said later.

"It's Eli. It's Eli," she cried, running from the bedroom and into the kitchen, and spinning around the table. "I just know he killed his son. I *know* it."

Diane Swartzentruber wasn't about to let Stutzman get away with anything. She had suspected him of killing his wife, of abusing his child—her mind flashed on the pornography she had found in Danny's bedroom. She had even heard the story of the murder in Texas. She got on the phone and began calling and calling. She called everyone she thought might help.

The next day, she called Abe Stutzman, who told her that he had read the *Reader's Digest* article three times.

"There was something about it," he told her.

Diane also called Eli Byler, who now farmed land near Grand Rapids, Michigan, to see what he knew. The last Byler had heard, Stutzman was somewhere in Texas.

"I thought by getting a hold of Eli Byler that I could call the police and say, 'Look for the sucker here,' " she later said.

She also called Gary Young, after picking up his name from the *Digest* piece. She told him that she'd call back if she found out anything more about Stutzman.

She dialed the Wayne County Sheriff's Office and left a message that she wanted to talk about Eli Stutzman.

It was Tim Brown, who was working the case in conjunction with the Nebraskans, who returned her call.

"I'm not going to talk with you. I know what you are—you're a faggot," she said, her voice rising through angry and tightened lips. "I want to speak with Sheriff Alexander."

Loran Alexander returned her call later that day. Swartzentruber was still angry, and she let the sheriff know it.

"What's the deal here? Brown is probably his boyfriend, and you're letting him run the investigation? What kind of deal is this? First the coroner and now this?"

The sheriff calmly assured her that Tim Brown was a good cop and doing a good job.

Headlines in Ohio newspapers dredged up more memories of Ida Stutzman and the fire. Wayne County Coroner J. T. Questel told a Canton reporter, "I didn't really like the way it looked, though there was no evidence of anything. There was an awful lot we never did uncover."

Diane Swartzentruber called Questel and gave him a blast of her anger.

"What's with these people?" she later asked. "They believed this liar?"

December 9, 1987

Azle, Texas, is the kind of place where realtors take out classified ads and hit heavy and hard on the words *Country Livin'*. It's the kind of place where cowboys drive pickup trucks from neat split-levels on the edge of town to jobs in Fort Worth.

The city's stationery features the motto: "Small enough to welcome you, large enough to serve you." Sure, more outsiders came every week, but with them came new friends and new businesses. But if being neighborly wasn't on a transplant's mind, Azle would be a good place to get lost.

No doubt Eli Stutzman thought so.

Police Chief Ted Garber had come to Azle after twenty years in law enforcement with the department in Garland, Texas, most recently heading the SWAT team. He had arrived a no-nonsense professional with a sense of humor and a slight touch of gray to his hair. After a couple of years in Azle, he had kept his humor, but his combed-back hair had turned the color of ash.

When he came to Azle he had had to "kick some butt"

and make a few changes. First, naturally, was a good housecleaning of the dead weight. He updated the criminal investigation division and developed an emergency response team.

Garber listened with interest to Gary Young when he called with the story of the boy left dead on Christmas Eve. Young was looking for Eli Stutzman in connection with the possible homicide and child-abuse case. Garber could hear the obvious personal concern and emotion in Young's voice.

Ted Garber wanted to catch this character Stutzman.

Some slob who dumps his kid off in a ditch is no class-C misdemeanor, no run-a-red-light kind of person, he thought. *This son of a bitch needs to be caught.*

A check with his records clerk turned up two Stutzman entries—one an Eli E. Stutzman, the other, Eli C. Stutzman. There were also different dates of birth. One incident involved a burglary in October, the other a stolen vehicle in November.

Records indicated a VCR, 20 videotapes, an answering machine, and a gold "Four Corners Rodeo" belt buckle had been stolen on October 16. Stutzman's truck had been recovered two days after it was stolen in November.

Garber considered simply passing the information on to an investigator, but he was sufficiently interested to pursue the case and play detective on his own.

He went out to the rundown house at the Toronto address but found no one home. He checked with neighbors, and no one seemed to know the man. *Owen Barker*, Stutzman's former landlord, did not know exactly where Stutzman had moved. Barker thought Stutzman might be in Dallas doing some construction work. There was a possibility that he was staying in the Cedar Springs area of Dallas.

Cedar Springs. Garber knew it as a faggot hangout outside of the Metroplex. *Leather and lace. Whips and chains.* Eli Stutzman hung out with a crowd Garber knew little of, beyond the standard, negative stereotypes.

He really didn't care to know more about those kind of people anyway.

Garber reported back to Young, telling him that Stutzman was gone and that no one knew where he was. Young didn't let it sit; he told Garber that he and Jack Wyant were on their way to Azle. Nobody back in Thayer County wanted the story to end with another cold trail.

Garber put the word out that he was looking for a light-blue Ford pickup with Texas plates, and a man named Eli Stutzman, known to his friends as "Junior."

On December 11, a warrant for Stutzman's arrest was finally issued. Officially, the charge was felony child abuse, though the Nebraskans knew that they had to prove the abuse happened in their state in order for the charge to stick. . . .

> Knowingly or intentionally cause or permit Daniel E. Stutzman, a minor child, to be placed in a position that endangers his life or health or deprived of necessary food, clothing, shelter or care.

The next day, Wyant and Young were in Azle, Texas, calling on Owen Barker. Barker had told Ted Garber he expected Stutzman back that weekend. He was even holding mail for him, including a letter from New Mexico.

At six feet three inches and three hundred pounds, Owen Barker was an immense man with gray eyes and blond hair who worked as a comptroller for a Fort Worth company. Wyant and Young sat in the man's crowded and dumpy house on Toronto Road.

Cats were everywhere.

Wyant took the lead in the interrogation. Barker said he had met Stutzman when they became pen pals through *The Advocate*. They had met for the first time in person when Stutzman and Danny had come down for a horse show in Fort Worth.

Barker was unsure whether it was February 1978 or 1979.

Stutzman and his boy had stayed in Azle for three or four days, and left when Stutzman got off the phone with news that his grandfather was ill and that he would have to leave right away.

"When did you next hear from Eli?" Wyant asked.

Barker again was uncertain, but thought it had been February 1986 when Stutzman called asking if Barker still remembered him and could he come visit.

Barker had told him to come on down.

Stutzman had arrived driving a gray Gremlin with New Mexico plates. He said that his car had broken down and that he had borrowed the Gremlin. Stutzman claimed that Danny was still in the care of the Barlows, in Wyoming.

"Why isn't your son with you?" Barker had asked.

"Danny's fair-skinned and blond and the other kids—Mexicans and Indians—tease him."

"Why didn't you bring him down here?" Barker recalled asking Stutzman.

"He likes it in Wyoming with the Barlows and their children. I'm going to get him later, when I'm settled in," Stutzman said.

In mid-June 1986, Barker and some friends made plans for a vacation to Guadalupe. Barker said he pressed Stutzman to have Danny come down to join them on the trip.

"It was around Father's Day," he recalled.

Barker stated that he went outside for five minutes or so after he talked to Stutzman about bringing the boy; when he returned, Stutzman was on the phone.

"I've got Danny here," Stutzman said, handing the phone to Barker.

"Danny, this is Owen. You looking forward to coming down here to go to Guadalupe?"

The answer from a child was, "Fine."

"I hope you'll enjoy Texas," Barker said.

"Okay," said the boy.

"Are you sure it was Danny Stutzman?" Wyant asked.

"I hadn't talked with Danny since 1979. But it sounded like a 9-year-old boy," Barker said.

Neither Wyant nor Young knew what to make of Barker's statement. He couldn't have been talking to Danny Stutzman, who had died six months before. But who was the little boy pretending to be Stutzman's son? What kind of person would put someone up to something like that?

But there was more.

Barker said that the day before Danny was to fly down to Texas, Stutzman called. "Danny was involved in a traffic accident on his way to the airport," he said. "He's in the hospital. You go on the trip without me, I'm driving up to Salt Lake City."

"Later, Eli called me and said he was at the hospital and it had taken him sixteen hours to get there," Barker told the Nebraskans.

Stutzman told Barker that Danny was conscious, though he had suffered head injuries.

Barker said he went ahead on the four-day trip. When he returned to his house on June 24, he was surprised to find Eli Stutzman inside.

"How's Danny?"

"He died," Stutzman said.

"You're kidding!"

Stutzman got mad and left. Still Barker wondered how it, everything, including a funeral, could have happened so fast.

Barker gave the investigators a couple of addresses that might help them find Stutzman. One was a bar called Cowboy City, the other a place in south Dallas—Stutzman had moved there on November 30. That was about the date Little Boy Blue's identity was being talked about all over Wayne County, Ohio.

An interview with the other family planning the trip to Guadalupe backed up Barker's story. So did phone records. No calls had been made to Wyoming during the time when Stutzman said Danny had died in the car wreck.

It left the Nebraskans to wonder who had helped Stutzman bluff Owen Barker with "Danny's" call?

Young and Wyant drove around the Metroplex looking

for Stutzman. The addresses Barker had given turned up nothing. The trip was a waste.

"We decided it was a fruitless venture . . . money not well spent and all this bullshit; we decided to come back," Wyant later recalled.

During the long drive back to Nebraska, Wyant and Young pulled over to watch what they thought were flying saucers. It turned out to be a Soviet satellite that had come apart, leaving a shower of lights and debris. Both men were discouraged. They had come so close to catching Stutzman, who could be anywhere now.

After Stutzman had been named as the man who had dumped his son in a ditch, the Amish pipeline bubbled with new and old rumors. Sometimes the grapevine seemed wild and ridiculously inaccurate; often it was dappled with truth.

"Eli told people he saw a dove just before his wife died."

Some Amish, particularly the Old Order groups, put faith in folktales of the visiting bird as a messenger of death.

"As a schoolboy, Eli used to twist the heads of kittens and cats until they choked to death."

Wasn't it Stutzman who had told people when he first left the Amish that he had been the victim of a terrible prank—a skinned cat hanging in his buggy?

"He started the fire at Keim's, just like he did the one that killed his wife."

Mose Keim had never thought so.

"Eli wrote a letter to his mother telling her it was true that he was homosexual. He wrote that he was closer to God than he ever had been."

Canton *Repository* newspaper reporter Dennis Webb got into the Stutzman story as a chance to work on something of national interest, away from the mundane stories he wrote for a county bureau. He never expected to become part of the story. He had been chasing down leads since the first word from Nebraska came that Little Boy Blue was Danny Stutzman, a former Amishboy from Dalton.

On December 12, he left a message for Stutzman on the answering machine belonging to his boss in Dallas.

A soft-spoken man called Webb's house asking if "David Summers" was there.

Joyce Webb answered the call and told the caller he had the wrong number.

A short period later the phone rang again.

"Is Dennis Webb there? This is David Summers."

The voice belonged to the same person on both calls—halting, with a definite trace of an Amish accent.

The man told Dennis Webb that he understood the reporter was looking for Eli Stutzman, and asked him why.

Webb filled him in on the Little Boy Blue story.

"Eli's out of the country," the man insisted. "He's in England now."

Webb didn't know what to make of the caller, first asking for David Summers, then saying he *was* David Summers.

"I think it was Eli Stutzman that I talked with," he later said.

Webb called Ted Garber, and later Jack Wyant, with the information.

Azle police chief Garber had a strange call of his own to contend with nine o'clock one Sunday night, when an informant called his office saying he, too, had spoken with a David Summers. He told the police chief that Eli Stutzman was using the Summers' name and was now hiding out up north somewhere in the county. Stutzman's P.O. box number was 405.

"Look for his pickup," the caller said.

Garber asked for more specifics, but either the man didn't know or flat refused to tell. As little information as it was, Garber decided to drive up Highway 730 to have a look around.

CHAPTER THIRTY-TWO

It was cold, windy, and rainy—an ugly combination just about anywhere, but somehow worse in nighttime Azle. Ted Garber, who by now could understand Gary Young's obsession with Eli Stutzman, figured he was crazy to be out combing the county for a phantom pickup. He smoked and flashed a spotlight on mailboxes and suspicious vehicles.

Turning off the paved road onto a dirt and gravel road, a street sign grabbed his attention: "Summer's Circle." Suddenly he knew.

Stutzman is using the street name.

At the end of a driveway joining a one-lane road through a trailer park shrouded in manzanita and live oak was Stutzman's pickup, parked in front of a trailer house. Garber shut off his headlights and verified that the plates were Stutzman's.

It was around midnight when he radioed the office to get some backup. Garber decided it would be best to stake out the place all night and arrest Stutzman in the morning. The wooded area made a nighttime arrest risky. It would be too easy for Stutzman to bolt out the back door and into the cover of the trees.

Officer John Lyons, a 25-year-old redhead with the deliberate walk of a military officer, came out to mark time with the chief until daylight. They took turns catching a bit of sleep, and Garber had Lyons make a coffee run down 730 to an all-night store.

In the meantime, he had the department run a crisscross check on the mailbox number in an effort to come up with a telephone number. They turned up a phone number belonging to Elvy Kenyon. A check on Kenyon's driver's license and prior arrests showed that he had been in the Azle jail two times on alcohol-related offenses.

Monday, December 14, 1987

Morning brought a new perspective to the trailer court. Stubborn, sodden oak leaves stuck on branches. The thick mesh of trees made Garber glad it was winter—in spring the olive-green-painted, single-wide trailer would barely be visible from the road. A Japanese lantern and a cherub kneeling in a birdbath decorated the front yard, which was enclosed by a chain-link fence.

It had been a good decision to wait. At the very least, Garber figured that if Stutzman ran, they could corral him in the yard.

At 7:00 A.M., Garber called for the day shift to come out to the trailer park to assist with the bust of a child killer. With all of the interest in this case, Ted Garber wasn't about to risk being known as the cop who let the father of Little Boy Blue escape.

At 7:45 A.M., officers encircled the mobile home, and a dispatcher called Kenyon's telephone number to let the occupants know that the trailer house was surrounded and to tell them to come out one by one with their hands on their heads. Garber knew this would accomplish one thing for certain. He would learn their attitude fast.

"Either they'd come out and say 'Okay,' or they'd refuse and say 'To hell with you, come on and get us,' " he later said.

Elvy Kenyon told the dispatcher that there were three men inside and that they had been sleeping.

"We need to get dressed first," Kenyon said.

When the front door swung open, three disheveled men

stepped outside into the morning drizzle. The second one out was Stutzman. To Garber, Stutzman looked small, almost frail—hardly a menacing child killer—but he knew looks mean nothing. Stutzman wore Levi's and a Western, snap-pocket, flannel shirt. His hair was cropped short and his face, clean shaven. Garber recognized him from the picture Gary Young had sent—the one taken by Dean Barlow in front of his Christmas tree just before Danny died.

Garber fixed his eyes on Stutzman and displayed a teletyped warrant for Felony IV Child Abuse.

If Stutzman had just been asleep, he woke up fast.

"I didn't have anything to do with that. Those charges aren't true," he said.

Garber turned to Kenyon. "I don't know what kind of charges will be brought against you," he said coolly.

Kenyon's ruddy face went white.

"I will want to talk with you later. Don't you run off now, Elvy Kenyon."

"Yes, sir."

Garber asked if Kenyon had ever heard of harboring a fugitive.

Kenyon looked sick. "Yes, sir."

Stutzman's pickup was impounded, searched, and taken to Wood's Auto Pound in Azle. It was clean.

Nothing unusual was found on Eli Stutzman. In fact, what *wasn't* on him was remarkable. His wallet held no photograph of Danny, no reminder of his lost son. Inside the wallet, Garber found Stutzman's phony social security card; his attempt to disguise his handwriting was obvious—it looked as though Stutzman had used his left hand to sign his name. In a ridiculous addition, he had written his new middle initial—"C"—after he had signed his name. It looked like an afterthought.

He did a little better with the signature on the Ohio driver's license, which had been issued on August 30, 1985. The signature still looked wrong. A plastic promotional card for a country-music station had been issued in the name of Junior Stutzman.

A business card belonging to a man who bought snakes raised Garber's eyebrow. He also found a Fort Worth doctor's business card. Later, he called the number, and the doctor said he had been treating Stutzman for a head injury. In addition, Stutzman had tested HIV positive.

"I ain't going to fuck in no sock," Stutzman had told Kenny Hankins in New Mexico.

Garber phoned Young with the news that Stutzman was now in custody. "Young was wound up real tight," Garber later said.

"Now we can put the case together and get this all resolved," Young said. Further, a fingerprint examiner at the state patrol's crime lab in Lincoln had confirmed what everyone knew: A palm print on the documents sent from Wyoming matched Little Boy Blue's.

Young asked Garber to interview Stutzman.

"He'll probably have an attorney by the time he gets up here," he said.

Garber was glad to comply. Stutzman was a monster, a man who had dumped his kid on the side of the road like yesterday's trash. Garber wanted to be certain that he didn't do anything that could hurt Nebraska's case. The interview would have to be totally by the book.

There were several times in the five hours that followed when Garber wished he could break a few rules—and maybe a few bones.

Stutzman was subdued, a little mousy even. Maybe even feminine, Garber thought, though he couldn't be sure if it was a prejudice against homosexuals that was working on him or the glaring indications of a stereotype. He had to be careful. He didn't want to focus on the subject's sexuality and have him get pissed off and freeze up during the interview. He led the suspect into the small interrogation room—a room Garber half-hoped the suspect would think "reeked of rubber hose and pipes."

The department called the room "the interview room"

when referring to it to outsiders. It sounded nicer, friendlier. Stutzman and Garber sat in straight-backed chairs, across a small, circular table.

After a few awkward moments, Stutzman agreed to talk, but only to Ted Garber. At 10 A.M., Ted Garber became the first law-enforcement officer to talk with Stutzman since Jerry Wiggins of the Travis County Sheriff's Office had taken his statement regarding Glen Pritchett's murder in 1985.

Garber didn't know it then, but he would also be the last police officer to talk to Stutzman without the suspect protected by the shield of a lawyer.

Later, in a report, Garber noted: "Mr. Stutzman appeared very distant and unemotional."

Stutzman told Garber that he would talk about his son's death on the condition that only Sheriff Young would hear the information. He did not want any reporters to get wind of his statement. He did not want publicity of any kind—good or bad.

Garber agreed. He started by asking about the long, jagged scar on Stutzman's forehead, just below his hairline. Stutzman said he had been hurt and hospitalized when a car he was working on fell on him.

Easing into the interview, the police chief told Stutzman that he was from New York and that his family had on occasion traveled to the Amish community in Pennsylvania. He asked question after question about the horse-drawn buggies, the beards, the horse-pulled farm equipment. Stutzman's responses were brief, but not to the point of being curt. He seemed to hold some esteem for the "down-to-earth, basic way of life" the Amish lived.

Stutzman told Garber the scenario of Ida's death, but the police chief didn't buy it. The lightning, the fire at midnight, the milk pails. It was all there, but it didn't make sense to Garber.

"Eli, you think I'm stupid."

Stutzman didn't react.

"Eli, do I look stupid to you? I'm not really stupid. I can tell when you're telling stories."

Stutzman half shrugged, but didn't say anything.

Garber continued. "You're telling me your wife went into a burning barn, and then when she came out she went back in all the way around to the other side of the barn. Why didn't she go in the same door she came out of? She was pregnant—why did she go in anyway?

"You killed her. She was a burden to you."

The statement jolted Stutzman, and he looked at the ceiling. Garber figured he was trying to buy time to come up with an excuse or a lie.

"I'm telling you the truth. This is your idea and this is mine. *And I was there*."

After his wife died, Stutzman told Garber, he had lost interest in the Amish way of life and left the Order.

Garber turned his attention to the Pritchett murder case.

"Are you a queer?" he asked.

Stutzman seemed surprised at the question.

"What has that got to do with anything?" he asked.

"Nothing, Eli. Just curious."

"Well, because I suck a dick every once in a while makes me a queer, then I guess I am."

Garber, who by his own admission is not exactly a gay-rights advocate, half smiled at Stutzman. "I guess you are, Eli. Don't you touch me!"

Stutzman was visibly angry and defensive. "What's wrong with being gay?"

"Nothing. It's perfectly normal," Garber said, his sarcasm subtle but unmistakable.

The interview went on. Stutzman said that in 1984 he and Danny had lived with Pritchett in a house in Austin. One night something terrible happened.

"Me and Danny were in bed, and I heard several people talking loudly in the front room. I was afraid to get up, so me and Danny stayed in bed. I heard a gunshot, and after a while, when things got quiet, I went into the front room and found everyone had left."

"Who was in the living room arguing that night?" Garber asked.

"I don't know."

Stutzman's delivery remained slow and quiet. He indicated that he and Danny had stayed in bed until morning, before getting up to see what had happened.

"Austin police began questioning me about this situation because my gun was used," he said.

"Why did you leave Austin shortly after the murder of your friend if you have nothing to hide?" Garber asked.

Stutzman thought for a moment. "That's a very good question."

Next was Danny's story. Garber felt that Stutzman had teetered on the edge of a confession throughout the interview. This was a chance to clear up a mystery, and it wasn't lost on him. He wished he could grab the guy by the throat and rough him up a little, like they did in the "good old days of police work"—just enough of a shaking to loosen Stutzman's tongue about the boy's death.

Maybe he could shake the lies right out of the man's throat.

After leaving Austin, Stutzman said that he and Danny stayed with some friends in the Azle–Fort Worth area. He would not say who the friends were. Danny, Stutzman said, was dropped off in Wyoming with some foster parents in July 1985.

In December 1985, Stutzman said he returned to Wyoming to pick up Danny for a cross-country trip to Ohio for the Christmas holidays.

"I still felt that Stutzman was not telling the truth on many pertinent points and that he was being very evasive. As we began talking about his son, Stutzman displayed a very indifferent attitude about his son and showed little, if any, emotion," Garber later wrote.

Stutzman explained that Danny was sick when he picked him up at the home of Dean and Margie Barlow. Stutzman was unclear, however, about exactly what had ailed the boy. Medication was provided by the Barlows.

"Danny seemed to get worse as we traveled. He would not eat very much."

"Why didn't you take him to a doctor?" Garber asked.

"I thought the boy would get better. He was quiet, sleeping on some luggage, wrapped in a blanket in the back."

Stutzman added that he and Danny stopped at a truckstop near Salina, Kansas, to eat. Danny went inside, but did not eat much. When they came back to the car, Stutzman said, he changed Danny into a pair of blue pajamas. The boy got into the back seat of the AMC Gremlin and wrapped a blanket around himself.

"As we were driving along the boy seemed to be sleeping. I would talk to the boy but he would not answer. I thought he was sleeping."

Stutzman was unable to pinpoint the exact time sequence, but sometime later he stopped the car to see how Danny was doing. He said he noticed that Danny had slid off the luggage and that his head had become wedged between the luggage and the side of the car. A blanket was wrapped around the child's head. As he shifted the boy's body, he noticed that his son's eyes had rolled back.

Stutzman's story and his emotionless delivery were too much for Garber. He slammed his open hand on the table and Stutzman jumped. "Yeah. You're the son of a bitch that put the blanket around his face and neck!"

Garber wanted to take the man apart.

Stutzman, now nervous, shook his head. "I freaked out," he said. "I didn't know what to do."

He lifted Danny back on top of the luggage and drove on.

"Was Danny alive at that point?" Garber asked.

"I don't know. Could have been. I've often wondered if he was."

Garber grew more frustrated. Stutzman's response indicated to him that if Stutzman had been unsure whether the boy was dead or alive, then surely his intent had been to kill Danny by dumping him in that frozen field.

"Why didn't you seek medical help?"

"I didn't know what to do. I freaked out," he reiterated.

Maybe he couldn't kill the boy outright. Maybe he tried to kill the boy in increments. Maybe the only way he could kill his boy was gently. He could have left it up to the frozen air to finish a job he'd started somewhere between Wyoming and Nebraska. Garber figured Stutzman must have known the boy would be dead in thirty minutes in those frigid conditions.

The police chief felt that Stutzman's defenses might be tenuous. He wanted an emotional reaction. He could see Stutzman's eyes clearing as he tried to focus and regroup. Garber thought he was trying to remember a story he had made up.

"Did you kill your son?"

For the first time, Stutzman showed some emotion. Tears welled in his eyes. It was the first time Garber saw that the man might have actually cared for his child.

"No, the boy was sick."

"Did you use the blanket to smother the boy?"

"No."

Stutzman fought for composure.

"Look at me!" Garber demanded. "Did you kill your son?"

Tears pushed at Stutzman's eyelids. "No. No, the boy was sick."

Stutzman said he drove for a long time, and, after he had pulled himself together, he decided to leave Danny, as he put it a moment later, "where God could find him." Stutzman described how he turned off a highway onto a side road and decided to leave his son.

Garber wanted details.

"I drove a ways, pulled over, and got Danny out from the back seat. I took him off to the side near a ditch, laid him down, and covered him with snow. I would have buried him, but I didn't have anything to dig with. I wanted to leave him where God could find him."

This was too much. Garber wanted to reach across the table and smack Stutzman. Better yet, he wanted to ram him into the wall. But the good old days were gone. Instead, he pushed on and asked another question.

"Was Danny alive when you threw him outside into that ditch?"

Stutzman tensed. "I didn't throw him. I laid him there."

"Sure, Eli. Was he alive when you *laid* him there?"

Stutzman paused. "That's a very good question. I don't think so, but he could have been."

He said he continued on to Ohio, where he lied to relatives about Danny's whereabouts. He also admitted he had lied when he later told people the boy had died in a car accident. None of that, of course, would be news to Gary Young.

"Why did you lie about Danny's death?" Garber asked.

Stutzman repeated himself. "That's a very good question."

"After you left Ohio, where did you go?"

"Back to Texas."

"Did you go back to Nebraska to the spot where you left Danny?"

"Yes," Stutzman said, his eyes now drying. "I went there to see if Danny was still there. He wasn't, so I figured someone had found him."

Garber was beat from twenty-four hours without sleep, and Stutzman didn't feel too good himself. He'd had too much coffee and too many cigarettes. Five hours had passed since they'd sat down in the little interrogation room. Garber wrapped up the interview.

"Sounds like the devil really got a hold of you, Eli."

Stutzman agreed. "Could be."

"I've been doing this for twenty-three years," Garber later said of the interview, "and Eli Stutzman is the hardest one I've talked to. I can usually bullshit you pretty good, and if you're crazy, I can get crazy to get you to talk. But this guy was tough. Tough like cold."

Garber filled Young and Wyant in on the interview and left them with a final thought. "When you get down here to pick him up, don't you be kissing him," Garber warned the Nebraskans. "He's got AIDS!"

When Wyant heard about Stutzman's statement that the boy might have been alive when his father left him, he recalled the day at the field. He had noticed that the snow had melted, leaving an indentation, almost a cradle, for Danny's head.

The boy was warm when he was laid there, he thought.

CHAPTER THIRTY-THREE

Gift to town: A slain boy's name

—USA TODAY

December 15, 1987

Gary Cutler, pumped up by the spotlight for the big interview with Stutzman and Jerry Wiggins, still angry they had delayed their interview because of a departmental group photo session, drove the long, flat drive to the Tarrant County Jail. It was the first time Travis County investigators and Stutzman had had a face-to-face since he'd hightailed it from Texas in June 1985.

Plenty had happened since then. Danny Stutzman's mysterious death had made the Pritchett case important enough to work on again.

It was a different Eli Stutzman than Wiggins had seen in Austin. Now he was cornered, and he seemed frightened. Right off, he admitted he had lied to Wiggins when he made his statement to the Travis County Sheriff's Office.

"I was there when it happened," he said softly. "It might have been my gun . . ."

The story he began to tell was the same one he had told Ted Garber the day before.

"Danny and I were in bed and I heard a gunshot . . ."

Just as he started to spill it, he was cut off. Without

warning, Rob Robinson, a lawyer, unexpectedly and dramatically broke into the room where they were holding the interview.

"I'm this man's attorney. The interview is over!"

Wiggins couldn't believe it. He flashed back to his days as a cop in Sherman when he had arrested Randall Silkwood, a man who had broken into a department store and stolen dozens of leather coats. The police had recovered all but a few of them.

"Silkwood pleaded guilty to several charges and Rob Robinson represented him," Wiggins once explained. "We were talking to the judge and letting him know that we had recovered most of the coats, but that there were a few missing. The judge looked at Robinson, then at Silkwood. Robinson was wearing a leather coat, and the judge asked him to take it off. The label had been cut out. Rob Robinson remembers the story differently."

"Frank sent me," Robinson said to Wiggins and Cutler, as if a surname were unnecessary.

"Frank?" Wiggins drew a blank.

"You remember Frank Hefner?"

The detective didn't. But he did know a Steve Hefner. Almost everyone in law enforcement in Grayson County, Texas, did.

Stephen Frank Hefner had been a Sherman attorney when he'd made headlines in the Mary Ellen Bader case.

In April 1984, Bader, a 55-year-old Sherman widow with a history of mental problems, retained Hefner and handed over $67,000 for "safekeeping" while her son was seeking through the courts to have his mother declared mentally incompetent, thus gaining control of her estate.

Shortly after giving the money to Hefner, the widow's small fortune vanished.

After considerable publicity, Hefner was convicted of third-degree theft and ordered to pay restitution to Bader.

Naturally, the Texas Bar followed the conviction with a proceeding of its own. Hefner was disbarred on September 17, 1985, for numerous violations of professional conduct, including taking client funds and charging excessive and unwarranted fees.

The Sherman *Democrat* summed up this embarrassing abuse of the legal profession in an editorial the following day: “Hefner is more to be pitied than reviled. His verdict was correctly rendered by a jury that saw him for what he is: a thief.”

As one close to the Texas Bar put it: “This guy is some kind of bad.”

Tall and wavy-haired, Robert K. Robinson—who had been one of Hefner’s co-counsels during the Bader affair—didn’t exactly have a sterling record, either. Though he had escaped the kind of attention that had nailed his client and good friend, the combative attorney had problems of his own. In matters unrelated to Hefner’s, the state bar handed him a five-year probated suspension on April 9, 1987. The complaints were excessive fees and refusing to return client funds.

Hefner disappeared for a while, resurfacing on November 9, 1987, when he and Rusty Porter formed HIC Associates.

Wiggins figured Stutzman wasn’t too careful about the company he kept. The truth was, he never had been.

Cutler and Wiggins left the Tarrant County Jail with little more than they had had two years before.

So, bombarded by the local and national media, Wyant and Young, both in street clothes, pulled a fast one and slipped out of Lincoln on the Lancaster County plane to extradite Stutzman to Thayer County. For the interview, Wyant even set up a video camera, but Stutzman, in chains and handcuffs, kept his mouth shut. He had said too much already and seemed to know it. “I will not talk to you about the case on the advice of my attorney,” he said in his quiet, clipped speech.

They were too late.

“By the time I got to talk to Eli, he’d pretty well shut

up. I sat next to him on the plane. I didn't badger him. But there was always the chance he would change his mind and say something off the cuff. I wanted to be there to get it," Wyant said.

Young tried to size up the elusive mystery man.

"Inside he might have been scared spitless, but he was cool," he later said. "Eli is smart. He would like us to think he doesn't know the ways of the English world. But he does. He used being Amish as a ploy to make people think he was naive."

On the flight back to Nebraska, Young wished he'd had a camera with him, though he didn't need a photograph to remember the scene.

"A tear rolled down Stutzman's cheek as we flew over Oklahoma City. I wondered if Stutzman's tears were because he got caught or because he was sorry for what had happened."

Young later wondered if the tears hadn't been solely for his benefit.

A greeting party of media buzzards was waiting at the sheriff's office, and the investigators and the prisoner raced to get into the garage ahead of them.

Stutzman asked if he could see Danny's grave. Young and Wyant, thinking it might break him down, obliged. His head lowered, Stutzman stood out in the Chester cemetery alone, next to "Matthew's" marker. If he looked straight past the trees on the edge of the cemetery, it was less than a mile to where he had put the boy.

"It's nice what the town did for the boy," Stutzman said.

If the scene seemed touching, some knew better. It was Stutzman manipulating the people around him—or at least trying to.

"Eli's dumb like a fox," Young later said.

After booking, Stutzman settled comfortably—and quietly—into a cell in Thayer County's jail. He requested Grecian Formula, cherry cough drops, Skoal chewing tobacco, and a prescription for Restoril, a sedative to be taken in the evening time.

He also asked for copies of the *Omaha World.*

Studying up? Young wondered.

The sheriff gave Stutzman a photograph of Danny when he asked for it.

That looks good, too. Why didn't he see fit to have a photo of his son in his wallet?

He had no trouble finding room for Frank Hefner's business card.

The Nebraska investigators were frustrated by the information provided by Garber's interrogation. Maybe more could have been dragged out of him, maybe even the truth, if he had been shown photographs of Danny's body.

"That might have shaken him up some," Wyant later said.

"When we went down there looking for him, if we could have found him first, I think I would have had a chance . . . but I didn't get to talk to him right away. Not taking anything away from Mr. Garber—he's a fine police officer, but he only had limited info on the case. It's hard. I might not know something that is important—he might jump all over some detail that I might not even remember. He only knew what we told him," Wyant said later.

Young and Stutzman confined their conversations to small talk. Meanwhile, Young and Wyant did their best to find the truck stop Stutzman had told Garber his boy had eaten at hours before his death.

"It was a needle in a haystack or worse," Young said. He talked with people at a couple of truck stops near Salina, but the exercise proved futile.

"Ever try waving a picture around in a restaurant two years after the fact? It doesn't go very far," Young later said.

In Lyman, Wyoming, the *Bridger Valley Pioneer* published an ambiguous statement of half-truths by Dean and Margie

Barlow, though their names were withheld from the December 17 edition.

> We hope people will respect our privacy as we are grieving over Danny, but we will make this statement.
>
> Danny's father, who was a casual friend, knew we had had foster children. He had met our family and knew we loved children. July, 1985, he asked if we would take care of Danny for a short period of time as he had run into some difficulties. The father and we went to a lawyer, who drew up guardianship papers, so we could enroll Danny in school and take care of any medical problems if they should arise.
>
> Danny was a loving, happy little boy who had the ambition to be a soccer player. He did well in school, but missed his father whom he loved very much.
>
> What we saw of his father was a soft spoken man who was very concerned about the welfare of his son.
>
> When his father notified us that his problems were resolved, and he would pick up Danny, we had no questions since we had initiated the guardianship. We wrote a note to the school and told them Danny's last day of school would be December 13 as his father was picking him up. Danny and his father left December 14. What transpired from that date on, we have no idea. We, too, are waiting for answers.

On the same day, Frank Hefner and his HIC associate Rusty Porter came up from Fort Worth and met with Stutzman for nearly two hours. They identified themselves as "investigators" from Texas.

"Eli Stutzman is a victim," Hefner proclaimed.

December 18, 1987
Dirty, thawed, and frozen snow covered the ground like burned sugar the morning of Stutzman's arraignment. Stutzman, dressed in jeans, a down vest, and tennis shoes, looked appropriately sullen as he walked from his cell to the courthouse.

It was the day before Gary Young and his family planned to leave for Ohio for Christmas vacation.

Court-appointed attorney Lyle Koenig, whose office was a door down from County Attorney Dan Werner's, sought the dismissal of Stutzman's $500,000 cash bond. No one was surprised when Judge J. Patrick McCardle let it stand.

After all, it had taken two years to get him to Thayer county. Who was going to take a chance on Stutzman disappearing again?

Werner still didn't have a felony child-abuse case, and he knew it. He only hoped that Young and Wyant would come up with something. The Christmas and New Year's holidays bought them some time.

The preliminary hearing was set for January 11.

Jean Samuelson's phones rang like old times after Stutzman was captured. This time, though, it was different. While many of the callers were reporters, some who called were friends of Thayer County's most celebrated prisoner.

"Eli has a lot of friends, a lot of people who care," she said later.

A man from Oklahoma called to speak on Stutzman's behalf. He said Stutzman had been planning to move in with him before he was picked up in Azle.

Samuelson met with Stutzman twice after the arraignment. The man she met was shy and remorseful, a gentle and cowering lamb. She was the shepherd.

Stutzman told her the reason he'd fled Austin was that one of the investigators had shoved a grisly photograph of Glen Pritchett's body in his son's face. "Danny was terrified, because they were showing him pictures and asking him questions about the murder," he said.

The answer made sense. If it were a normal thing occurring in the household—like his father's homosexuality—it wouldn't have shaken him so. Unaccustomed details of a death would hit the child hard.

Samuelson didn't know it had been the homosexual-oriented questions directed to Danny, which Stutzman had mentioned to others like Wanda Sawyer and the Barlows, that had been his impetus to leave Austin.

At first, he denied that he was gay, but the woman gently pursued the truth.

"Eli, I've got two of your friends that have told me you are. Tell me the truth."

He finally did.

Stutzman told her that he didn't use drugs, that it had been murder victim Glen Pritchett who was the user and dealer.

When they discussed the story about Danny's death on the way to Ohio, she wondered why he hadn't called the police.

Stutzman looked blank. "Why would I do that?"

"Why didn't you call the hospital?"

"You don't call the hospital . . . he was already dead. You call family together. You call people together," he said. "Why would I call the police? What could they do?"

He knew he had to face his family, and the thought was unbearable. His father had told him, *cursed* him, that when he left the Order he and Danny would both die on the outside.

"It was the price we would pay for leaving the Amish," he said.

Samuelson wondered if Danny's death had been the result of an allergic reaction to medication. She knew some kids were allergic. Stutzman told her he had given pills to Danny at six in the evening, and at midnight he had gone back and shaken his son's foot over and over, and he'd been dead. His eyes were rolled back and white.

"When he told me the story, he wept the entire time," she later recalled. "He had to use Kleenex after Kleenex."

"Why is death stalking me?" Stutzman asked between tears.

He talked about his grandmother dying.

"She was the only one who loved me," he said, his eyes now red from tears.

He told Samuelson about the barn fire.

"He talked about the fact that the bull could have killed him. . . . He had to get all of the animals out. He carried his wife across the road into the ditch.

"He's a haunted man," Samuelson later said.

Stutzman and his tears had drained her. He had presented himself as a naive and misunderstood man—a victim of some kind of media witch hunt. Samuelson desperately wanted to believe his story.

She later described Stutzman. "He's not somebody who invites you into his life easily. He was wracked with pain over Danny, but he also had a huge pride. Gigantic pride. 'I will not show who I am to other people.' Not the hurt part."

From his cell, Stutzman wrote the following to Dean and Margie Barlow:

> Dear [Dean], [Margie] and all:
>
> How are you all? I am sure you heard on the news what took place today in court so I won't waste any ink. A lady by the name of Rev. Jean Samuels [sic] was here today. She would really like to talk to you all. She did Danny's funeral services and sure seems to be real nice. So I gave her your address so she'll probably drop you a line. I understand she now lives in Harvard. I don't know what else to write so I'll close for you. Please write if you like. . . .
>
> Sincerely,
> Eli Stutzman
> Sheriff's Office

> P.S. I would like to know about the exact date was that I left your house with Danny. I do remember it was on a Saturday morning before Christmas but I don't know what day of the month it is. Also what day of the week was Christmas in 1985? I would like a statement from you of what you feel was the kind of relationship between Danny and I.

The postscript, of course, was the reason for the letter.

On December 19, 1987, the Young family drove east to Urbana, Ohio, for Christmas. Gary Young made a detour from his in-law's place in Urbana and poked around the Amish Country of Wayne and Holmes counties, looking for leads to the Stutzman case.

In Mount Eaton, Dr. Elton Lehman showed him Stutzman's medical records and filled him in on the story of Ida's death, the barn fire, and Stutzman's mental breakdowns.

Young also picked up copies of Stutzman's driver's-license forms, noting how Stutzman had apparently used his left hand for his signature. Young figured Stutzman had done the fake initial and birth date and obtained a second social security number in order to "lose himself in the computer."

"Maybe the middle initial was C so that later, if someone asked, he could say 'it was a clerical mistake—it should have been E.' "

No one Young talked with ever referred to Stutzman as "Junior."

Trailed by a photographer and a reporter from *People*, Young visited the cabinet shop of Abner Petersheim, in Dalton, and met the young Amishman who had first wondered if Little Boy Blue could be Danny Stutzman. The Amishman described how, after Petersheim had told him about the story in *Reader's Digest*, it had come to him that the child in the story must be Danny Stutzman.

"After what Abner told me and what I saw, there were too many coincidences that fit together," he said.

When he returned to Hebron, Gary Young had more questions than answers. Where Eli Stutzman was concerned, that seemed to be par for the course.

Everyone, of course, wanted answers. Ohio, for Ida's death; Texas, for Glen Pritchett's; Colorado, even, for the two murders they had been sitting on for two years; and Nebraska, for Danny.

Young wondered if the bunch of them shouldn't hold their breath. Stutzman wasn't talking and there didn't seem to be any evidence.

The media attention on Thayer County heated up again after Stutzman's arrest. Tom Brokaw and Dan Rather introduced segments about Stutzman on the evening news. The NBC report even featured a family portrait of the Barlows—though it didn't name them.

To everyone, they were the kindly foster family from Wyoming. Nobody thought to ask how it was they had come to know Eli Stutzman.

December 21, 1987

Sitting in his smoke-choked office at the state patrol office in Lincoln, Investigator Wyant played it nice and easy when he got Kenny Hankins on the phone at his Four Corners trailer home.

Hankins told Wyant that he had first met Stutzman in 1981, when Stutzman lived on his ranch. Wyant wanted to know how close Hankins and Stutzman were, and a nervous and intimidated Hankins sweated the answer. He didn't want anyone to know his personal life.

"I can't say we were too close. We were on and off friends," he said.

Wyant asked Hankins if he had any recollections of Danny Stutzman. Hankins indicated that he had seen the boy "seven or eight" times and that the boy had always been healthy and seemed happy.

"When was the last time you saw Danny?"

Hankins searched his memory. "The last time would have been 1985, when Eli was working up at Chuck Freeman's place in Aztec. Eli and Danny lived up at the ranch in Cedar Hill."

He also described the visit—in his report, Wyant noted April 1986—during which Stutzman had told him that Danny had died in a car accident in Wyoming.

"One thing that made me feel uncomfortable about it was that he didn't seem to show any emotion when he was telling me about his boy dying like that. Didn't seem right," Hankins said.

Hankins further advised the Nebraska investigator that Stutzman had told him a man in Texas had been killed with his gun. Furthermore, he said that his attorney had told him to "get out of the state or he would be arrested for murder."

The last line of Wyant's report was chilling: "Hankins also made a statement that Eli told him that because of the resentment to the Amish faith Eli told him that he would rather see Danny dead than for Danny to go back to Eli's folks."

Wyant wondered if that could be the motive.

Hankins said he thought Stutzman had been at the Nebraska funeral for Little Boy Blue.

"We videotaped it, and Eli Stutzman wasn't there," Wyant responded.

"But you were looking for a man. You should have been looking for a *woman*."

Hankins knew Stutzman sometimes went in drag. Not often, but he had seen him in a dress a couple of times.

"I think he was keeping an eye on Danny being found. I really felt that's why he went back, that he was back for the funeral," Hankins later said.

Durango police detective Bill Perreira contacted Thayer County sheriff's deputy Bill McPherson with a little tidbit about a couple of murders he was working on—the victims were men named David Tyler and Dennis Slaeter.

A doctor from the Four Corners area had seen a television news broadcast of Stutzman's capture and indicated that Stutzman was a man who had worked on his house.

"We're wondering if you can put Stutzman in our area about the time of the murders—November and December 1985?"

McPherson said he could, and made arrangements with the state patrol's criminal investigation division to have Stutzman's prints sent down to Colorado.

While McPherson was fielding calls and digging into the Stutzman story in the sheriff's absence, a photo opportunity took place at the Chester cemetery. Funeral director Lon Adam's wife, Dixie, posed in front of Matthew's marker, now etched with Daniel E. Stutzman's name and date of birth.

Cameras clicked and rolled as Mrs. Adams choked with emotion.

At the same time, old lovers listed in Stutzman's address book were being milked for funds with the persistence of a telemarketing firm.

"Please help us defend Eli in Nebraska. Send whatever you can," the man who identified himself as Stutzman's lawyer told Al Jorgensen.

Jorgensen wrote out a check for $50. The Eli Stutzman that he knew would never have harmed his boy. Then again, there was that letter Stutzman had sent on the day he picked up his boy; Jorgensen kept it in a file box with the others. It was a letter that the police would never see.

"I must admit," Jorgensen later said, "I was disturbed by the letter's contents."

Christmas cookies again piled up, and hot mulled cider still steamed back by the sink, but Christmas Eve in the Thayer County Sheriff's Office was decidedly different in 1987 than it had been two years before when Danny Stutzman's body was found in Chester.

As Stutzman had been two years ago, Gary Young was in Ohio celebrating Christmas. This year found Eli Stutzman in the Thayer County Jail.

Stutzman, the father of Little Boy Blue, sat in his cell eating a tray of goodies the Reverend Bill Anderson had brought in. Stutzman, who had found God again—or at least wanted those around him to think so—requested a copy of the Book of Psalms.

"Amen!" was inscribed on the jail sign-in sheet by the faithful who brought the book to him.

Christmas Eve gave Young a few minutes to sit back and think. Everything had happened so fast.

I wish I could just stop the world for a few minutes, he thought. *Give me a minute to catch up!*

More stories about Stutzman and the murder in Texas got the attention of the Amish and *Englischers* who had known Eli Stutzman.

"Eli Stutzman was making drug runs to the Mexican border."

"Danny was sexually abused."

"Eli's construction business was only a front."

Later, when Wayne County sheriff's deputy Tim Brown's work on the Stutzman case came under fire from people like Diane Swartzentruber, who assumed he and Stutzman had been more than friends, the deputy was already in too deep.

"He lived with Stutzman, for God's sake, and he says he's not gay? Right!"

Brown had even been on television. *People* magazine had interviewed him. He was a cop, he *had* to talk with them. The sheriff's department hadn't instructed him not to. Besides, he was running around—just ahead of the press—interviewing those who knew Stutzman—people he said wouldn't talk to anyone but him.

He gave all of his information to Captain Jim Gasser, who funneled reports to Nebraska and Texas investigators.

"My job comes first. If it were a minor thing . . . but murder, no way. I wasn't going to do anything to cover for him. I don't want any shadows on me," Brown later said.

CHAPTER THIRTY-FOUR

December 28, 1987

When state patrol investigator Jack Wyant flew into Lyman, Wyoming, he had reservations at a mom-and-pop motel, and the idea that Dean and Margie Barlow were holding the key to the mystery of Little Boy Blue.

Over the phone, the Barlows had seemed reluctant, even asking if they should have an attorney present. They were frightened. Maybe it was the result of their conversations with a relentless Gary Young, who had made them feel as though he thought they had something to hide. Young *did*, of course, but he didn't mean to come across as brusque. He had a job to do.

For Dean Barlow, 39, a slender six-footer, the events unfolding must have been his worst nightmare. His sexual secret would be told, exposed, put up on the front page of the local paper. His wife, Margie, a small, reddish-blond woman seven years older than her husband, couldn't have liked the situation any better. Yet throughout the interview she displayed a cooler and more articulate manner than her husband. Margie taught creative writing at Western Wyoming Community College in Rock Springs.

It was mid-afternoon when Wyant arrived at their neat house on Lincoln Street. The Barlows were guardedly friendly. As they had told Amos Gingerich when he and the other Amish had come to Wyoming, they wanted answers, too.

Before the interview began they made it clear they didn't think Danny had been murdered by his father.

Wyant set up his tape recorder and sized up the subjects. Dean Barlow seemed agitated. There was good reason for that, and Wyant knew it. He asked Barlow how Stutzman had come into his life.

Barlow hesitated.

"I met Eli in Durango, Colorado. That's the only thing that's kind of private and I don't want to discuss," Barlow said rather dramatically, as though he had practiced the words.

Wyant planned to corner the man later, away from his wife, which he did when Margie left the room.

"I don't care if you like to suck . . . I have a murder to solve . . ."

Barlow admitted he and Stutzman had sex, but it had been only "one time."

He didn't volunteer, however, that he and Stutzman had met through a magazine.

Barlow said the next time he saw the Stutzmans was when they came up from Texas for Christmas 1983. After that, they lost contact. Accordingly, he was surprised to hear from Stutzman when in late June or early July 1985 he called to see if the Barlows could take Danny. He was having trouble with the police regarding the murder of an employee.

Barlow reasoned that Stutzman had called the Barlows because he knew they had been foster parents in Hawaii and Colorado. Barlow also said he had been a "Big Brother" in Hawaii for eight years.

Wyant let the fidgety schoolteacher ramble before asking for details about Texas.

"Danny had gone through a pretty brutal session with an investigator," Barlow said, "and Danny had been upset about it." Barlow explained that Stutzman had wanted to "get Danny out of Austin as quickly as possible. There was some question about a rifle. Later he told us it was not his gun that killed his employee."

"Did he say who had been killed?"

"A guy from Wyoming. He had paid him two weeks earlier to go back to Wyoming to be with his family." Stutzman had never indicated to Barlow that Glen Pritchett had been his roommate.

Barlow picked up steam. "This sounds real crazy. I questioned him at the time. He said his lawyer in Texas told him to leave Austin and take Danny to Colorado."

When Barlow had picked Danny and Eli up at the Greyhound station in Salt Lake City, the boy and his father were carrying only a couple of small bags between them.

Stutzman had signed over two checks totaling $1,950 for Danny's care and clothing. He told the Barlows that he knew who the killer was and was going to look for him in Denver and Ohio.

"He said a private investigator in Denver was looking for this guy," Barlow said.

Wyant asked why the Barlows had let such a bizarre story pass as truth. Why hadn't they questioned Stutzman more thoroughly?

"It was an awkward topic—we didn't want to be rude and ask him too much," Dean Barlow said.

Stutzman said he had signed over his checking account to his Austin attorney.

"At the time it seemed real bizarre," Barlow conceded.

I'm sure it did, Wyant thought.

Barlow said Stutzman left on July 5 or 6.

"He seemed real anxious to leave," he said.

Wyant asked if Stutzman's story had seemed genuine.

"We never questioned his honesty until all of this. We never thought he was lying. My impression was that he was the Quaker Oats guy on the Quaker Oats box—strong Amish, kind, sensitive," Dean Barlow said.

Wyant later wondered if Barlow had been in love with Stutzman. The way the Wyoming man protected and talked about Stutzman, it was like a man talking about the woman he loved.

Yet Margie Barlow's statements mirrored her husband's.

"I think he's naive and he doesn't understand the ways of the world," she said softly, sitting next to her husband as he defended Stutzman.

Maybe she didn't know about the two of them, but, of course, she *had* to.

Dean Barlow told Wyant that he had gone with Stutzman when he purchased eastbound bus tickets, but that he hadn't paid any attention to the man's destination.

And Danny Stutzman, for one, hadn't known how long his father was going to be gone.

"Just a few weeks," Stutzman had told the boy before he left on the Greyhound. He told the Barlows that enrolling Danny in school wouldn't be necessary—he'd take care of his problems and be back for Danny.

Wyant coolly flipped the tape over.

Occasionally Stutzman called to have Barlow wire money through the Western Union office at the Evanston, Wyoming, bus station. Stutzman had arranged it so that he would pick the funds up by giving his mother's maiden name: Susan Miller. The mother whose illness had been an excuse wherever Stutzman went had come in handy again.

A mouse scurried across the floor, provoking a tension-releasing laugh. Dean Barlow laughed the hardest.

Wyant, who didn't know about the parties in Colorado and was still trying to see if a case could be made for felony child abuse, asked what kind of a father Stutzman had been.

It was Margie Barlow who took the lead.

"Kids would ask him why his father left him, why he was here, but he would never answer," she said. " 'My dad's the best,' he'd say."

"Danny *missed* his father," Barlow added. "At the end of every phone conversation Danny would cry. 'How long before you come and get me?' "

Maybe it had never occurred to the Barlows just *why* Danny Stutzman had cried after every call. What was it that

Eli Stutzman had said to his boy? Was he threatening the boy?

Sam Miller said Danny knew about the murder in Texas—he was sitting in the truck when Stutzman confessed to it, and the boy showed no reaction—yet the Barlows maintained Danny never mentioned it.

Not a single word, they said.

Margie and Dean Barlow said they had liked Danny. "Danny was a cuddlebug. He would jump in our laps." Indeed, he was so much of a "cuddlebug" that one of the Barlow children became jealous of the attention Danny got from his parents.

Wyant turned his attention to the events leading to the boy's death.

"Eli told us and Danny that he'd be picking Danny up to take him to Ohio for Christmas."

Barlow said Stutzman had called December 13 to tell them he was on his way to get Danny. That was the same day he had mailed the letter to Jorgensen telling him Danny probably wouldn't be with him.

The Barlows had been surprised, they said, because Stutzman had changed his plans and would be taking the boy out of school before his third-grade class party.

But, as usual, Stutzman had a convincing reason.

"He said his mother had problems with her lungs," Dean Barlow said.

"He felt that his mother would die," Margie added.

Because Danny always got so excited, the Barlows said they waited until the last minute to tell him that his dad was planning to get him.

Stutzman showed up after dark, driving the Gremlin, the same day.

The Texas murder was on Dean Barlow's mind, and he asked about it.

"He said that it was cleared up. The guy had been arrested and convicted. It was the fastest murder trial I'd ever heard of," Barlow said.

Stutzman said he expected to be in Ohio in two days.

It was another lie, of course. Stutzman had planned to stay with Yost and Jorgensen before showing up in Ohio.

Wyant, unfortunately, didn't know any of that. Jorgensen and Yost were unknown to the investigator and would remain so, though both men had read about the Little Boy Blue story in the paper when Stutzman was arrested. Neither man came forward.

"He was going to leave Danny with his folks for Christmas," Barlow said.

That, of course, didn't fit with what Stutzman had told others. He hated the Amish. He would never allow Danny to stay with his parents.

"He's kind of gotten away from the language . . ." he had written in the letter to Jorgensen that he mailed the day before he and Danny left Wyoming for Ohio.

Wyant focused on the boy's health. The Barlows had suggested numerous times to Gary Young that the boy had been ill.

Margie Barlow explained that Danny had complained of a sore throat and been diagnosed with hemopholis, a viral infection similar to strep, and had been given a prescription for Ceclor on December 11 for twenty-one pills, to be given over seven days.

When Stutzman got the boy, Margie Barlow had told him about the virus and its treatment. "I wrote instructions for the medicine, and made it clear that Danny needed another throat swab," she told Wyant.

Wyant probed. "His general health . . . would you describe him as getting better?"

"Yes," Margie answered quickly.

Wyant thought it was worth checking out. But he didn't think Danny had died of a virus.

Father and son slept at the Barlows', and left before 8:00 A.M. on December 14. Before leaving, Stutzman gave Dean and Margie an Amish quilt as a thank-you for all they had done.

Later, around January, Dean Barlow said he and Stutzman spoke again. Barlow asked about Danny and about an

Amish china hutch Stutzman had said he would have made for them. Stutzman said he had enrolled Danny in a Mennonite school in Benton, Ohio, and was working at Troyer's Cabinet Shop. Margie Barlow also got on the line and asked if Stutzman had had Danny's school records forwarded from Wyoming. Stutzman said the Mennonites didn't require any records.

"How did Danny like his gifts—the soccer ball and the Garfield?"

"Danny enjoyed them. *Loved them.*" Stutzman had said.

Wyant asked if the Barlows had heard from Stutzman after January.

They said they had, in April 1986.

Margie had wanted to know if the Mennonite school was doing anything for Danny's speech.

Stutzman indicated that progress was being made and that the boy was improving.

Like the first time, when the Barlows asked to speak with Danny, Stutzman claimed he was at church or at the neighbors' playing.

"Why hasn't Danny written?"

"I'll remind him," Stutzman promised.

At the end of June 1986, the Barlows said Stutzman called to say that he and Danny were going to take a vacation trip to California, and that Stutzman would bring the hutch with him then.

"Have you heard from my in-laws?" Stutzman asked.

"No, why?" Barlow said.

"I just wanted to know."

Barlow asked for Stutzman's phone number, and the former Amishman gave the first three digits before stopping and saying he was very difficult to reach.

After hanging up, Barlow called his wife, who was out of town visiting relatives at the time. "I just got a really strange call from Eli," he said.

The Barlows indicated that they had spoken with Stutzman a couple of times since his confinement in the Thayer

County Jail, but that they were reluctant to give any information about those calls. Wyant pursued it, and finally Dean Barlow agreed.

"There's no information that I have that could hurt Eli," he said.

Eli Stutzman had cried on the phone, telling them the story of Danny dropping dead in the middle of the night—the *second* day after he left Lyman.

Stutzman mentioned the blue sleeper.

"Eli told us the sleeper was a Christmas present for Danny," Barlow explained.

Barlow had called Stutzman's attorney and told him about Danny's illness, but the attorney didn't seem interested.

"He said he knew 'the boy wasn't sick enough to die.' "

The attorney said that people in Texas had the Gremlin and that it was the car's faulty exhaust system that had killed Danny. The boy had died of asphyxiation related to carbon monoxide poisoning.

Barlow said the Nebraska attorney was getting his information through a man named Robinson, in Texas.

More than two hours had passed when Wyant got up to leave. The picture of Stutzman as a pathological liar and manipulator had become even more clear. Wyant felt that the Barlows had been honest, but had held something back.

"We don't think there is any way on the face of this earth that Eli killed Danny. No way," Dean Barlow said.

"We're after the truth," Wyant said. "I'm sure that if and when it goes to court you'll be in court as a witness."

"I hope not." Barlow said, with an annoying burst of nervous laughter.

Wyant leaned forward. "If you have nothing to hide there is no reason to be nervous."

He got the approval necessary for obtaining Barlow's bank records and Danny's medical records. The next day he picked up copies of Danny's December 11 prescription from the drugstore in Lyman and paid a visit to Dr. Jane Wuchinich's office at the Bridger Valley Health Services.

"Dr. Jane," as they called her, was on vacation, but an associate provided records indicating that Danny's throat had been swabbed for culture on December 10.

The medical records backed up what Dean and Margie Barlow had told him.

Wyant went on to Kemmerer and picked up microfilmed copies of the checks Stutzman had signed over to the Barlows. A trip to the bus station to find out where the money for "Susan Miller" had gone proved futile.

Wyant flew out of Salt Lake City thinking he didn't have anything to make a case against Stutzman.

"By then I was getting to know Eli real good," Wyant said later.

With the Danny Stutzman/Little Boy Blue mess out in the open and the rumors around Wayne County burning like a tire fire, Diane Swartzentruber took to her telephone again. This time she called Gary Cutler in Austin.

She and Chris had visited with Amos Slabaugh again, and the story of the Texas murder, mixed in with some wild innuendo, was being discussed at feed mills, barn raisings—anyplace the Amish gathered.

Diane told Cutler that Sam H. Miller, a young man from the Freeport/Newcomerstown area, had been in Austin around the time of Pritchett's murder. He had since gone into the navy.

"He found bloody clothes in a closet, hidden under some things. He got frightened and left."

She told Cutler she was going to go see the Amish again to see what else she could learn.

"I was a go-between for the Amish who didn't want to get involved. If they didn't speak up, he was going to get away with it and kill more and more people," she said later.

The homicide investigator appreciated the lead, though it was not a particularly good one. After all, Diane Swartzentruber had said other rumors circulating included one about a woman, a girlfriend of Stutzman's, who had died thirty days before he was captured in Azle. Additionally, word had it that two other men—"bosses of Stutzman's"—had died mysteriously, too.

Gary Cutler needed to trace Diane Swartzentruber's information to its source—which meant Sam Miller. When Miller had been interviewed in Texas he had made no mention of the "bloody clothes." What his questioners didn't know was that Stutzman had made his comments about killing Pritchett *after* he gave his statement to the sheriff. The comments were made, in fact, in Stutzman's truck on his way home from the sheriff's office.

Though new information was finding its way to Travis County, in some ways investigators had even less than they did in June 1985. The rifle Stutzman gave to Jerry Wiggins ended up on a destruction order signed by Judge Jon Wisser.

"Ballistics didn't match, but you try telling that to a jury. 'We accidentally chopped up the potential murder weapon.' Right. That sounds real bad," Wiggins later said.

CHAPTER THIRTY-FIVE

Travis County homicide detective Jerry Wiggins had to sit back down when a TV reporter called him and announced that Stutzman had signed over book, movie, and television rights to disbarred attorney Frank Hefner. It was unbelievable.

But it was true. The next day Hefner was spouting off on TV and in the paper. When asked who had hired him and HIC, the lawyer-turned-con-turned-investigator-turned-movie-magnate indicated it had been Rob Robinson.

Not Rob Robinson again. Wiggins thought. *Eli Stutzman sure knows how to pick 'em.*

Movie rights would pay Stutzman's legal bills.

"He doesn't have a lot of resources," Hefner explained to a *Dallas Morning News* reporter. "We thought it would be of economic value to help pay for his defense. It's like looking around and all you see on your dresser is the watch your grandfather gave you, and you see what you can get for it."

Hefner proclaimed Stutzman innocent and indicated that HIC had retained Omaha attorney William Gallup. Court-appointed Lyle Koenig was out.

The agreement between Stutzman, HIC, and Robinson raised a few eyebrows at the Texas State Bar in Austin, and in Thayer County, Nebraska.

"If there is such an agreement—and I haven't seen

one—I have grave questions as to whether it's ethical or not. My concerns aren't directed so much to Mr. Stutzman as to the attorney in this matter," Dan Werner told reporters hanging around the county courthouse.

Gallup told reporters he had asked that the felony charges against Stutzman be reduced to the misdemeanor "abandoning a human body." Stutzman would plead guilty to the charge, he said.

Dan Werner didn't say a word about that.

Sheriff Young shook his head when he heard that the defense attorney might contest that Danny had died of carbon monoxide poisoning caused by a leaky exhaust system.

He knew that the Lincoln and St. Louis autopsies had indicated carbon monoxide levels no greater than what might be absorbed during normal car travel.

Stutzman smothered his son, he thought.

Wyant still believed that Danny had been alive when he was put outside to freeze. He focused on Stutzman's statement to Ted Garber conceding that Danny might have been alive when left in the ditch in Chester.

Either scenario was possible, and as the Nebraskans came to know Stutzman, either was likely.

The leaky exhaust was typical Stutzman—a convenient excuse.

"We have the car. We have pictures. We can prove it," Frank Hefner later claimed.

December 30, 1987

With Stutzman awaiting his hearing, Ted Garber decided to dig a little deeper. The news media had stirred up a thick, wretched pot. Phone calls from the media after Stutzman's arrest had been continuous, and, Garber thought, a little annoying. Garber liked media attention, but a call from an out-of-state reporter at the ungodly hour of 2:00 A.M.?

Garber called Elvy Kenyon in for an interview. A tape recorder whirred as the two began speaking about Stutzman. It was 3:03 P.M.

At 48, Kenyon looked older than his age, the inevitable

result of sunshine and his share of beer. He said he and Stutzman, both carpenters, were drinking buddies who had met two years before. They had worked on two or three jobs together in Dallas.

"I wrecked my car and he give me a ride, and he was working in Dallas and I worked in Dallas a time or two. So I worked over at Dallas with him on a job," he said.

He told the police chief that they had met when Stutzman had just returned from a trip to Colorado, driving the Gremlin.

"What did you do?" Kenyon recalled asking, just making small talk with a person he said had just happened along.

"He said, 'My boy was in a car wreck.' The boy's name was Danny. And it bumped his head and—he had a word for it—blood clot."

Garber pressed for details: "Did he tell you where this wreck was, where this wreck occurred?"

"I think he said Colorado. Now I'm not for sure on that. But he said his godfather and his little boy were in the wreck, too. I didn't have no reason to doubt him. And the boy died. That was the whole deal on his family then."

The boy's body, Stutzman told Kenyon, had been sent to New Mexico for burial.

Garber wondered why Kenyon believed such a story. Why would a man send a body all the way to New Mexico for burial? It wasn't the boy's home; his family wasn't there. Garber thought it was a stupid lie—the kind that could easily be disproved with a telephone call.

Stutzman had said that his house on Toronto was sold and that he needed a place to stay, and Kenyon had offered his place as long as they split groceries and utilities.

Stutzman had moved in a week or two before he was arrested.

When the word got out through the local media that the police in Nebraska were looking for a man named Eli Stutzman who was believed to be in the Dallas–Fort Worth area,

Kenyon said Stutzman was quick to place the blame somewhere else.

"Tell me in as much detail as you can when you saw the article in the paper about him and his son. What happened then?" Garber asked.

"He went down and got the Sunday paper, and he brought the paper back, and I looked at the paper. He said, 'That's a lie. That's not me. That's my cousin!' "

"There are lots of Amish named Eli Stutzman," Stutzman said. "It's a cousin of mine that they are looking for."

Kenyon confronted him. "Eli, tell me the truth. That's you. I thought you told me your boy died in an accident in Colorado."

"I didn't want to tell you the boy died on the way to Ohio. What they are saying is not the way it was. It didn't happen that way. It's not true."

Kenyon had no way of knowing if his friend was lying or telling the truth this time.

But the picture in the paper *was* his.

"I said, 'Well, you better go down to the police and tell them and straighten things out.' "

Stutzman said he would, after he got hold of his lawyer.

"Eli got on the phone and talked with someone who he said was his lawyer, and then he got off the phone and said that his lawyer told him he would meet him down at the police Monday morning.

"And the next thing, y'all were here."

"Do you remember what attorney that was? Did he ever tell you?"

"No. I don't believe he ever said his name. But he told me that he was a real-estate attorney, and he recommended him to somebody else."

"As time went along, what happened? Was there any mention about his son?"

"No. He showed me a picture of him one time. He said, 'This is Danny.' That's the only time he discussed anything about his boy."

"There was no more mention of the boy after, other than when he showed you the picture?"

"That was all."

"At what point did he tell you the truth, that he was lying to you?"

"That was the next time I talked to him. That was on the telephone. He said, 'Well, I lied to you. I'm sorry I lied to you and got you in trouble.' "

"He called you from the jail?"

"Yeah."

"That was the first time that you heard from him straight out that he had been telling you stories?"

"Yeah. That's what he told me. 'I lied to you, it didn't happen the way I told you, but it didn't happen the way it was in the paper.' "

Kenyon didn't know what to believe.

"Did he ever tell you how it happened?"

Kenyon said he didn't ask. "I didn't say 'Hey, man, did you do what they said or not?' "

Garber wanted to learn more about the attorneys Stutzman had hired.

"When did the attorney from Dallas—did he mention the name Robinson?"

"Yeah."

Kenyon was being helpful within his own limits. He did not volunteer anything. Garber had to ask even the most obvious and tedious follow-up. "What did he say?"

"He said that was his attorney, and he was gonna take care of everything."

"Did Eli tell you about signing over any rights to this attorney?"

"He told me that they had some contracts for him to sign. I don't know what he called them . . . just contracts."

"Did they have anything to do with book rights or story rights?"

"Yeah, book rights."

"Since all of this has come down, you mentioned to me that an attorney or some representatives from an attorney in Dallas had come out to your house. You want to tell me what the situation was?"

"That was on his pickup. I bought the pickup from Junior."

"And Junior is who?"

"Eli. I bought the pickup from him. And y'all had impounded it here in Azle, and the attorneys or the guys from Dallas or whoever they are—they was going to pick up the pickup.

"So I give up the title—he left the title and everything with me—so they could go pick up the truck. And I done paid him four hundred dollars on it, and I was going to pay the rest of it when they bring the title back. They brought the pickup but they didn't bring the title back."

"Did they say anything to you in regards to testimony?"

"They said I might have to go up as a character witness."

"Did he express any remorse to you about the situation with his son?"

Kenyon said they hadn't talked about that, and the interview was over at 3:25 P.M.

CHAPTER THIRTY-SIX

The Nebraskans were going to plead Eli Stutzman on two misdemeanors—abandoning a body and concealing a death. *Two lousy misdemeanors*. When he heard the news, Azle police chief Ted Garber winced hard. It was a joke. He knew that Stutzman was a killer.

Garber considered calling Gary Young. Words ran through his head: *This is your business and I don't want to tell you your business, but you need to pursue this. This is a murder. The man is a killer. He told me the boy might have been alive when he put him in the field.*

As far as Garber could see, they were going to slap a killer on the wrist and send him off for a few months of time.

"Knowing Eli, he'd probably think prison was some kind of vacation," he later said.

January 11, 1988

Chuck Kleveland did an about-face on the concrete steps of the Thayer County Courthouse on the morning of Stutzman's hearing. He had come to renew a vehicle license, but was confronted by the commotion of a group of media people. The man who had found Danny Stutzman's body didn't want to answer any more questions about how he had felt and what he had done two Christmases ago. He was not, he later said, a hero.

Inside the courthouse, Stutzman, in jeans and flannel shirt, sat facing the spectators and attorneys; his face was ashen and his eyes rarely met the gaze of others. He looked the part of a spectator—a farmer or a mechanic or anyone else from the community. Word had sifted through the courtroom: Eli Stutzman was going to plead guilty and, more important, he was going to tell his story.

The legal rigmarole went quickly. County Attorney Werner acknowledged that he and Bill Gallup had agreed Stutzman would plead guilty to the misdemeanors. Though there had been no plea bargain, Werner indicated that the state had agreed to dismiss without prejudice the child-abuse charge. As a part of the agreement, Stutzman would take the stand.

Young and Wyant, sitting with the other spectators in Judge Pat McCardle's courtroom, were finally going to hear Stutzman's side of the story.

Gallup eased into his questioning of Stutzman. "Now, did there come a point in time when you left your son with some people in Wyoming?"

"Yes."

"When was that?"

"That was in July of 1985."

"And how did you happen to leave him with those people?"

"Because of some things I needed to take care of in a couple of different places. I felt it would be better to leave him with some friends rather than be going from place to place."

"Before you picked up your son, and before you had gone off to Wyoming, had you had some religious problems with your family?"

"Yes."

"What was that over, briefly?"

"Just disagreements in—disagreements with different rules of the church."

"And this caused some dissension between you and your father, for example?"

"Right."

"Did that lead you to leave the family?"

"Right."

"Now, when did you pick up your son in Wyoming?"

"On December 14, in 1985."

"And what were you driving?"

" '75 AMC."

"What was the general condition of the car?"

"It had close to a hundred thousand miles on it, so it was not in A-1 condition. It ran fairly good."

Stutzman said he had put down the backseat of the Gremlin so that Danny would have more room. He gave him a sleeping bag to curl up with.

"What was your son's condition when you left Wyoming? Had he been treated for any illness?"

"Yes."

"What?"

"He was on medication." Stutzman explained that Dean and Margie Barlow had given him a prescription and told him how to administer the medication.

Stutzman said he had mapped out a route to Ohio via U.S. 81. He said he took 80 at first.

"I was looking for a place to cut across to 70, which is the route I used traveling back and forth to—from Colorado to Ohio. It seemed like 81 was the most appropriate route to cut across."

The truth was that 81 provided a direct route to John Yost's place.

Gallup led Stutzman like a horse.

"At some point in the trip, did you notice anything unusual about your son, at any point, or notice that he wasn't alert, or what happened if anything?"

"In the afternoon he complained a little bit about not feeling real good and I suggested stopping, not continuing, for seeing a doctor, and he said he just wanted to lay down and he would be fine."

Stutzman moved some luggage and toys so that the boy would have room to stretch out.

"What eventually drew your attention to the back of the car?"

"Well, later, late in the evening, during the night—I believe it was time for his medication—I reached back while driving and got a hold of him and I couldn't get him awake."

Gallup looked concerned. "He didn't respond to touch?"

"Right. He did not respond. So I pulled over to a—to see what it was about. I was shocked to see that there was no response at all."

Gallup questioned Stutzman about his medical training, and the witness said that he had been a hospital orderly and knew the techniques of CPR and heart massage.

"So, then, would you relate to the judge what, if anything, you did when you found your son didn't respond to your touch?"

"I was shocked. I could not believe finding him that way."

"What did you do?"

"I—"

Gallup told him to speak up.

"I tried desperately to revive him."

Stutzman said that he tried mouth-to-mouth resuscitation and heart massage, but that nothing worked. The boy was dead, and Stutzman didn't know what to do. He was somewhere on U.S. 81, close to Chester, Nebraska. He drove to a place off the main road.

"I had difficulty facing the fact that he had died. I couldn't understand, couldn't figure out why he died, or would have died under the circumstances."

"I pulled off the main road and made another turn or two and found a place in a valley, up in a valley, where I thought there was nobody else around, and I spent some time, quite a bit of time there praying, and I tried again to revive him and I just—"

Gallup cut him off. "Did you think at any time that

maybe this was due to the disfavor of your God for the way you had left the church? Was that something that was bothering you?"

The defendant shook his head. "No, I can't tell—I don't remember that crossing my mind, that I felt guilty because of my past in any way."

Stutzman thought he stayed in the valley for several hours, trying to figure out what to do with the body in the back of the Gremlin.

"I knew that I could go and try and, you know, find a phone and get an emergency squad, but I did have feelings that maybe the facts would be against me."

"What?"

"The facts would be against me from my family."

Stutzman's voice was so soft, Gallup again asked him to speak louder.

"I thought the fact about my family might be against me, that I was not taking proper care of him. I feared for that . . . and I had a big difficulty realizing what had happened and why it would have happened. I could not understand why it would have happened."

Stutzman said he continued home to Ohio, where he told a number of people different stories about Danny's whereabouts and death.

"I guess I did not want to face the fact that he actually had died. I had difficulty accepting that."

Gallup wrapped it up. "As you sit there right now, you don't know what caused your son's death, is that a fair statement?"

"Right."

Gallup reminded Stutzman that a Saint Louis pathologist had favored the conclusion that Danny had died a natural death.

"Would that help let you sleep a little better?"

"Yes, I believe so."

. . .

It was Dan Werner's turn, and though he was glad for the chance to confront the accused, he wished that he'd had more time to prepare. Maybe information would have come to light possibly leading to an investigation that would result in an abuse or murder charge.

"Mr. Stutzman, let's go back a little bit. You left Danny with foster parents in Wyoming, is that right?"

"Friends, so to speak."

Stutzman said that he and Danny had left Austin, Texas, and arrived at the Barlows', in Lyman, Wyoming, where he left his son.

"Why did you leave Danny with the Barlow family?"

"I was preparing to move, and I was afraid that because of moves . . . I would probably not be able to avoid having to change schools, not be able to keep him in one school for the first half of the school year. And another reason was because of a roommate of mine . . . his body was found, I was informed—had been informed recently, and I was questioned, I had given a statement, and my son was also questioned, and it left a bad effect on him by some of the questions he was asked by the law."

Stutzman said his roommate had left Texas, and that he had no idea he was missing until the sheriff came calling.

Werner asked why Stutzman and his son had left Austin.

"Because of the psychological effect it left on him, some of the questions that were asked. Plus I had planned on moving, had some things to take care of in the Durango area."

After leaving Danny with the Barlows, Stutzman saw friends in Ohio, before returning to Texas. He spent most of his time with Owen Barker in Azle. A month later, he left for Durango to complete some ranch business. He said he did some remodeling for Chuck Freeman.

Stutzman said that he had planned to pick up Danny and spend Christmas in Ohio and then return to Texas.

Werner made his move. He was looking for the *why* of Danny Stutzman's death.

"Mr. Stutzman, do you resent your Amish upbringing?"

"No, I don't."

"Do you ever recall telling Mr. Chuck Freeman that you resented your Amish upbringing?"

"I may have mentioned that I didn't get the education I could—probably would—have benefited from. But as far as the strict rules, being brought up, I have no—"

Werner cut short Stutzman's ramblings.

"Do you recall telling Mr. Freeman that you did not wish to see your son brought up in the Amish faith?"

"Yes, I felt he had—"

Again, Werner interrupted the defendant.

"Were you concerned at that point in time that your parents might get custody of Danny?"

"I would not know any reason why."

Now *the* question.

"Did you tell Mr. Freeman that you would rather see Danny dead than being brought up as Amish?"

Stutzman shook his head. "I don't remember making that statement."

The county attorney continued to push his scenario of Little Boy Blue's death. Stutzman said that he had returned to Wyoming on December 13 and that he and Danny had left the following morning. Danny seemed to be "in good health and spirits," but he had a virus and was on medication for it.

Margie Barlow gave the boy the medication that night, before bedtime, and told Stutzman that it was required four times a day. Stutzman and Danny stopped for a haircut on their way out of Lyman.

"Then you went directly to 80, is that correct?"

"Filled up with gas. Bought some soft drinks and got a few breakfast things and we ate in the car."

"And after leaving there, did you stop again anywhere before getting to Nebraska?"

"Not other than for gas or food. Whether we did before

we hit Nebraska, I am not sure. I don't remember the distance."

Werner, knowing the boy's stomach was empty at the autopsy, zeroed in on the meals the Stutzmans might have had on their trip across the plains. Stutzman said that Danny had been munching off and on and hadn't eaten a real meal until evening.

Stutzman said he was certain they had stopped to eat in the evening, though he couldn't recall the name of the restaurant.

"It was a truck stop where they serve smorgasbord-style food." He believed it was in Nebraska.

"He did not eat everything that he had dished himself out, but he ate better than I expected."

"Up until this point in time, was he feeling fairly well, or how would you describe his health?"

"In the afternoon he had some complaints, but it didn't seem to be serious, according to him. But then in the evening, after he had laid for several hours, he told me he felt a lot better and agreed to eat."

"And when you ate at this truck stop, do you remember how long a drive it was before you reached 81 from that truck stop?"

Stutzman shook his head. It had probably been dusk when he pulled into the truck stop for dinner. They ate, and he filled the car up with gas. Danny sat in the front seat.

"We didn't leave right away," Stutzman added. "I had him change into some pajamas so that he could get in the back."

Stutzman said that they talked before Danny fell asleep in the back of the Gremlin. Stutzman said that he checked on him a short time later and that he was still sleeping. Stutzman drove on, occasionally getting out of the car for fresh air.

When Stutzman turned south on U.S. 81, traveling through Thayer County to U.S. 70, Danny was still curled up in back. Stutzman said he had given the boy his medication at six and at noon.

"Now, Mr. Stutzman, do you recall speaking with Ted Garber after your arrest in Texas?"

Stutzman looked confused. "Ted Garber, a detective?"

"In Azle, Texas?"

"Oh, yes."

"After your arrest and before you were brought up here?"

Stutzman nodded.

"Now," Werner continued, "you just told me that you were in Nebraska and stopped at a large truck stop near Salina, Kansas, to eat, is that right?"

"I do remember Salina, Kansas, the following morning."

"The following morning?"

"Yes, but not while I had my son with me."

"And you stated to him that Danny got out, but didn't eat very much. But you have told me today that Danny ate fairly well at the truck stop. Which is correct?"

Again Stutzman seemed confused, and his voice was nearly inaudible. "He dished out—what he dished out for himself, he did not eat all of it."

It was about midnight—time for Danny's medication, Stutzman said—when he tried to wake him.

"I reached back, I got a hold of his leg, and he wouldn't wake up. So I pulled over and reached back again and couldn't figure it out. So I got out of the car and went around the back of the car and opened the back end where he had his head back there. And I noticed right way, or shortly, the look on his face—there was something wrong."

"What did you notice about his face?" Werner asked.

"His eyes were, like, rolled back in his head, and his complexion did not look like it normally does."

"What did his complexion look like?"

"White."

"What did you do?"

Stutzman said he tried mouth-to-mouth resuscitation. But Danny remained still, his eyes rolled back.

Werner retraced what had been said in court that morning. The Stutzman car was somewhere off U.S. 81 when this happened. Stutzman couldn't recall exactly how long he had driven by then.

"Do you remember any towns in the area?"

"No, I really don't. I do remember—I remember some landmarks and stuff, and I do—"

"What type of landmarks?"

"One of the things I remember that was close by was a cemetery."

Stutzman said that after he noticed Danny was not moving and couldn't be awakened, he felt for a pulse. He tried mouth-to-mouth and heart massage numerous times.

But nothing worked.

"And what did you do after you had done all of these things?"

"I got back in the car and went on a little ways and decided to pull off the main road."

"How far did you go? How far is a little ways?"

Stutzman was uncertain, but conceded it had probably been less than a mile.

"Mr. Stutzman, when you noticed his eyes rolled back, when you couldn't get a pulse, why did you not seek help for Danny at that time?"

"That's what I keep—still keep asking myself today. I had difficulty believing that it had happened. I could not figure out why it happened. I wish now I would have."

"Could Danny have been alive at that time?"

"I don't think it is possible. Well, I'm not going to swear to it, but I don't think so at all, because at the time there was no pulse and I spent several—at least several more hours with him after that, and he never did breathe during that time."

"This was after you pulled off the road that you spent several hours with him?"

"Yes."

"Were you outside the car when you spent that time with him?"

"I kept him in the car until I left him. But, yes, I did get out of the car some of the time."

"Could Danny have been alive when you placed him in that ditch?"

"I don't see any way possible."

"Do you recall Officer Garber asking you that question down in Azle, Texas, after your arrest?"

"No, I don't."

Werner probed further. "Do you recall telling Garber when asked, was Danny alive when you put him in the ditch, do you recall telling him, 'That is a good question. I don't think so, but he could have been?' "

"No, I don't recall that."

"Did Danny have a T-shirt, a wrestling T-shirt?"

"From Wyoming?" Stutzman looked puzzled.

Werner handed Stutzman a photograph, marked as exhibit number three. He asked if the shirt had been Danny's.

Stutzman studied the photograph for a moment, then asked if it was a child's size.

"Did Danny have a T-shirt like that?"

Stutzman shrugged it off. "I don't recall. But it is possible. He had a lot of different T-shirts with a lot of different emblems. . . . It is possible. I don't know."

"Did you buy a T-shirt like that for Danny?"

"I don't recall buying a T-shirt with Panther Wrestling on it."

"Did you throw out a T-shirt like that in the country?"

"I don't remember throwing anything out."

Werner changed the direction of his cross-examination. "What type of toys did Danny have?"

"That he was playing with? He had all kinds of toys."

Werner asked him to describe some, and Stutzman responded that Danny had some video games. He also had a soccer ball on that trip two years ago.

"Do you remember him playing with any toys that were blue in color, with kind of a metallic paint?" Werner asked.

"Blue? No, I don't."

"Mr. Stutzman, did you kill Danny?"

The room was so quiet that no one had difficulty hearing the man's response.

"No, I did not."

"Did you help Danny die in any way?"

"No."

"Do you remember anything else about Danny's death that you haven't told us about?"

"No, not that I can think of. Only thing I can say, it's real tragic. I still, to this day, don't know why or exactly what—"

"Did—what did you do when you placed him in the ditch?"

Again, Stutzman was very quiet. "I told him another prayer. I decided to leave him and let God take care of him."

He said he pulled off the road, parked, and carried the boy's limp body to a ditch and covered him with snow. He got back on the main road and headed south. He said he didn't report the boy's death because he could not bear what had happened.

"I guess I didn't want to face my friends and family, realizing what had happened. I couldn't figure out *why*."

Werner asked how many days had passed between Stutzman and Danny leaving Wyoming and Danny's death, and Stutzman told him that Danny had died the same day.

"I left there on a morning and he died during that night, and I left him."

Did Stutzman know on what day he had arrived in Ohio?

"It was towards—I would say either—probably either Thursday or Friday."

"Where did you go—did you go directly to Ohio after you left Thayer County?"

"I did spend some time—I had difficulty continuing on. What I had in mind—I lost the holiday spirit, and spent some time in motels."

Lost the holiday spirit? The statement was so ludicrous

that some spectators might have laughed had the case not been so grim.

"Do you remember where?"

"I suppose I could find it or look it up. I don't remember the names right offhand."

Stutzman said that he remembered spending some time in his car and that he did not get a motel room every night. He said he did not recall getting a room until the night after Danny died.

Questioned further, however, Stutzman could not recall the motels or anything about them.

With good reason. There hadn't been any.

Stutzman told how he had lied about his son's death when he arrived in Ohio. He also said he had lied to the Barlows, telling them that Danny was enrolled in an Ohio school.

After the holidays, Stutzman said he went to the Azle, Texas, area, where he lived with Owen Barker.

Werner asked, "What did you tell Owen Barker about Danny?"

"I believe I told him Danny was with the Barlow family."

"Is there a time when you told Owen Barker that Danny had died?"

"Yes."

"Did you have Owen Barker speak with someone and tell him—have Owen Barker speak with someone on the telephone and tell him that it was Danny?"

"Repeat that again, if you would?"

"Remember Father's Day of about 1986?"

Stutzman nodded.

"At the time you spoke to Danny on the telephone, according to Mr. Barker, and had Mr. Barker speak with someone whom you said was Danny, is that correct?"

Stutzman disagreed. "Not to my knowledge. I remember him talking to Danny while I was there, but it was prior to

Danny's death. But that particular Father's Day, I don't know."

Werner asked if Stutzman had ever called anyone on the phone and pretended it was Danny he was talking to.

Stutzman admitted it was possible. "I know it was on my mind a lot, and I was trying to cover the fact at that point that he had died."

Werner entered into evidence the letter from Stutzman to his former in-laws as exhibit number four. Stutzman confirmed that he had written it.

"Now, Mr. Stutzman, on several occasions now at least, you've told us that you lied about Danny's death, telling people what was not true. Did you ever tell anyone the truth about Danny's death?"

"Yes. Last month. Yes, since I realized his body has been found."

The judge couldn't hear the answer, so Stutzman repeated his response. He added that it was the court and a reporter to whom he had told the truth. He had also told his attorney and a couple of others from Texas.

He never told anyone else.

"Did Danny die in that blue sleeper, then, that he was wearing when you placed him in the ditch?"

"Yes."

"Did you clean him up any before you placed him in the ditch, do anything to him?"

"The only thing is him washing up after he ate. That's all I remember."

"Mr. Stutzman, before you took the stand, you took an oath to tell the truth. What does that mean to you?"

"What I say is the truth."

Werner asked for a brief recess, and the court granted him five minutes.

Next, Werner focused on a letter, exhibit number five. It was the letter to Eli's parents with a British return address.

"Did you write your parents a letter indicating that it was from England, in 1987?"

"I don't know. I've heard different things about that, and I'm not real sure what that is about."

Werner showed Stutzman copies of the letter and the envelope and asked him to review them. "Do you recall that now?"

"I recall writing this to my mother, but there is something wrong with this here, I don't know what happened." Stutzman indicated the return address.

"Well, the letter states that you're working with horses. In November of 1987, were you working with horses?"

"Yes."

"The wording on the envelope, is that your wording? Is that your writing?"

Stutzman nodded. "Yes. It is to my parents, but this is not." He indicated the return address. He said that he had some friends who lived at that address, but that it had been several months since he had corresponded with them.

Wyant and Young knew that Interpol had reported there was no such address.

Werner offered the letter as an exhibit, and Gallup objected, stating that the defendant could not identify the letter's return address. The court received the exhibit anyway.

Bill Gallup had some brief additional questions. He touched on his client's training as an orderly in a hospital.

"Did you see dead people as you worked as an orderly in a hospital?"

"Yes."

"You are of the opinion, when you saw your son and placed him in that field, that he was dead, is that correct?"

"That's correct."

"To the best of your knowledge, as a person with some medical training, is that true?"

"Right."

Werner had no further questions, though he did request

that the court accept into evidence exhibit number six, which included reports by Jack Wyant and Ted Garber.

The judge instructed Werner to present his argument for sentencing.

"Well, Your Honor, I cannot conceive of abandoning a body or concealing a death in a situation . . . more severe than this one. And I believe that the court is aware of the situation through the reports, through the testimony, through the pleas.

"And I would ask that the court announce a sentence in accordance with the facts of this case."

Gallup backpedaled.

"Your Honor, I think that the tone of this whole proceeding was probably set the other night, when my wife told me she got a couple of phone calls from what appeared to be elderly people, saying that her husband better not get the child killer off.

"And I mention that because there has been a misconception that Mr. Stutzman has been accused of killing his son, and the State has never made that contention, although the general perception about that has been that he killed his son."

Gallup said that since the ground was frozen, the defendant couldn't have dug a grave. What he did was not unnatural for someone with only an eighth-grade education. Considering that Stutzman had lost his son, was only 36 years old, and had never had a brush with the law beyond a few traffic tickets, Gallup asked for leniency.

He stressed that the appropriate sentence for the two misdemeanors was thirty days in jail, meaning that Stutzman should be released in a couple of days—given that he'd been held in Thayer County Jail for twenty-eight days already.

Werner was permitted the last word.

"This is a case where we, as far as the State is concerned, and sentencing, everything is true that Mr. Stutzman has said, but we do not know why Danny died, how Danny died, or where, precisely, Danny died. And we do not know whether Danny was alive or dead when he was placed there."

The judge stated for the record, in case of appeal, the court's impression of the defendant.

"He was, in the court's opinion, very matter-of-fact, controlled. He did not shift in his chair under cross-examination. Oftentimes he covered his mouth on the part of his responses, and there was, the court noted, almost a complete lack of emotion."

Judge McCardle sentenced Stutzman to one year for the charge of abandoning of a human body, and six months for that of concealing a death, the counts to run concurrently.

As Stutzman was led back to jail, it seemed to be over. But it wasn't, not for Thayer County and not for Eli Stutzman.

Wyant and Young left the courtroom feeling frustrated and angry.

"I knew he was lying," Wyant said.

AFTERWORD

Eli Stutzman's day of reckoning with Texas law was played out in the chilly environs of an air-conditioned Travis County courtroom in July 1989 when the former Amishman was finally tried for the 1985 murder of roommate Glen Pritchett.

In what had become typical of his erratic and self-righteous behavior, Stutzman fired his court-appointed attorney only a few weeks before the trial. He feigned outrage when he told friends that the Austin lawyer had said he could do a better job if Stutzman slipped him ten thousand dollars under the table. Stutzman retained Houston-based Connie Moore and Debra Hunt with funds provided by the remarkable and unlikely alliance of conservative Mennonite supporters and a former gay lover.

The defendant's thinner appearance and graying hair prompted those who knew he carried the AIDS virus to speculate that the disease was taking its deathly toll. The truth was less malevolent. Travis County Jail food was not agreeable, and he no longer had his Grecian Formula.

The prosecution's case was circumstantial and slight and everyone knew it. No physical evidence tied Stutzman to Pritchett's murder. No gun. Absolutely nothing. Moore and Hunt conceded that their client was a liar, but argued that that didn't make him a killer.

Stutzman seemed preoccupied, at times even detached,

as he slumped in his chair. His eyes never met those of his accusers as they took the witness stand: Sawyer, Ruston, Hankins, and Miller.

Travis County assistant district attorneys Carla Garcia and Maryanne Powers argued that Stutzman's Nebraska convictions be admitted because the defendant's actions in both cases had been so strikingly similar that they should be considered "signature crimes." The rural deposition of the body, the elaborate cover-ups, and the phone conversations with the victims—after they were dead—were among the points the attorneys enumerated.

A courtroom spectator scribbled a cue-card-like message on a scrap of paper: *"They were both dumped in a ditch!"*

Presiding judge Jon Wisser, who ironically had been the same judge who signed the destruction order on Stutzman's rifle, rejected the motion. Wisser did permit the jury to hear that Danny Stutzman was deceased, but nothing further.

"Well, we've lost it," Garcia said in the hallway, after learning that Travis County's Little Boy Blue trump card could not be played before the jury.

The defense offered no witnesses. Moore and Hunt did not feel compelled to refute what they perceived to be a weak case. The state, they said, had simply failed to prove the charge beyond a reasonable doubt.

The verdict was swift and surprising to the spectators, who half-expected that Stutzman might go free. But after a lunch of cheeseburgers and Cokes, the jury returned a guilty verdict on the fourth day of the trial.

Stutzman was sentenced to forty years in the Texas Department of Corrections at Huntsville.

Connie Moore broke down later. "If they can convict him on such a circumstantial case, they can make a case on anyone. You or me. Anyone—for any crime."

She was not the only one who left the capital city of Texas, bitterly disappointed.

Disbarred attorney Frank Hefner and partner Rusty Porter came to the trial banking on a not-guilty verdict and armed with a news release stating that HIC Associates had sold film rights to Stutzman's story for a figure in "excess of $500,000." Without an innocent man—persecuted by the media and a victim of the naïveté of an Amishman—HIC didn't have rights worth anything. A rights contract with a convicted killer was in violation of state law.

After the verdict, prosecution witness Wanda Sawyer paid a visit to the convicted murderer. Incredibly, she still considered him a friend. They even touched hands through the glass divider.

"He said he suffered a severe memory loss because of a car accident. He couldn't remember anything before 1985."

Stutzman said he had been planning a trip with his Mennonite supporters to see Danny's grave, and Wanda Sawyer was moved, as Stutzman had surely meant her to be.

Stutzman declined all media interviews, claiming that *People* magazine had done a hatchet job and twisted his words when the weekly published a follow-up to its "Death of an Unknown Boy" feature story, in February 1988.

Though Eli Stutzman is in prison, the story of the former Amishman's dark descent continues. Some wonder if it will ever end.

In 1990 Stutzman emerged as a key suspect in the Colorado murders of David Tyler and Dennis Slaeter. Durango detective Tony Archuleta plowed through the files of the stalled investigation, launched a relentless series of interviews, and uncovered more information linking Stutzman and Tyler. He also faced the same frustrating problem that had dogged others working Stutzman-related cases. Many witnesses were reluctant or outright refused to come forward because they were gay and feared being labeled homosexual.

That conspiracy of fear and silence helped lead Danny Stutzman to the Nebraska cornfield.

From their pastoral settlements, the Amish still wonder and talk among themselves about Ida Stutzman's death.

They refuse to pass final judgment—only God can—and many decline to make definitive statements about her death. Most are diplomatic and simply say they "fear Eli killed Ida."

Stutzman is a diabolical star in a community that abhors media attention. Murder committed by an Amishman has but a single precedent in the history of the religious order.

Former Wayne County sheriff Jim Frost offers no help in sorting out the truth. He told a journalist in 1989 that he couldn't recall any details of the night the pregnant woman died.

Wayne County coroner J. T. Questel has told several reporters that he "blew" the case at the time of the original investigation.

Gary Young remains Thayer County's sheriff, with plans to run for another, possibly final, term. He looks back on his most famous case with frustration and the regret that he might have missed something during the investigation. When he looks at Eli Stutzman he sees the eyes of a killer.

The Reverend Jean Samuelson, now pastor of a huge church in Aurora, still prays for the wayward Amishman.

"I think he's kind of naive and innocent. Certainly he got into some bad stuff," she said in 1990. "He's got a vulnerability."

But vulnerability is a trait Stutzman has practiced. Today he fine-tunes the charade from prison. His letters open with prolonged passages from Scripture and words about his love for God, though some recipients get the impression that the words are copied from a Sunday schoolbook. He is studying drafting and algebra, with his eye on earning a college degree.

And as has been his habit at least since he was 21, Stutzman continues to walk the tightrope of two worlds, excluding people from both sides. He paints the picture he wants people to see—innocent Amishman, sexual maniac, good father, religious scholar. Even after all he's been through, Eli Stutzman still thinks no one will catch on. But he is wrong.

"He told me he was offered thousands of dollars for movie rights and he flushed the letter down the toilet," said a Mennonite man who visited Stutzman at the prison in Lincoln, Nebraska.

Another's experience was the converse.

"Stutzman now tells me he wants $100,000 for the rights! I keep telling him I can't come up with that kind of money. No one can," complained a Hollywood-based producer who corresponded with Stutzman in an effort to put together a deal.

The father also persists with easily disproved fabrications about his son's death. Now he no longer talks about the Gremlin's faulty exhaust system, but rather hints of a conspiracy.

"Court records about Danny's death have been sealed in Nebraska. I want to know how my son died," he wrote to New Order Amishwoman Liz Chupp in June 1990. "Five children died in Wyoming of a rare disease the same year Danny died."

Both statements are untrue.

Questions remain and continue to haunt. Did Danny die at the hands of his father? Investigators affirm the idea with conviction and authority—though the allegation can't be proved. Stutzman's actions and statements point to foul play. Why didn't he seek help from a farmhouse, or from others in the truck stop cafe where he might have stopped for coffee and composure? It would seem to be the natural reaction for a father with a sick child. The idea that his Amish upbringing left him with no basis for dealing with the outside world is ludicrous and insulting. Eli Stutzman was far from naive. One reason for his inaction might be that Stutzman knew that hospital authorities would want to know who he was, and would possibly learn that he was wanted in Texas for questioning. Stutzman couldn't risk that. If Danny had to die, so be it. Eli Stutzman wasn't going to jail for anything or anyone.

Just how did Danny die? Of course, a natural death is plausible, and no medical evidence exists that doesn't support that possibility. Murder is also a possibility. Pathologists concede that suffocation could have caused Danny to die. Stutzman himself suggested the scenario of Danny suffocating in the back as the boy lay pressed up against the luggage with a sleeping bag or blanket wrapped around his head. If there had been a struggle and the boy had suffered some trauma to his face when and if he were smothered, such evidence, of course, had been lost by the time the body was found. Half of Danny's face, including the mouth and nose, had been gnawed away by field mice.

Freezing to death is the scenario favored by state patrol investigator Jack Wyant. He feels that Stutzman left the boy outside in the subzero temperature to die. Danny might have been weakened or unconscious, or Stutzman could have just *told* the boy to lie down until he told him to get up. The boy had been abused so much and for so long that it is likely he would have been compliant.

The freezing scenario makes sense. Stutzman's Gremlin was seen by a Thayer County sheriff's deputy at Foote's early the morning Danny was dumped. Was Stutzman passing time with plans to return to the field to make sure Danny had succumbed? If he wasn't, then why the stop at Foote's? One would have thought he'd want to get the hell out of Thayer County. Did he need the time to pull himself together to run through the skiing story? Not likely, as there was plenty of time for that on the way to his lover's place near Salina, Kansas.

There is also the matter of the letter Stutzman sent to the Missouri man while on his way to Wyoming to pick up the boy. *"My son may not be coming with me . . ."*

Stutzman might have been planting the seed as he had with Ida's death, when he told Amos Gingerich that Ida's heart was giving her trouble when she did chores. Prosecutors and cops first saw the note in 1990 and immediately considered it the "best piece of evidence." It's the kind of document that Jack Wyant could have pushed into Stutzman's face when he was being interrogated: "Why did you do it? You planned it!"

But Wyant didn't know about the letter. And he didn't know about the Kansas or Missouri men.

The wrestling T-shirt remains an intriguing piece of the puzzle. Found a mile from the dump site, it had on it blue paint particles—the same color as the interior of the so-called Levi's-style Gremlin—that matched the particles on the sleeper. At the hearing, Stutzman denied that he had seen the shirt before. Why? Why was it left on the side of the road? He said he never got out of the car before he left Danny where "God could find him." Yet it must be another lie. What happened at the side of the road that would have caused Stutzman to get out of the car, and the shirt to fall out?

The sleeper continues to baffle. The boy was too old, too sophisticated to wear such a babyish garment. Stutzman purchased it in New Mexico before he left to get Danny—after he knew that the boy wouldn't be with him when he got to Missouri. If it was part of a plan, what role did it play? In Stutzman's anxious state, had he felt compelled to return Danny to an earlier time, a time when the boy was younger and no threat to his father's life-style? Besides Eli Stutzman, who knows?

Some non-Amish said they had heard that the boy was left in the sleeper because the Amish always bury their dead in a blue shroud. It makes for a nice theory, but it is untrue.

If, for the sake of argument, Danny was murdered, what was his father's motive? Texas investigators feel that Danny had knowledge of the murder in Texas and that Stutzman had to shut him up. Sam Miller's testimony before the grand jury validated that supposition when he said that the boy was in the truck as Eli and Sam returned from being questioned at the sheriff's office. It was then that Stutzman admitted his guilt while Danny looked on, unfazed. Yet, if the motive was that Danny knew too much, why did Stutzman take the boy to Wyoming, where he could have told anyone?

If Danny hadn't, in fact, talked about the murder, as Dean and Margie Barlow told Jack Wyant and Gary Young, it wouldn't be so extraordinary. Danny had been a victim of child abuse, and compliance to a parent's demands or threats is routine in such cases.

The motive might have been simpler. Eli Stutzman didn't want the boy, but he didn't want the Amish to raise him. Stutzman, as evidenced by his personal letters back home to friends in Ohio, continued to play the game of a good, but misunderstood man. He couldn't have Danny ruin him in the eyes of the people he believed still admired him. Danny had knowledge of the murder. At his father's bidding, Danny had participated in and seen much of the gay life-style.

The renegade Amishman wasn't exaggerating when he told Kenny Hankins that he'd rather see his son dead than be raised by the Amish.

Ida Stutzman's death, though equally sinister, is easier for many to comprehend. Stutzman, a mentally unstable gay man trapped in the rigid world of the Amish *Ordnung*, might have seen only one way out of his marriage. His fabrications and embellishments of the story of the barn fire are as incriminating as the incredibly unlikely sequence of events the day the pregnant woman died.

Later, when he wrote to another Amish widower, he told the man that the police had determined that lightning caused the fire, and that a doctor had determined that she had suffered a heart attack. Both were stories that *he* originated. Both were part of a setup to get him away from Ida, and away from the Amish.

Was Stutzman mentally ill, or was he merely adept at manipulation? It's interesting to speculate. From the time he left the notes for Mose Keim to find, or wrote the letters to himself at Stoll Farms, he found elaborate setups effective. He knew that such tactics made him the subject of sympathy rather than disdain. The night of his breakdown, one year after Ida's death, smacks of a setup—it was perhaps Stutzman's finest performance. If he had told the Gingeriches he wanted them to leave, he would be admitting he no longer wanted an Amish life. Stutzman didn't want to look bad. A breakdown was his answer.

Pathological liars often embellish falsehoods with unnecessary details to prove their words are the truth. Stutzman did this repeatedly and recklessly.

It was five years ago this Christmas season that Chuck Kleveland found the boy in the blue sleeper. Five years ago, amid darkness and the howls of wind and drifting snow, the nightmare of an abused child ended when his father's car crossed the state line into Kansas.

Danny Stutzman has been dead half as long as he lived.

Toys and flowers still decorate his tiny grave and pay tribute to the victim of the dark and dangerous life ordained by his father. The dead boy's spirit calls for the truth, and someday that spirit might even be answered.

As Jack Wyant once said, drawing on a cigarette and surveying the volumes of Little Boy Blue notebooks he keeps handy in his office, "Someone, somewhere, knows."

A MESSAGE FROM THE AUTHOR

Of all the subjects of my books, I probably have had more consistent interest from readers about Eli Stutzman and the crimes portrayed in *Abandoned Prayers*. In the fourteen years since the book was first released, I have received thousands of inquiries about the Amishman who dumped his son's body in rural Nebraska. Most want to know if he died in prison, as if such a demise would be fitting retribution. They are uniformly disappointed when I tell them Stutzman is very much alive. Outrage follows when I report that in the spring of 2003 he made parole and was released by the Texas Department of Corrections.

For more on Stutzman and an update on other characters in the book, please visit my web site *www.greggolsen.com*.

—Gregg Olsen
Olalla, Wash.
2003

Howard Petrella

Number-one *New York Times* and *USA Today* bestselling author GREGG OLSEN has written more than thirty books, including *Lying Next to Me, The Last Thing She Ever Did,* and two novels in the Nicole Foster series, *The Sound of Rain* and *The Weight of Silence.* Known for his ability to create vivid and fascinating narratives, he's appeared on multiple television and radio shows and news networks, such as *Good Morning America, Dateline, Entertainment Tonight,* CNN, and MSNBC. In addition, Olsen has been featured in *Redbook, People,* and *Salon,* as well as in *The Seattle Times,* the *Los Angeles Times,* and the *New York Post.* Both his fiction and nonfiction works have received critical acclaim and numerous awards, including prominence on the *USA Today* and *Wall Street Journal* bestseller lists. Washington state officially selected his young adult novel *Envy* for the National Book Festival, and *The Deep Dark* was named Idaho Book of the Year.

A Seattle native who lives with his wife in rural Washington state, Olsen's already at work on his next thriller. Visit him online at www.notoriоususa.com.